D1536854

Human Resource Management
Essential Perspectives

Consulting Editors

Robert L. Mathis
University of Nebraska at Omaha

John H. Jackson
University of Wyoming

SOUTH-WESTERN College Publishing

An International Thomson Publishing Company

Acquisitions Editor: Charles McCormick
Developmental Editor: Judy O'Neill
Production Editor: Shelley Brewer
Production House: Lachina Publishing Services
Cover Design: Jennifer Lynne Martin
Marketing Manager: Joe Sabatino
Manufacturing Coordinator: Sue Kirven

Library of Congress Cataloging-in-Publication Data

Human resource management : essential perspectives / consulting
    editors, Robert L. Mathis, John H. Jackson.
        p.   cm.
    Includes bibliographical references and index.
    ISBN 0-324-00207-6
    1. Personnel management.   I. Mathis, Robert L.,
II. Jackson, John Harold.
HF5549.H7854   1998
658.3--dc21   98-21500
                                                                        CIP

1 2 3 4 5 6 7 8 9 WE 6 5 4 3 2 1 0 9 8

Printed in Canada

I(T)P
International Thomson Publishing
South-Western College Publishing is an ITP Company. The ITP trademark is used
under license.

Contents

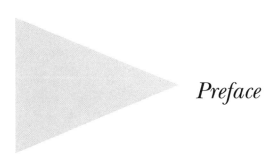

Preface

The importance of HR issues for managers and organizations is evident every day. As indicated by frequent headlines and news media reports on downsizing, workforce shortages, sexual harassment, union activity, and other topics, the management of human resources is growing in impact throughout the United States and the world. Many individuals are affected by HR issues and consequently must become more knowledgeable about HR management. Those interested in the field of HR management must know more about the nature of various HR activities. Every manager's HR actions can have major consequences for organizations. This book has been prepared to provide a concise overview of HR management for students, HR practitioners, and others in organizations.

Currently, there is no book covering the essence of HR management in a concise and focused manner. Many HR texts that cover the field are over 500 pages. The shorter books that are available tend to be heavily academic in nature, not as practical, or cover only specific functional areas (compensation, benefits selection, training, and so on). Clearly, a need exists for a moderately priced overview of HR management that both HR practitioners and traditional students can use. In addition, this book presents information in a way that makes sense to various industry groups and professional organizations. Finally, this condensed view of HR management also addresses the tremendous interest in U.S. practices of HR management in other countries, making it a valuable resource for managers worldwide.

This book covers all the essential HR activities. It reviews important laws and regulations and provides an overview of information that is used typically by practicing HR professionals. By publishing the book in softcover, it can be used in conjunction with other softcover books in workshops, seminars, and college/university courses. The test bank and instructor's manual offer the academic market unique resources for a softcover book.

As consulting editors, it is our belief that this book and others that may follow will be useful and interesting resources for those desiring an overview of the important issues and practices in HR management. It is our hope that this book will contribute to more effective management of human resources in organizations.

Robert L. Mathis, SPHR
John H. Jackson
Consulting Editors

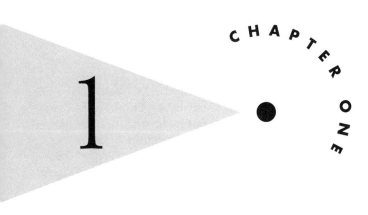

CHAPTER ONE

Strategic Human Resource Management and Planning

Human resource (HR) management is a key ingredient affecting organizational competitiveness and its ability to fulfill its mission. The effectiveness of an organization in providing a product or service that fits customers' needs is critical if it is to survive. That product or service is provided in part (or entirely) by people. Employees are not only among the most important resources a firm has, they also are among the most expensive and sometimes the most problematic. Organizational human resources have grown as a strategic interest to upper management recently because effective use of people in the organization can provide a *competitive advantage* both domestically and abroad. **Human resource (HR) management** deals with the design of formal systems in an organization to ensure the effective and efficient use of human talent to accomplish the organizational goals.

▶ HR MANAGEMENT AND COMPETITIVE ADVANTAGE

The activities that focus on HR management can provide a direct contribution to organizational performance. Such a contribution can be positive or negative, depending on the effectiveness of the design and implementation of the HR policies and systems. Human resources are frequently "underutilized" because employees often perform below their potential. The design of HR activities can affect the effectiveness and efforts of employees by influencing their jobs, skills, and motivation.

Goals of HR Management

While a CEO's goals for HR management are usually to have productive employees that contribute to a competitive advantage for the organization, HR executives concern themselves with the more specific objectives necessary to reach those goals. A recent national survey identified the top concerns of HR executives. The most important concerns identified were productivity, quality, and service.[1]

Productivity. Improving productivity has become even more important as global competition has increased, particularly when technology keeps changing. Organizations are discovering that the traditional approach of cutting costs, specifically labor costs, may be counterproductive in some cases because some human resources may hold the keys to productivity improvement. Productivity can be generally identified as the amount of output per employee.

Quality and Service. Because human resources are the ones producing the products or services offered by an organization, they must be included in identifying any quality and service blockages and redesigning operational processes. Involving all employees, not just managers, in problem solving often requires a change in corporate culture, leadership styles, and HR policies and practices. But as more and more managers have discovered, the quantity and composition of human resources available to organizations today are dramatically different from those in previous decades.

The push for quality that followed Japan's successful competitive moves into the United States has become a way of life in some firms. Total quality management (TQM), an approach championed by W. Edwards Deming, focuses on employee communication, continuous improvement, training, and worker involvement, among other HR-oriented issues.

Strategic and Operational Roles of HR Management

At the heart of the evolution of HR management is the fact that there are two major roles associated with the management of human resources in organizations. As Figure 1–1 shows, those roles are the strategic role and the operational role. HR management began as an operational function, but its strategic role is growing.

Strategic Role of HR Management. The strategic role of HR management emphasizes that the people in an organization are valuable resources representing a significant investment of organizational efforts. These human resources can be a source of competitive strength if they are managed effectively.

Strategically, then, human resources must be viewed in the same context as the financial, technological, and other resources that are managed in organizations. HR supply and demand must be viewed from a strategic standpoint.

Operational Role of HR Management. Operational activities are both tactical and administrative in nature. Compliance with equal employment opportunity and other laws must be ensured, applicants must be interviewed,

► **FIGURE 1–1**   **HR Management Roles**

Role	Focus	HR Often Reports to	Typical Activities
Strategic	Global, long-run, innovative	CEO/ President	• Human resource planning • Tracking evolving legal issues • Assessing workforce trends and issues • Engaging in community economic development • Assisting in organizational restructuring and downsizing • Advising on mergers or acquisitions • Managing compensation planning and strategies
Operational	Administrative, short-term, maintenance-oriented	Corporate Vice-President of Administration	• Recruiting and selecting for current openings • Conducting employee orientation • Reviewing safety and accident reports • Resolving employee complaints and grievances • Administering employee benefits programs

new employees must be oriented to the organization, supervisors must be trained, safety problems must be resolved, and wages and salaries must be administered. In short, a wide variety of activities typically associated with the day-to-day management of people in organizations must be performed efficiently and appropriately. It is this collection of activities that often has been referred to as "the personnel function," and the newer strategic focus of HR management has not eliminated it. However, instead of performing both roles, many HR practitioners are, unfortunately, continuing to perform only the operational role. This emphasis still exists in some organizations partly because of individual limitations and partly because of top management's resistance to an expanded HR role.

► THE CURRENT ENVIRONMENT OF HR MANAGEMENT

The environment in which HR management takes place is very much in a state of flux. Changes are occurring rapidly across a wide range of issues. Some of the more visible changes present challenges to HR management and are discussed next:

▶ Economic and employment shifts
▶ Education and training
▶ Organizational restructuring
▶ Demographics and diversity
▶ Balancing work and family

Economic and Employment Shifts

Several economic changes have occurred that have altered employment and occupational patterns in the United States. A major one is the shift of jobs from manufacturing and agriculture to service industries and telecommunications. Additionally, pressures from global competitors have forced many U.S. firms to close facilities, adapt their management practices, and increase productivity and decrease labor costs in order to become more competitive. For instance, in a recent two-year period, over 3.7 million jobs were eliminated by major U.S. firms. Over half of the jobs cut were in manufacturing, indicating that significant shifts in industries and occupations continue to occur.

Occupational Projections to 2005.   The U.S. economy increasingly has become a service economy, and that shift is expected to continue. Over 80% of U.S. jobs are in service industries, and most new jobs created by the year 2005 also will be in services. It is estimated that manufacturing jobs will represent only 12% to 15% of all U.S. jobs by that date. From 1990 to 2005, the number of service jobs will increase 35%, while the number of manufacturing jobs will decrease 3%.

Service-sector jobs generally include jobs in industries such as financial services, health care, transportation, retailing, fast food and restaurants, legal and social services, education, and computer systems. The fastest-growing occupations in terms of percentage are predominately in the computer and health-care fields. Another facet of change is the pattern of job growth or shrinkage in firms of varying sizes. Whereas many large firms have cut jobs by reducing their workforces, many smaller firms have continued to create jobs.

Education and "Knowledge Jobs".   Many occupational groups and industries will require more educated workers in the coming years. The number of jobs requiring advanced knowledge is expected to grow at a much more rapid rate than the number of other jobs. This growth means that people without high school diplomas or appropriate college degrees increasingly will be at a disadvantage, as their employment opportunities are confined to the lowest-paying service jobs. In short, there is a growing gap between the knowledge and skills required by many jobs and those possessed by employees and applicants. Several different studies and projections all point to the likelihood that employers in many industries will have difficulties obtaining sufficiently educated and trained workers.

Education and Training

Quite simply, there is an education and training crisis in the United States that increasingly will affect the quality of the human resources available to employers.

One estimate by the American Society for Training and Development (ASTD) is that close to half of the U.S. workforce (about 50 million workers) need or will need new or enhanced workplace training to adapt to the myriad of job and technological changes that are occurring.

Increased emphasis on remedial education and job training for employees will be a continuing HR management concern. Implications are as follows:

▶ New training methods, such as interactive videos and individualized computerized training, will grow in usage.
▶ Training for future jobs and skills must be available for employees at all levels, not just managers and professionals.
▶ More accurate skill assessment for existing employees and jobs will be critical. Screening applicants for specific skills will be necessary.
▶ Remedial and literacy training will be offered by more employers.
▶ Employers increasingly will become active partners with public school systems to aid in the upgrading of the skills of high school graduates.

Organizational Restructuring

Many organizations have "rightsized" either by: (1) eliminating layers of managers, (2) closing facilities, (3) merging with other organizations, or (4) outplacing workers. A common transformation has been to make organizations flatter by removing several layers of management. Three ideas related to such organizational restructuring are reengineering, downsizing, and outsourcing.

Reengineering.   **Business process reengineering (BPR)** is the fundamental rethinking and redesign of work processes to improve cost, service, and speed. Reengineering work involves an attempt to rethink and redesign the way work gets done. The idea is to make improvements in cost, quality, service, and speed. Reengineering is seen as part of a "clarification" of lines of business; the clarification involves deciding on the *core business* and diverting investment away from marginal activities.

Downsizing.   **Downsizing** is an intentional strategy to reduce costs—most often through a reduction in payroll. One of the reasons for downsizing has been the past practice of American businesses to accumulate employees. The human cost associated with downsizing has been much discussed in the popular press: a survivor's mentality for those who remain, unfulfilled cost saving estimates, loss of loyalty, and many people looking for new jobs.[2]

Outsourcing.   Related to clarification of the core business through downsizing and reengineering is outsourcing, a practice that is growing rapidly. **Outsourcing** is contracting with another organization to provide operations that previously were handled internally. An example is hiring a janitorial firm to keep the building clean instead of hiring janitors. The process both eliminates and creates jobs as tasks are shifted from one organization to another.

Managers note several advantages of outsourcing: the company is not as likely to end up with an out-of-date system that it cannot afford to upgrade, there is less up-front financial commitment, and there is no long-term commitment. But outsourcing has definite downsides as well.

First, unions *do not* like outsourcing, and unionized firms face a fight over the practice. For example, General Motors and the United Auto Workers have had major disagreements on outsourcing. Further, the payoffs from outsourcing may be less than expected. For example, typically consultants promise savings averaging 20% to 40%, but one firm found that average savings for outsourcing were around 9%. There are other problems as well. Southern Pacific Railroad suffered through many computer breakdowns after outsourcing its computers to IBM. General Electric was late introducing a new washing machine because production was delayed by a key contractor to which GE had contracted work.[3] Critics note, too, that increasingly fragmented work cultures result from the presence of lower-paid individuals working for contractors who simply get the work done with little enthusiasm or attention to quality.

Demographics and Diversity

The U.S. workforce has been changing dramatically. It is more diverse racially; by 2000, nearly a third of the workforce will be members of racial minority groups. Further, women are in the labor force in much greater numbers than ever before, now composing close to 50% of the workforce. The age distribution has changed as well, and the average age of the workforce is now considerably older than before. In addition, today's employees have different expectations about their roles in the workplace and different work values.

Balancing Work and Family

For many workers in the United States, balancing the demands of family and work is a significant challenge. While this was always a concern in the past, the 1980s saw major growth in the number of working women and dual-career couples. Family composition also is changing in the 1990s.

Family Composition. Just as the workforce and population have become more diverse, so too have the living patterns and household composition of families. According to data from the U.S. Census Bureau, families and households today can be described as follows:

► The number of married couples who are childless or without children living at home exceeds the number of couples with children at home by 3 million.
► 60% of all U.S. households will have no children at home by 2010.
► Dual-career couples compose 58% of all married couples, representing 30.3 million couples.
► Households headed by a single parent make up 27% of all families, with women heading most of these households.
► Single-parent households are less prevalent among whites than among other racial/ethnic groups.
► About two-thirds of all women with children under age six are in the workforce, and 55% of all women with children under age three are working.

▶ Both men and women are marrying at later ages, with the median age of first marriage for men about 27 and for women about 24.

▶ A majority of both men and women aged 18 to 24 still live with their parents or are considered dependents.

These statistics reveal that the traditional pattern (in which the father works, the mother stays home, and there are several children) exists only in some families and in the misperceptions of some managers who think that it is widely prevalent. Actually, the "traditional family" represents only about 10% of modern American households.

Care of Dependents.   To respond to changes in the composition of families, employers are facing growing pressures to provide "family-friendly" policies and benefits. The assistance given by employers ranges from maintaining references on child-care providers to establishing on-site child-care and elder-care facilities. Elder-care benefits are offered by some employers because about one-third of all workers have significant responsibilities for caring for elderly relatives, and these responsibilities can detract from job performance and increase absenteeism. Finally, legislation requiring employers with at least 50 workers to provide up to 12 weeks of unpaid parental/family leave is required by the Family and Medical Leave Act.

Changes in Family and Work Roles.   The decline of the traditional family and the increasing numbers of dual-career couples and working single parents place more stress on employees to balance family and work. For instance, many employees are less willing than in the past to accept relocations and transfers if it means sacrificing family or leisure time. Organizations that do get employees to relocate often must offer employment assistance for spouses. Such assistance can include contacting other employers, providing counseling and assistance in resume development, and hiring employment search firms to assist the relocated spouse. Balancing work and family concerns has particular career implications for women, because they tend to interrupt careers for child rearing more than men do.

▶ HR MANAGEMENT ACTIVITIES

As Figure 1–2 depicts, HR management is composed of several groups of interrelated activities. All managers with HR responsibilities must consider legal, political, economic, social, cultural, and technological forces when addressing these activities. The activities are as follows:

▶ HR planning and analysis
▶ Equal employment opportunity compliance
▶ Staffing
▶ HR development
▶ Compensation and benefits
▶ Employee and labor/management relations

▶ **FIGURE 1-2** **HR Management Activities**

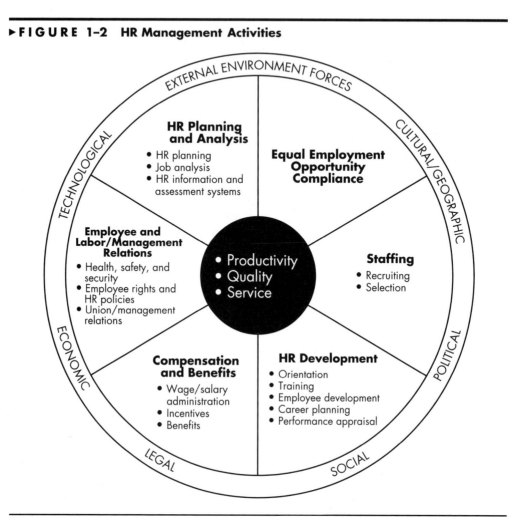

HR Planning and Analysis

HR planning and analysis activities have several facets. Through *HR planning,* managers attempt to anticipate forces that will influence the future supply of and demand for employees. *HR analysis* comprises information, communications, and assessment systems that are vital to the coordination of HR activities.

Equal Employment Opportunity Compliance

Compliance with equal employment opportunity (EEO) laws and regulations affects all other HR activities. For instance, strategic HR plans must ensure sufficient availability of a diversity of individuals to meet *affirmative action* requirements. In addition, when recruiting, selecting, and training individuals, all managers must be aware of EEO requirements.

Staffing

The aim of staffing is to provide an adequate supply of appropriately qualified individuals to fill the jobs in an organization. *Job analysis* is the foundation for the staffing function. From job analysis information, *job descriptions* and *job specifications* can be prepared to *recruit* applicants for job openings. The *selection* process is concerned with choosing the most qualified individuals to fill jobs in the organization.

HR Development

Beginning with the *orientation* of new employees, HR training and development also includes *job-skill training*. As jobs evolve and change, *retraining* is necessary to accommodate technological changes. Encouraging *development* of all employees, including supervisors and managers, is necessary to prepare organizations for future challenges. *Career planning* identifies paths and activities for individual employees as they develop within the organization. Assessing how well employees are doing their jobs is the focus of *performance appraisal.*

Compensation and Benefits

Compensation rewards people for performing organizational work through *pay, incentives,* and *benefits.* Employers must develop and refine their basic *wage and salary* systems. Also, *incentive programs* such as gainsharing and productivity rewards are growing in usage. The rapid increase in the costs of *benefits,* especially health-care benefits, will continue to be a major issue.

Employee and Labor/Management Relations

The relationship between managers and their employees must be handled effectively if both the employees and the organization are to prosper together. Whether or not some of the employees are represented by a union, activities associated with employee *health, safety,* and *security* must be addressed in all organizations. To facilitate good employee relations, *employee rights* must be addressed. It is important to develop, communicate, and update HR *policies and rules* so that managers and employees alike know what is expected. In some organizations, *union/management relations* must be addressed as well.

▶ ORGANIZING THE HR UNIT

HR management as an organizational function traditionally was viewed as a *staff* function. Staff functions provide advisory, control, or support services to the *line* functions. Line functions are those portions of the organization directly concerned with operations resulting in products or services. Line authority gives people the right to make decisions regarding their part of the work flow; however, traditional staff authority only gives people the right to advise the line managers who will make the decisions.

HR Management Costs

As an organization grows, so does the need for establishing an HR department, especially in today's climate of increasing emphasis on human resources. As might be expected, the number of HR-unit employees needed to serve 800 employees is not significantly different from the number needed to serve 2,800 employees. The same activities simply must be provided for more people. Consequently, the cost per employee of having an HR department is greater in organizations with fewer than 250 employees, as Figure 1–3 shows.

Outsourcing HR Activities

In a growing number of organizations, some specialty HR activities are being outsourced to outside providers and consultants. For example, one firm with 1,500 employees has many processing activities related to employee benefits performed by a service bureau instead of hiring two full-time benefits technicians. Portions of HR activities that are most frequently outsourced are:

▶ 401(k) savings plan administration
▶ Employee assistance plans

▶**FIGURE 1–3   Costs of the HR Function**

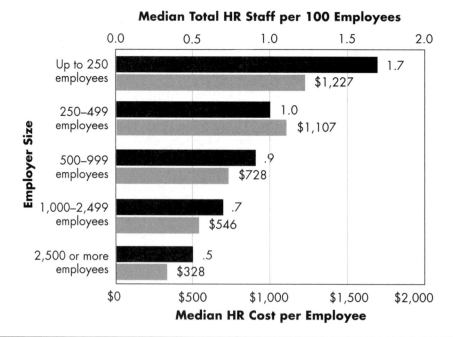

Source: Adapted from *Bulletin to Management (BNA Policy and Practice Series)*, SHRM Survey no. 62, (June 26, 1997):10. Copyright 1997 by The Bureau of National Affairs, Inc. (800-372-1033) <http://www.bna.com>

- ▶ Relocation services
- ▶ Employee benefits administration
- ▶ Management development programs
- ▶ Skills training for employees
- ▶ Payroll administration

▶ ORGANIZATIONAL STRATEGY AND HR PLANNING

Strategic planning must include planning for human resources to carry out the rest of the plan. Figure 1–4 shows the relationship among the variables that ultimately determine the HR plans an organization will develop.

The competitive organizational strategy of the firm as a whole becomes the basis for **human resource (HR) planning,** which is the process of analyzing and identifying the need for and availability of human resources so that the organization can meet its objectives.

Whatever strategy an organization chooses, it must deal with changes in basic relationships within the economy. One such change in today's business environment involves staffing levels during economic downturns and upturns—an area obviously important in HR planning.

At the heart of HR planning is the knowledge gained from scanning the external environment for changes. Scanning especially affects HR planning because each organization must draw from the same labor market that supplies all other employers. Some of the more significant environmental factors are workforce composition and work patterns, government influences, economic conditions, and geographic and competitive concerns.

▶ FIGURE 1–4 Factors That Determine HR Plans

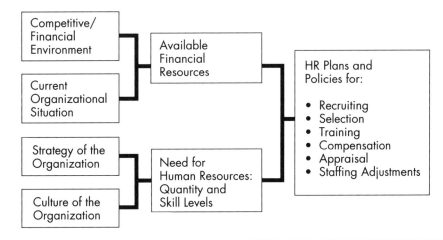

Workforce Composition and Work Patterns

Changes in the composition of the U.S. workforce combine with the use of contingent workers and alternative work schedules to create a workplace very different from that of a generation ago. HR planners need up-to-date information on these changes.

In the past, temporary workers were used for vacation relief, maternity leave, or peaks of workload. Today "contingent workers" (temporary workers, independent contractors, leased employees, and part-timers) represent 20% of the workforce. Many employers operate with a core group of regular employees with critical skills and then expand and contract the workforce through the use of contingent workers.

This practice requires determining staffing needs and deciding in advance which employees or positions should form the "core" and which should be more fluid. At one large firm, about 5% of the workforce is contingent. The company sees contingent employees as a way to stabilize the workforce. Instead of hiring regular workers when work piles up and then firing them when the work is finished, the company relies more on temporary workers and independent contractors. Productivity is measured in the output per hour. Thus, if employees are paid only when they are working (as contingents are), overall productivity increases.

Government Influences

Another major element that affects labor supply is the government. Today, managers are confronted with an expanding and often bewildering array of government rules as regulation of HR activities has steadily increased. As a result, HR planning must be done by individuals who understand the legal requirements of various government regulations.

Economic Conditions

The general business cycle of recessions and booms also affects HR planning. Such factors as interest rates, inflation, and economic growth help determine the availability of workers and figure into organizational plans and objectives. Decisions on wages, overtime, and hiring or laying off workers all hinge on economic conditions.

Geographic and Competitive Concerns

Employers must consider the following geographic and competitive concerns in making HR plans:

▶ Net migration into the area
▶ Other employers in the area
▶ Employee resistance to geographic relocation
▶ Direct competitors in the area
▶ Impact of international competition on the area

▶ INTERNAL ANALYSIS OF JOBS AND PEOPLE

Analyzing the jobs that will need to be done and the skills of people currently available to do them is the next part of HR planning. The needs of the organization must be compared against the labor supply available.

Auditing Jobs

The starting point for evaluating internal strengths and weaknesses is an audit of jobs currently being done in the organization. A comprehensive analysis of all current jobs provides a basis for forecasting what jobs will need to be done in the future. A planner should examine the following questions:

- ▶ What jobs now exist?
- ▶ How many individuals are performing each job?
- ▶ What are the reporting relationships of jobs?
- ▶ How essential is each job?
- ▶ What jobs will be needed to implement the organizational strategy?
- ▶ What are the characteristics of anticipated jobs?

Much of the data to answer these questions should be available from existing organization charts. However, determining how essential each job is may require some judgment on the part of planners.

Auditing Skills

As planners gain an understanding of current jobs and the new jobs that will be necessary to carry out organizational plans, they can make a detailed audit of current employees and their skills. The basic source of data on employees and their skills is the HR records of the organization. Increasingly, employers are making use of a computerized human resource information system (HRIS) to compile such records.

HRIS and Organizational Skills Inventories. Human resource information systems (HRISs) have numerous applications. They are most frequently used for routine and time-consuming tasks such as payroll, record keeping, and benefits administration. By integrating different data bases, HR has been able to add such valuable applications as **skills inventories,** which can be used to identify existing skills throughout the organization. That information can be the basis for determining which additional skills will be needed in the future workforce. Planners can use skills inventories to determine long-range needs for recruiting, selection, and training, as well as the feasibility of making bids for new work.

Content Skills Inventories. In general terms, a skills inventory should consist of:

- ▶ Individual employee demographics (age, length of service in the organization, time in present job)

▶ Individual career progression (jobs held, time in each job, promotions or other job changes, pay rates)
▶ Individual performance data (work accomplishment, growth in skills)

All the information that goes into an employee's skills inventory affects the employee's career. Therefore, the data and their use must meet the same standards of job-relatedness and nondiscrimination as those used when the employee was initially hired. Furthermore, security of such information is important to ensure that sensitive information is available only to those who have specific use for it.

▶ FORECASTING

The information gathered from external environmental scanning and assessment of internal strengths and weaknesses is used to predict or *forecast* HR supply and demand in light of organizational objectives and strategies. **Forecasting** uses information from the past and present to identify expected future conditions. Projections for the future are, of course, subject to error.

HR forecasting should be done over three planning periods: short range, intermediate, and long range. The most commonly used planning period is *short range,* usually a period of six months to one year. This level of planning is routine in many organizations because very few assumptions about the future are necessary for such short-range plans. These short-range forecasts offer the best estimates of the immediate HR needs of an organization. Intermediate and long-range forecasting are much more difficult processes. *Intermediate* plans usually project one to five years into the future, and *long-range* plans extend beyond five years.

Forecasting the Need for Human Resources (Demand)

The main emphasis in HR forecasting to date has been on forecasting organizational need for human resources, or HR demand. Forecasts of demand may be either judgmental or mathematical. However, even the best mathematical methods still require considerable judgmental human input.

The demand for employees can be calculated on an organization-wide basis and/or calculated based on the needs of individual units in the organization. For example, to forecast that the firm needs 125 new employees next year might mean less than to forecast that it needs 25 new people in sales, 45 in production, 20 in accounting, 5 in HR, and 30 in the warehouse. This unit breakdown obviously allows for more consideration of the specific skills needed than the aggregate method does.

Forecasting Availability of Human Resources (Supply)

Not only the need for human resources but also their availability must be identified. Forecasting the availability of human resources considers both *external* and *internal* supplies. Although the internal supply is easier to calculate, it is important to calculate the external supply as well.

The external supply of potential employees available to the organization can be estimated based on the following factors:

- ▶ Net migration into and out of the area
- ▶ Individuals entering and leaving the workforce
- ▶ Individuals graduating from schools and colleges
- ▶ Changing workforce composition and patterns
- ▶ Economic forecasts for the next few years
- ▶ Technological developments and shifts
- ▶ Actions of competing employers
- ▶ Government regulations and pressures
- ▶ Factors affecting persons entering and leaving the workforce

▶ MANAGING A HUMAN RESOURCE SURPLUS

With all the data collected and forecasts done, an organization has the information it needs to develop an HR plan. Such a plan can be extremely sophisticated or rather rudimentary. Regardless of its degree of complexity, the ultimate purpose of the plan is to enable managers in the organization to match the available supply of labor with the forecasted demands in light of the strategies of the firm. If the necessary skill level does not exist in the present workforce, employees may need to be trained in the new skill, or outside recruiting may need to be undertaken. Likewise, if the plan reveals that the firm employs too many people for its needs, workforce reductions may be necessary.

Downsizing

The 1980s saw the introduction of a trend toward downsizing, which has continued through the 1990s. **Downsizing** is reducing the size of an organizational workforce. A wave of merger and acquisition activity in the United States has often left the new, combined companies with redundant departments, plants, and people. Another cause for downsizing is the need to meet foreign competition and cut costs. There are several alternatives to immediate downsizing. Attrition, early retirement buyouts, and layoffs are the ones most frequently used.

Attrition and Hiring Freezes.   *Attrition* occurs when individuals who quit, die, or retire are not replaced. With this approach, no one is cut out of a job, but those who remain must handle the same workload with fewer people. Unless turnover is high, attrition will eliminate only a relatively small number of employees. Therefore, employers may use a method that combines attrition with a freeze on hiring. This method is usually received with better employee understanding than many of the other methods. It is usually the first method used to downsize.[4]

Early Retirement Buyouts.   Early retirement is a means of encouraging more senior workers to leave the organization early. To provide an incentive, employers make additional payments to employees so that they will not be penalized too much economically until their pensions and Social Security benefits take effect.

Such voluntary termination programs, or buyouts, entice employees to quit with financial incentives. They are widely viewed as ways to accomplish workforce reduction without resorting to layoffs and individual firings.

Layoffs.   Layoffs occur when employees are put on unpaid leaves of absence. If business improves for the employer, then employees can be called back to work. Layoffs may be an appropriate downsizing strategy if there is a temporary downturn in an industry. Nevertheless, careful planning of layoffs is essential. Managers must consider the following questions:

▶ How are decisions made about whom to lay off (seniority, performance records)?
▶ How will call-backs be made if all workers cannot be recalled at the same time?
▶ Will any benefits coverage be given workers who are laid off?
▶ If workers take other jobs, do they forfeit their call-back rights?

Companies have no legal obligation to provide a financial cushion to laid-off employees; however, many do. When a provision exists for severance pay, the most common formula is one week's pay for every year of employment. Larger companies tend to be more generous. Loss of medical benefits is a major problem for laid-off employees. But under a federal law (COBRA), displaced workers can retain their medical group coverage for up to 18 months, and up to 36 months for dependents, if they pay the premiums themselves.

Outplacement

Outplacement is a group of services provided to displaced employees to give them support and assistance. It is used most often with those involuntarily removed because of plant closings or elimination of departments. A variety of services may be available to displaced employees. Outplacement services typically include personal career counseling, resume preparation and typing services, interviewing workshops, and referral assistance.

▶ EVALUATING HR PLANNING

HR planning is a critical part of managing human resources in an organization. If it is poorly done, there may be too few people to staff the company or, conversely, massive layoffs may be necessary—with all the attendant problems. If HR planning is done well, the following benefits should result:

▶ Upper management has a better view of the human resource dimensions of business decisions.
▶ HR costs may be less because management can anticipate imbalances before they become unmanageable and expensive.
▶ More time is available to locate talent because needs are anticipated and identified before the actual staffing is required.

▶ Better opportunities exist to include women and minority groups in future growth plans.

▶ Development of managers can be better planned.

To the extent that these results can be measured, they can form the basis for evaluating the success of HR planning. Another approach is to measure projected levels of demand against actual levels at some point in the future. But the most telling evidence of successful HR planning is an organization in which the human resources are consistently aligned with the needs of the business over a period of time.

▶ HR MANAGEMENT AS A CAREER FIELD

A wide variety of jobs can be performed in HR departments. As a firm grows large enough to need someone to focus primarily on HR activities, the role of the **HR generalist** emerges—that is, a person who has responsibility for performing a variety of HR activities. Further growth leads to adding **HR specialists,** who are individuals who have in-depth knowledge and expertise in a limited area. Intensive knowledge of an activity such as benefits, testing, training, or affirmative action compliance typifies the work of HR specialists.

Professional Associations

The broad range of issues faced by HR professionals has made professional involvement important. For HR generalists, the largest organization is the Society for Human Resource Management (SHRM). Public-sector HR professionals tend to be concentrated in the International Personnel Management Association (IPMA). Other major functional specialty HR organizations exist, such as the International Association for Human Resource Information Management (IHRIM), the American Compensation Association (ACA), and the American Society for Training and Development (ASTD). A listing of these associations is shown in Appendix B.

Certification

One of the characteristics of a professional field is having a means to certify the knowledge and competence of members of the profession. The most well-known certification program for HR generalists is administered by the Human Resource Certification Institute (HRCI), which is affiliated with SHRM. Certification by HRCI is available at two levels; both levels have education and experience requirements, as noted in Appendix D. The body of knowledge of the HR field, as used by the HRCI, is contained in Appendix D. This outline reveals the breadth and depth of knowledge necessary for HR professionals. Additionally, those who want to succeed in the field must update their knowledge continually. Reading HR publications, such as those listed in Appendix A, is one way to do this.

Additional certification programs sponsored by other organizations exist for both specialists and generalists. For specialists, the most well-known programs include the following:

▶ Certified Compensation Professional (CCP), sponsored by the American Compensation Association.
▶ Certified Employee Benefits Specialist (CEBS), sponsored by the International Foundation of Employee Benefits Plans.
▶ Certified Benefits Professional, sponsored by the American Compensation Association.
▶ Certified Safety Professional, sponsored by the Board of Certified Safety Professionals.
▶ Occupational Health and Safety Technologist, given by the American Board of Industrial Hygiene and the Board of Certified Safety Professionals.

Regardless of the certification attained, those individuals who are certified demonstrate their professional commitment and competence. Also, certification may enhance job and career prospects.

▶ SUGGESTED READINGS

1. Fitz-Enz, Jac. 1997. *The 8 Practices of Exceptional Companies: How Great Organizations Make the Most of Their Human Assets.* New York: AMACOM.
2. Gardiner, Gareth S. 1996. *21st Century Manager: Meeting the Challenges and Opportunities of the New Corporate Age.* Princeton, NJ: Peterson's/Pacesetter Books.
3. Richards, Dick. 1995. *Artful Work: Awakening Joy, Meaning, and Commitment in the Workplace.* San Francisco: Berrett-Koehler.
4. Ulrich, Dave, Mike R. Losey, and Gerry Lake. 1997. *Tomorrow's H.R. Management: 48 Thought Leaders Call for Change.* New York: John Wiley & Sons.

▶ NOTES

1. "HR Pros Less Worried About Benefits Costs," *Benefits & Compensation Solutions,* September 1995, 47.
2. "Workers See Pain, No Gain in Downsizing," *Omaha World Herald,* December 24, 1995, G1, and Del Jones, "Managers Study Up for Downsizing," *USA Today,* January 19, 1996, 1B.
3. S. E. O'Connell, "Outsourcing: A Technology Based Decision," *HR Magazine,* February 1995, 35, and J. C. Spree, "Addition by Subtraction," *HR Magazine,* March 1995, 38.
4. AMA Survey on Downsizing, 1994 (New York: American Management Association, 1994), 3.

Organizational Success and HR Management Effectiveness

Despite economic statistics and statements from politicians, many employees do not feel that the economy is sound or that they are important to their employers. As organizational mergers, restructuring, and "rightsizing" have spread throughout many industries, more and more employees believe that the loyalty and effort they have shown are not being returned by their employers. Consequently, there is a need to transform the relationships between organizations and individuals.

A recent poll by *Business Week* found that over 75% of the respondents rated large corporations *poor* or *fair* at providing job security and showing loyalty to their employees.[1] Although unemployment in the United States has stayed low, the primary reason is that many "rightsized" employees have taken jobs having lower pay and/or are working in multiple part-time jobs.

Similar problems have been noted in a number of other developed countries, such as Great Britain, France, and Germany. But those countries have many more governmental restrictions on employers eliminating jobs and workers. Therefore, a growing number of European employers have moved jobs to countries where wages and benefits costs are lower and productivity is higher. As a result, in Europe, economic growth has slowed, unemployment has climbed, and many younger workers cannot find jobs.

Downsizing, reengineering, and "delayering" have done recognizable damage to loyalty. The older hierarchical approach offered career progression in a single firm. Job security allowed large firms to demand sacrifices such as moving families regularly. It also allowed the companies to invest in training and development of their employees, confident they would not immediately go to another firm. But it is clear that the "one-company-for-life" attitude that existed during the period from 1950 to 1990 definitely has changed.

▶ THE PSYCHOLOGICAL CONTRACT

The long-term economic health of most organizations depends on the efforts of employees with the appropriate knowledge, skills, and abilities. One concept that has been useful in discussing employees' relationship with the organization is that of a **psychological contract,** which refers to the unwritten expectations that employees and employers have about the nature of their work relationships. Both tangible items (such as wages, benefits, employee productivity, and attendance) and intangible items (such as loyalty, fair treatment, and job security) are encompassed by psychological contracts between employers and employees. Many employers may attempt to detail their expectations through employee handbooks and policy manuals, but those materials are only part of the total "contractual" relationship.

Traditional Psychological Contract

In the "good old days," employees exchanged their efforts and capabilities for a secure job that offered rising wages, comprehensive benefits, and career progression within the organization. But as organizations have downsized and cut workers who have given long and loyal service, a growing number of employees question whether they should be loyal to their employers.

There are two general forces pushing for changes in organizations and hence in the psychological contract in the developed countries, such as the United States, France, Germany, Australia, and Japan. One force is the pressures caused by *globalization* and maintaining international competitiveness. The other force is *technology,* which is driving changes in many industries.

Transforming the Psychological Contract

The transformation in the psychological contract mirrors an evolution in which organizations have moved from employing individuals just to perform tasks, to employing individuals expected to produce results. Rather than just paying them to follow orders and put in time, increasingly employers are expecting employees to utilize their skills and capabilities to accomplish organizational results.

In a competitive environment, many organizations do not succeed over the long term. Those that do succeed need ongoing contributions from the human resources in the organization to become successful and continue their success over time. The remainder of this chapter will utilize the conceptual model shown in Figure 2–1. This model depicts the linkages, beginning with individual and job characteristics, that lead to job satisfaction and organizational commitment. Also, organizational outcomes are affected. The outcomes— productivity, quality, and service—are reflections of the broader goals by which organizational success is measured.

►FIGURE 2-1   Model of Individual/Organizational Performance

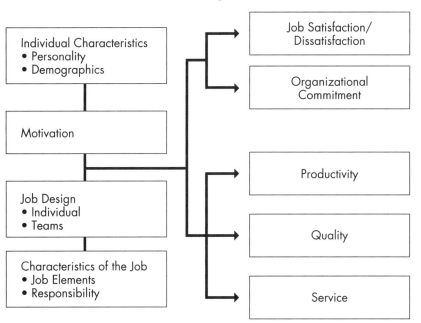

► INDIVIDUALS AND JOBS

The behaviors that employers look for in individuals rest on motivation. **Motivation** is the desire within a person causing that person to act. People usually act for one reason: to reach a goal. Thus, motivation is a goal-directed drive, and as such, it seldom occurs in a void. The words *need, want, desire,* and *drive* are all similar to *motive,* from which the word *motivation* is derived.

Approaches to understanding motivation differ because many individual theorists have developed their own views and theories. They approach motivation from different starting points, with different ideas in mind, and from different backgrounds. No one approach is considered to be the "correct" one. Each has contributed to the understanding of human behavior.

Individual responses to jobs vary. A job may be fascinating to one person but not to someone else. Also, depending on how jobs are designed, they may provide more or less opportunity for employees to satisfy their job-related needs. For example, a sales job may furnish a good opportunity to satisfy social needs, whereas a training assignment may satisfy a person's need to be an expert in a certain area. A job that gives little latitude may not satisfy an individual's need to be creative or innovative. Therefore, managers and employees alike are finding that understanding the characteristics of jobs requires broader perspectives.

Designing or redesigning jobs encompasses many factors. **Job design** refers to organizing tasks, duties, and responsibilities into a productive unit of work. It involves the content of jobs and the effect of jobs on employees. Identifying the components of a given job is an integral part of job design.

Consequences of Job Design

Jobs designed to take advantage of these important job characteristics are more likely to be positively received by employees. Today, more attention is being paid to job design for three major reasons, all of which can reduce turnover and absenteeism and thus costs:

▶ Job design can influence *performance* in certain jobs, especially those where employee motivation can make a substantial difference.
▶ Job design can affect *job satisfaction*. Because people are more satisfied with certain job configurations than with others, it is important to be able to identify what makes a "good" job.
▶ Job design can affect both *physical and mental health*. Problems such as hearing loss, backache, and leg pain sometimes can be traced directly to job design, as can stress and related high blood pressure and heart disease.

Because of the effects of job design on performance, employee satisfaction, health, and many other factors, many organizations are changing or have already changed the design of some jobs.

Alternative Work Schedules and Arrangements

The traditional work schedule, in which employees work full time, 8 hours a day, 5 days a week at the employer's place of operations, is in transition. Organizations have been experimenting with many different possibilities for change: the 4-day, 40-hour week; the 4-day, 32-hour week; the 3-day week; and flexible scheduling. According to the Bureau of Labor Statistics, about 60% of all employers have adopted some flexibility in work schedules and in the location of work. Changes of this nature require some major adjustments for organizations, but in some cases they have been very useful. They allow organizations to make better use of workers by matching work demands to work hours. Workers are helped to balance their work and family responsibilities; ultimately, everyone benefits—the employer, the employee, and society at large.

Flextime.   In a type of schedule redesign called **flextime,** employees work a set number of hours per day but vary starting and ending times. The traditional starting and ending times of the eight-hour work shift can vary up to one or more hours at the beginning and end of the normal workday. Flextime allows management to relax some of the traditional "time clock" control of employees.

Compressed Workweeks.   Another way to change work patterns is with the **compressed workweek,** in which a full week's work is accomplished in fewer than five days. Compression simply alters the number of hours per day per employee, usually resulting in longer working times each day and a decreased number of days worked per week.

Working at Home and Telecommuting.   A growing number of people in the United States do not leave home to go to work. One estimate is that about 40 million U.S. workers work at home on job-related tasks at least part time, including corporate employees working at home after hours. According to some estimates, over 8 million workers earn all of their income at home.

Telecommuting is the process of going to work via electronic computing and telecommunications equipment. Many U.S. employers have telecommuting employees or are experimenting with them, including such firms as American Express, Travelers Insurance, and J.C. Penney Co. Other types of nontraditional work arrangements have been labeled in various ways.

Jobs and Teams

Typically, a job is thought of as something done by one person. However, where it is appropriate, jobs may be designed for teams. In an attempt to make jobs more meaningful and to take advantage of the increased productivity and commitment that can follow, more organizations are using teams of employees instead of individuals for jobs.

Special-Purpose Teams and Quality Circles.   Several types of teams are used in organizations today that function outside the scope of members' normal jobs and meet from time to time. One is the **special-purpose team,** which is formed to address specific problems and may continue to work together to improve work processes or the quality of products and services. Often, these teams are a mixture of employees, supervisors, and managers. Another kind of team is the **quality circle,** a small group of employees who monitor productivity and quality and suggest solutions to problems.

Production Cells.   Another way work is restructured is through the use of production cells. As used in a number of manufacturing operations, **production cells** are groupings of workers who produce entire products or components of products. As many as fifty employees and as few as two can be grouped into a production cell, and each cell has all necessary machines and equipment. The cells ultimately replace the assembly line as the primary means of production.

Self-Directed Work Teams.   The **self-directed work team** is composed of individuals who are assigned a cluster of tasks, duties, and responsibilities to be accomplished. Unlike special-purpose teams, these teams become the regular entities in which team members work.

HR Activities and Teams.   Self-directed work teams are not created easily, nor do they always operate effectively. The greatest problem is that teams may be created for incorrect reasons, such as to follow the latest management fad or because they work well at a competing company. Set up improperly, the teams may not function effectively. Some team members may withdraw or become reluctant to voice dissent, and legitimate concerns may be ignored in the rush to create teams.[2] The following guidelines may be useful for the establishment of teams in an organization.

▶ Match teams with the organizational culture
▶ Train individuals to be on teams
▶ Make compensation team-based

The growing use of teams and other changes in working arrangements are designed to foster greater employee job satisfaction and organizational commitment, which hopefully will lead to enhanced productivity, quality, and service. Job satisfaction and organizational commitment are examined next.

▶ JOB SATISFACTION AND ORGANIZATIONAL COMMITMENT

The characteristics of individuals and jobs interact through the perceptions, expectations, and experiences that people have in organizations. Ultimately, all of those factors affect job satisfaction and the commitment that individuals make to work organizations.

Job Satisfaction

In its most basic sense, **job satisfaction** is a positive emotional state resulting from evaluating one's job experiences. Job *dis*satisfaction occurs when these expectations are not met. For example, if an employee expects clean and safe working conditions on the job, then the employee is likely to be dissatisfied if the workplace is dirty and dangerous.

Job satisfaction has many dimensions. Some include satisfaction with the work itself, wages, recognition, rapport with supervisors and co-workers, and organizational culture and philosophy. Each dimension contributes to an overall feeling of satisfaction with the job itself, but the "job" is defined differently by different people.

There is no simple formula for predicting a worker's satisfaction. Furthermore, the relationship between productivity and job satisfaction is not entirely clear. The critical factor is what employees expect from their jobs and what they are receiving as rewards from their jobs. Although job satisfaction itself is interesting and important, perhaps the "bottom line" is the impact that job satisfaction has on organizational commitment, which affects the ultimate goals of productivity, quality, and service.

Organizational Commitment

If employees are committed to an organization, they are more likely to be more productive. **Organizational commitment** is the degree to which employees believe in and accept organizational goals and desire to remain with the organization. Several types of organizational commitment have been identified.[3]

▶ *Affective commitment:* how strongly the individual identifies with and is involved in the organization
▶ *Continuance commitment:* the perceived consequences of leaving the organization

▶ *Normative commitment:* the responsibility that individuals feel toward the organization and its goals

A logical extension of organizational commitment focuses specifically on continuance commitment factors, which suggest that decisions to remain with or leave an organization ultimately are reflected in employee absenteeism and turnover statistics. Individuals who are not as satisfied with their jobs or who are not as committed to the organization are more likely to withdraw from the organization, either occasionally through absenteeism or permanently through turnover.

▶ ABSENTEEISM

Employees can be absent from work for several reasons. Clearly, some absenteeism is unavoidable. People do get sick and have family issues such as sick children that make it impossible for them to attend work. This is usually referred to as *involuntary* absenteeism. However, much absenteeism is avoidable; it is called *voluntary* absenteeism. Often, a relatively small number of individuals in the workplace are responsible for a disproportionate share of the total absenteeism in an organization.

Measurement of Absenteeism

Controlling or reducing absenteeism must begin with continuous monitoring of the absenteeism statistics in work units. Such monitoring helps managers pinpoint employees who are frequently absent and departments that have excessive absenteeism.

Various methods of measuring or computing absenteeism exist. One formula for computing absenteeism rates, suggested by the U.S. Department of Labor, is as follows:

$$\frac{\text{Number of person-days lost through job absence during period}}{(\text{Average number of employees}) \times (\text{Number of workdays})} \times 100$$

(This rate can be based on number of hours instead of number of days.)

Control of Absenteeism

Controlling voluntary absenteeism is easier if managers understand its causes more clearly. Nevertheless, there are a variety of thoughts about reducing voluntary absenteeism. Organizational policies on absenteeism should be stated clearly in an employee handbook and stressed by supervisors and managers. The policies and rules an organization uses to govern absenteeism may provide a clue to the effectiveness of its control.

Absenteeism control options fall into three categories: (1) discipline, (2) positive reinforcement, and (3) a combination of both. A brief look at each follows.

▶ *Disciplinary approach.* Many employers use a disciplinary approach. People who are absent the first time receive an oral warning, but subsequent absences bring written warnings, suspension, and finally dismissal.

▶ *Positive reinforcement.* Positive reinforcement includes such methods as giving employees cash, recognition, time off, or other rewards for meeting attendance standards. Offering rewards for good attendance, giving bonuses for missing fewer than a certain number of days, and "buying back" unused sick leave are all positive methods of reducing absenteeism.

▶ *Combination approach.* Combination approaches ideally reward desired behaviors and punish undesired behaviors. One of the most effective absenteeism control methods is to provide paid sick-leave banks for employees to use, up to some level. Once that level is exhausted, then the employees may face the loss of some pay if they miss additional work unless they have major illnesses for which long-term disability insurance coverage would begin.

Another method is known as a *"no-fault" absenteeism* policy. Here, the reasons for absences do not matter, but the employees must manage their time rather than having managers make decisions about excused and unexcused absences. Once absenteeism exceeds normal limits, then disciplinary action up to and including termination of employment can occur.

Some firms have extended their policies to provide a *paid time-off (PTO)* program in which vacation time, holidays, and sick leave for each employee are combined into a PTO account. Employees use days from their accounts at their discretion for illness, personal time, or vacation. If employees run out of days in their accounts, then they are not paid for any additional days missed. The PTO programs generally have reduced absenteeism, particularly one-day absences, but overall, time away from work often increases because employees use all of "their" time off by taking unused days as vacation days.

▶ TURNOVER

Turnover occurs when employees leave an organization and have to be replaced. Excessive turnover can be a very costly problem, one with a major impact on productivity.

Turnover often is classified as voluntary or involuntary in nature. *Involuntary turnover* occurs when an employee is fired. *Voluntary turnover* occurs when an employee leaves by his or her own choice and can be caused by many factors. Causes include lack of challenge, better opportunity elsewhere, pay, supervision, geography, and pressure. Certainly, not all turnover is negative. Some workforce losses are quite desirable, especially if those workers who leave are lower-performing, less reliable individuals.

Measurement of Turnover

The turnover rate for an organization can be computed in a number of different ways. The following formula from the U.S. Department of Labor is widely used. (*Separations* are people who left the organization.)

$$\frac{\text{Number of employee separations during the month}}{\text{Total number of employees at midmonth}} \times 100$$

Common turnover figures range from almost zero to over 100% per year, and normal turnover rates vary among industries. Organizations that require entry-level employees to have few skills are likely to have higher turnover rates among those employees than among managerial personnel. As a result, it is important that turnover rates be computed by work units. For instance, one organization had a companywide turnover rate that was not severe—but 80% of the turnover occurred within one department. This imbalance indicated that some action was needed to resolve problems in that unit.

Control of Turnover

Turnover can be controlled in a number of ways. During the *recruiting* process, the job should be outlined and a realistic preview of the job presented, so that the reality of the job matches the expectations of the new employee. A good way to eliminate voluntary turnover is to *improve selection* and to better match applicants to jobs. By fine-tuning the selection process and hiring people who will not have disciplinary problems and low performance, employers can reduce involuntary turnover.

Good *employee orientation* also will help reduce turnover, because new employees are more likely to leave than employees who have been on the job longer. *Compensation* also is important. A fair and equitable pay system can help prevent turnover. *Career planning* and *internal promotion* can help an organization keep employees, because if individuals believe they have no opportunities for career advancement, they may leave the organization.

Finally, voluntary turnover may be linked to personal factors that are not controllable by the organization. This is particularly true with part-time workers. Among the many reasons employees quit that cannot be controlled by the organization are the following: (1) the employee moves out of the geographic area, (2) the employee decides to stay home for family reasons, (3) the employee's spouse is transferred, or (4) a student employee graduates from college.

Even though some turnover is inevitable, organizations must take steps to control turnover, particularly that which is caused by organizational factors such as poor supervising, inadequate training, and inconsistent policies. HR activities should be examined as part of turnover control efforts.

▶ ORGANIZATIONAL PRODUCTIVITY, QUALITY, AND SERVICE

The performance of organizations significantly affects their survival and their growth or decline. In the competitive environment that exists in many industries today, the performance of the organization often is linked to the performance of the human resources in that organization. At the organizational level and even at the national level, productivity is one means of determining competitiveness.

Productivity

Productivity is a measure of the quantity and quality of work done, considering the cost of the resources it took to do the work. It is also useful to view productivity as a ratio between inputs and outputs. This ratio indicates the *value added* by an organization or in an economy.

Global Competitiveness and Productivity.   At the national level, productivity is of concern for several reasons. First, high productivity leads to high standards of living, as symbolized by the greater ability of a country to pay for what its citizens want. Next, increases in national wage levels without increases in national productivity lead to inflation. This means an increase in costs and a decrease in purchasing power. Finally, lower rates of productivity make for higher labor costs and a less competitive position for a nation's products in the world marketplace.

Organizations and Productivity.   Productivity at the level of the organization ultimately affects profitability and competitiveness in a for-profit organization and total costs in a not-for-profit organization. Decisions to close (or open) plants often are the result of productivity concerns.

Perhaps none of the resources for productivity are so closely scrutinized as human resources. Many of the activities undertaken in an HR system deal with individual or organizational productivity. Pay, appraisal systems, training, selection, job design, and incentives are HR issues concerned with productivity very directly.

A useful way to measure organizational HR productivity is by **unit labor cost,** or the total labor cost per unit of output, which is computed by dividing the average wages of workers by their levels of productivity. Using the unit labor cost, it can be seen that a company paying relatively high wages still can be economically competitive if it can also achieve an offsetting high productivity level.

Individual Productivity.   The productivity of an individual depends on: (1) the person's innate *ability (A)* to do the job, (2) the level of *effort (E)* that he or she is willing to exert, and (3) the *support (S)* given that person. The relationship of these factors, widely acknowledged in management literature, is that *performance (P)* is a result of effort times ability times support $(P = E \times A \times S)$. Performance is diminished if *any* of these factors is reduced or absent. HR management has a role in each factor.

Recruiting and selection are directly connected with the first factor, which involves choosing the person with the right talents and interests for a given job. The second factor, the effort expended by an individual, is influenced by many HR issues, such as compensation, incentives, and job design. Organizational support, the third factor, includes training, equipment provided, and knowledge of expectations. HR activities involved here include training and development and performance appraisal.

In summary, productivity is an important means of measuring the performance of national economies, organizations, and individuals. Another important factor affecting organizational competitiveness is quality.

Quality

Quality must be closely tied to productivity. The alternative may be to trade off quality of production for quantity of production. Currently, goods and services produced by some organizations in various nations suffer from an image of poor quality as a result of this very trade-off. As it relates to U.S. organizations, some observers blame the problem on the failure of U.S. manufacturers to make quality a first priority.

Organizations throughout the world are proceeding on the quality front in many different ways, ranging from general training of workers on improving and maintaining quality to better engineering of products prior to manufacturing. One way in which organizations have focused on quality is by using international quality standards.

A set of quality standards called the ISO 9000 standards has been derived by the International Standards Organization in Geneva, Switzerland. These standards cover everything from training to purchasing and are being implemented widely in European countries. Companies that meet the standards are awarded a certificate. The purpose of ISO 9000 certification is to show that an organization has documented its management processes and procedures and has a trained staff so that customers can be confident that organizational goods and services will be consistent in quality.

Total Quality Management (TQM)

Many organizations that have made major improvements in the quality of their operations have recognized that a broad-based quality effort has been needed. **Total Quality Management (TQM)** is a comprehensive management process focusing on the continuous improvement of organizational activities to enhance the quality of the goods and services supplied. TQM programs have become quite popular as organizations strive to improve their productivity and quality.

At the heart of TQM is the concept that it is *customer focused,* which means that every organizational activity should be evaluated and analyzed to determine if it contributes to meeting customers' needs and expectations. Another characteristic of TQM is the importance of *employee involvement.* Often, quality improvement teams or other group efforts are used to ensure that all employees understand the importance of quality and how their efforts affect quality. *Benchmarking* is another facet of TQM, in which quality efforts are measured and compared with measures both for the industry and for other organizations. It is hoped that providing measurement information to quality teams will help to make continuous improvements in quality a part of the organizational culture.

Service

Delivering high-quality customer service is another important outome that affects organizational competitiveness. Service begins with the design of the product or service and ultimately is reflected in customers' satisfaction with the product or service. Consequently, organizations working to enhance their competitiveness must work to enhance service.

Dimensions of Service.   Service is much like beauty: It is difficult to define, but people know it when they see it. The dimensions of service and the relative importance of each dimension are depicted in Figure 2–2.[4] Below, the factors are described briefly in order of importance.

▶**FIGURE 2–2 Dimensions of Customer Service and Relative Importance of Each Dimension**

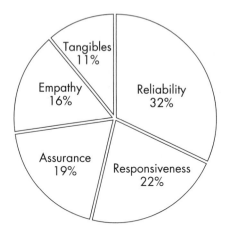

Source: Based on information in L. L. Berry, A. Parasuraman, and V. A. Zeithami, "Improving Service Quality in America: lessons Learned," *Academy of Management Executive,* May 1994, 32–45.

▶ *Reliability.* The product/service performs dependably and accurately, as promised.
▶ *Responsiveness.* The organization provides assistance to customers in a timely manner.
▶ *Assurance.* Knowledgeable employees create trust and confidence in customers.
▶ *Empathy.* Individualized attention is given to customers, which reflects the organizational care and concern about meeting customer expectations.
▶ *Tangibles.* Telecommunications and other equipment is easily used, and the appearance of physical facilities and employees creates positive images.

HR's Role in Service. In many organizations, service quality is affected significantly by the employees who interact with customers. To have human resources who can provide high-quality service, *employee selection* is critical. The individuals who deliver service to customers must have the requisite knowledge, skills, and abilities. Also, a key HR activity is *training.* Once individuals have been selected, they must receive training both in the technical facets of products or services and in providing customer service. Ongoing training in customer service must be provided also.

▶ HR MANAGEMENT EFFECTIVENESS

There is a myth of long standing that one cannot measure what the human resources function does. That myth has hurt HR departments in some cases because it suggests that any value added by HR is somehow mystical or magical. None of that is true, and HR—like marketing, legal, or finance—must be evaluated based on the value it adds to the organization. Defining and measuring HR effectiveness is not as straightforward as it might be in some more easily quantifiable areas, but it can be done.

However, identifying the relevant constituency is somewhat easier where the HR function in an organization is concerned. The other departments, managers, and employees are the main "customers" for HR services. If those services are lacking, too expensive, or of poor quality, then consideration may have to be given to outsourcing some HR activities.

Like other organizations and entities, HR departments must set goals and measure effectiveness. The following general concerns are common to all:

- ▶ Acquiring resources
- ▶ Producing proper outputs
- ▶ Conforming to codes of behavior
- ▶ Performing administrative tasks

- ▶ Using resources efficiently
- ▶ Investing in the organization
- ▶ Satisfying varying interests

The HR department is an organization within an organization. What it does (or does not do) affects the whole system. To function effectively, HR needs a vision as to what it does and whom it serves. That perspective should unify the HR staff and provide a basis for making decisions. HR can position itself as a partner in an organization, but only by demonstrating to the rest of the organization that there are real links between what it does and organizational results.

Human Resource Records

Many organizations, regardless of size, are addressing the need for more detailed and timely data and information on which to base HR decisions and measure effectiveness. Federal, state, and local laws require that organizations keep numerous records on employees. The requirements are so varied that it is difficult to identify exactly what should be kept and for how long. Generally, records relating to employment, work schedules, wages, performance appraisals, merit and seniority systems, and affirmative action programs should be kept by all employers who are subject to provisions of the Fair Labor Standards Act. Other records may be required on issues related to EEO, OSHA, or the Age Discrimination Act. The most commonly required retention time for such records is three years.

The result of all the legal restrictions is that many employers are establishing several separate files on each employee. The following files may be established:

1. Current file containing only the last few years of employee-related information
2. Confidential file containing such items as reference letters and promotability assessments
3. Confidential medical file as required by the ADA
4. Individual personnel file containing older information and nonconfidential, nonmedical benefits documents

One view of HR record-keeping activities is that HR records serve as important documentation should legal challenges occur. Disciplinary actions, past performance appraisals, and other documents may provide the necessary "proof" that employers need to defend their actions as job related and nondiscriminatory. Records and data can also provide a crucial source of information to audit or assess the effectiveness of any unit, and they provide the basis for research into possible causes of HR problems.

Jac Fitz-Enz, who studies HR effectiveness, has suggested some measures to check the effectiveness of the HR function. The measures are shown in Figure 2–3. Note how each requires accurate records and a complete human resource information system.

A problem organizations often face with HR record keeping is the inability to retrieve needed information without major difficulties. A solution is a well-designed resource information system (HRIS).

Human Resource Information System (HRIS)

A **human resource information system (HRIS)** is an integrated system designed to provide information used in HR decision making. Although an HRIS does not have to be computerized, most are.

The first purpose of an HRIS is to improve the efficiency with which data on employees and HR activities is compiled. Many HR activities can be performed more efficiently and with less paperwork if automated. The second purpose of an HRIS is to provide HR information more rapidly and more easily for use by management in making decisions.

HR management has grown in strategic value in many organizations; accordingly, there has been an increased emphasis on obtaining and using HRIS data for strategic planning and human resource forecasting, which focus on broader HR effectiveness over time.

▶**FIGURE 2–3   Possible Measures of HR Effectiveness from HR Records**

- Revenue per employee
- Expense per employee
- Compensation as a percentage of revenue
- Compensation as a percentage of expenses
- HR Department expense as a percentage of company expenses
- HR Department expense per company employee
- Benefits cost as a percentage of compensation
- Retiree benefit cost per retiree

- Cost of hires
- Time to fill jobs
- Workers' compensation cost per employee
- Absence rate
- Turnover rate
- Ratio of job offers to acceptances
- "Customer" satisfaction with HR

Source: Adapted from Jac Fitz-Enz, *How to Measure Human Resources Management* (New York: McGraw-Hill, 1995), 33.

There are many uses for an HRIS in an organization. The most basic use is the automation of payroll and benefits activities. Many other HR activities can be affected by the use of an HRIS, as Figure 2–4 notes.

▶ ASSESSING HR EFFECTIVENESS

This section describes some specific approaches to measuring HR effectiveness. A study of 968 large and medium-sized firms in 35 U.S. industries looked at accounting profits, productivity, employee turnover, and human resource practices. A solid relationship was found between the best HR practices and reduced turnover and increased employee productivity. Further, those practices enhanced profitability and market value of the firms studied. A high-quality, highly motivated workforce is hard for competition to replicate. It is an advantage that improves organizational performance, and it comes from effective HR management.[5]

▶ FIGURE 2–4 Uses of HRIS

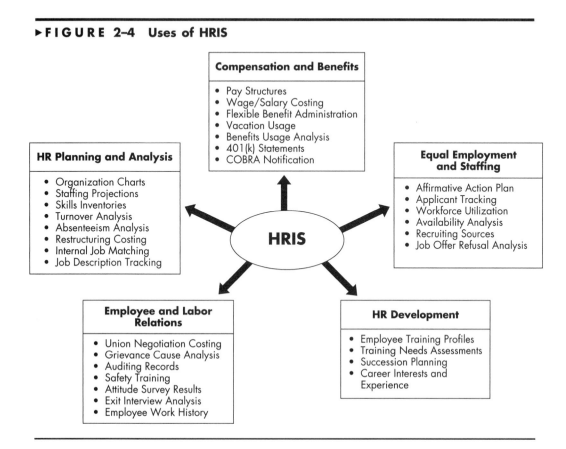

Using HR Research for Assessment

HR research is the analysis of data from HR records to determine the effectiveness of past and present HR practices. Such research data can be used in the following ways:

▶ Monitoring current HR activities
▶ Identifying HR problem areas and possible solutions to these problems
▶ Forecasting trends and their impact on HR management
▶ Evaluating the costs and benefits of HR activities

Conducting research is often crucial to solving HR problems because it is difficult to make good decisions without appropriate information. HR professionals must research and analyze current HR practices to ensure that future HR programs and activities are more effective. Many managers are intimidated by the word *research* and its academic connotations. But research can be quite simple and straightforward, as when an employer uses a questionnaire to ask employees about work scheduling options.

Employee and Attitude Surveys.   One type of research uses questionnaires to give employees opportunities to voice their opinions about specific HR activities. Employee opinion surveys can be used to diagnose specific problem areas, identify employee needs or preferences, and reveal areas in which HR activities are well received or are viewed negatively. New ways to obtain employee survey information include electronic mail (e-mail) surveys and interactive telephone surveys using touch-tone responses.

A special type of research is the **attitude survey,** which focuses on employees' feelings and beliefs about their jobs and the organization. By serving as a sounding board to allow employees to air their feelings about their jobs, their supervisors, their co-workers, and organizational policies and practices, these surveys can be starting points for improving productivity. Some employers conduct attitude surveys on a regularly scheduled basis (such as every year), while others do it intermittently.

Exit Interviews.   A research interview is an alternative to a survey and may focus on a variety of problems. One widely used type of interview is the **exit interview,** in which those who are leaving the organization are asked to identify the reasons for their departure. This information can be used to correct problems so that others will not leave. HR specialists rather than supervisors usually conduct exit interviews, and a skillful interviewer can gain useful information. A wide range of issues can be examined in exit interviews, including reasons for leaving, supervision, pay, training, and the best-liked and least-liked aspects of the job. Exit interviews are usually voluntary for employees who are leaving. Most employers who do exit interviews use standard questions so the information is in a format that allows summarizing and reporting to management for assessment.

Benchmarking for Assessment

One approach to assessing HR effectiveness is **benchmarking,** which compares specific measures of performance against data on those measures in "best practices" organizations. As applied to HR activities, benchmarking comparisons let the HR staff know how their activities and accomplishments compare with those in other organizations. HR benchmarking can lead to:

▶ Identifying areas where performance can be improved
▶ Evaluating HR policies and practices
▶ Comparing practices to "best practices and results"
▶ Setting performance goals to narrow the gap between current practices and best practices

To do benchmarking, planning is required, evaluation methods must be established, best practices must be identified, and changes must be implemented based on the gaps that are identified.

HR Audit

One general means for assessing HR effectiveness is through an HR audit, similar to a financial audit. An **HR audit** is a formal research effort that evaluates the current status of HR management in an organization. Through the development and use of statistical reports and research data, HR audits attempt to evaluate how well HR activities have been performed.

An HR audit begins with a determination by management of the objectives it wants to achieve in the HR area. The audit compares the actual state of HR activities with these objectives, as the sample audit in Figure 2–5 does.

▶**FIGURE 2-5 Sample HR Audit Checklist**

HR Audit

This HR management audit allows you to rate the extent to which an organization has basic HR activities in place and how well they are being performed. In deciding upon your rating, consider also how other managers and employees would rate the activities. The total score provides a guide for actions that will improve HR activities in your organization.

Instructions: For each of the items listed below, rate your organization using the following scale:

VERY GOOD (complete, current, and done well)	3 points
ADEQUATE (needs only some updating)	2 points
WEAK (needs major improvements/changes)	1 point
BASICALLY NONEXISTENT	0 points

I. LEGAL COMPLIANCE

____ **1.** Equal employment opportunity (EEO) requirements
____ **2.** Immigration reform
____ **3.** Health and safety (OSHA)
____ **4.** Wage and hour laws (FLSA)
____ **5.** Employment-at-will statements
____ **6.** Privacy protection
____ **7.** ERISA reporting/compliance
____ **8.** Family/medical leave (FMLA)

II. OBTAINING HUMAN RESOURCES

____ **9.** Current job descriptions and specifications
____ **10.** HR supply-and-demand estimates (for 3 years)
____ **11.** Recruiting process and procedures
____ **12.** Job-related selection interviews
____ **13.** Physical exam procedures

III. MAINTAINING HUMAN RESOURCES

____ **14.** Formal wage/salary system
____ **15.** Current benefits programs/options
____ **16.** Employee recognition programs
____ **17.** Employee handbook/personnel policy manual
____ **18.** Absenteeism and turnover control
____ **19.** Grievance resolution process
____ **20.** HR record-keeping/information systems

IV. DEVELOPING HUMAN RESOURCES

____ **21.** New employee orientation program
____ **22.** Job skills training programs
____ **23.** Employee development programs
____ **24.** Job-related performance appraisal
____ **25.** Appraisal feedback training of managers

____ **TOTAL POINTS**

HR Audit Scoring

Evaluate the score on the HR audit as follows:

60–75 HR activities are complete, effective, and meeting legal compliance requirements.

45–59 HR activities are being performed adequately, but they are not as complete or effective as they should be. Also, it is likely that some potential legal risks exist.

30–44 Major HR problems exist, and significant attention needs to be devoted to adding to and changing the HR activities in the organization.

Below 30 Serious potential legal liabilities exist, and it is likely that significant HR problems are not being addressed.

Source: Developed by Robert L. Mathis, Mathis & Associates, L.L.C., 1429 North 131st Avenue Circle, Omaha, NE 68153. All Rights Reserved. No part of this audit may be reproduced, in any form or by any means, without written permission from Mathis & Associates.

▶ SUGGESTED READINGS

1. Caruso, Lane S. 1996. *Selecting and Managing an Outsourcing Provider.* Scottsdale, AZ: American Compensation Association.
2. George, Stephen. 1997. *Uncommon Sense: Creating Business Excellence in Your Organization.* New York: John Wiley & Sons.
3. Holt, John, Jon Stamell, and Melissa Field. 1996. *Celebrating Your Mistakes.* Burr Ridge, IL: McGraw-Hill/Irwin Professional Publishing.
4. Jeffries, Elizabeth. 1996. *The Heart of Leadership: Influencing by Design.* Dubuque, IA: Kendall-Hunt.
5. Moran, Mark, and Alexander Padro. 1997. *The Internet Answer Book for Human Resource Professionals.* Orange Park, FL: Moran Associates.
6. Pfeffer, Jeffrey. 1998. *Human Equation: Building Profits by Putting People First.* Cambridge, Mass.: Harvard Business School Press.
7. SHRM Issues Management Survey Program. 1997. *SHRM® Work and Family Survey.* Alexandria, VA: Society of Human Resource Management.

▶ NOTES

1. Michael J. Mandel, "Economic Anxiety," *Business Week,* March 11, 1996, 50–56.
2. P. M. Mulvey, J. F. Veiga, and P. M. Elsass, "When Teammates Raise a White Flag," *Academy of Management Executive,* February 1996, 40–49.
3. N. Allen and J. P. Meyer, "Organizational Commitment: Evidence of Career Stage Effects?" *Journal of Business Research* 26 (1993), 49–61.
4. L. L. Berry, A. Parasuraman, and V. A. Zeithami, "Improving Service Quality in America: Lessons Learned," *Academy of Management Executive,* May 1994, 32–45.
5. M. Zigarelli, "Human Resources and the Bottom Line," *Academy of Management Executive,* May 1996, 63.

Equal Employment

The workforce today is composed of individuals of differing races, ages, cultural and geographic origins, abilities and disabilities, and genders. In addition, varied lifestyles, personalities, family arrangements, and other factors affect individual performance. In summary, people do differ from each other; **diversity** recognizes that people have different characteristics. Therefore, the concept of diversity should be viewed broadly, as Figure 3–1 indicates. Any of these factors can create conflict between people at work, which is why organizations have addressed diversity as a strategic human resource issue.

▶ DIVERSITY

Diversity is seen in demographic differences in the workforce. The shifting makeup of the U.S. population accounts for today's increased workforce diversity as many organizations follow projections by the U.S. Labor Department.[1]

Organizations today have been seeing the effects of these trends for several years. A more detailed look at some of the key changes follows.

- ▶ Total workforce growth will be slower between 1996 and 2006 than in previous decades.
- ▶ Only one-third of the entrants to the workforce between 1990 and 2005 will be white males.
- ▶ Women will constitute a greater proportion of the labor force than in the past, and 63% of all U.S. women will be in the workforce by 2005.
- ▶ Minority racial and ethnic groups will account for a growing percentage of the overall labor force. Immigrants will expand this growth.

▶FIGURE 3-1 Dimensions of Diversity

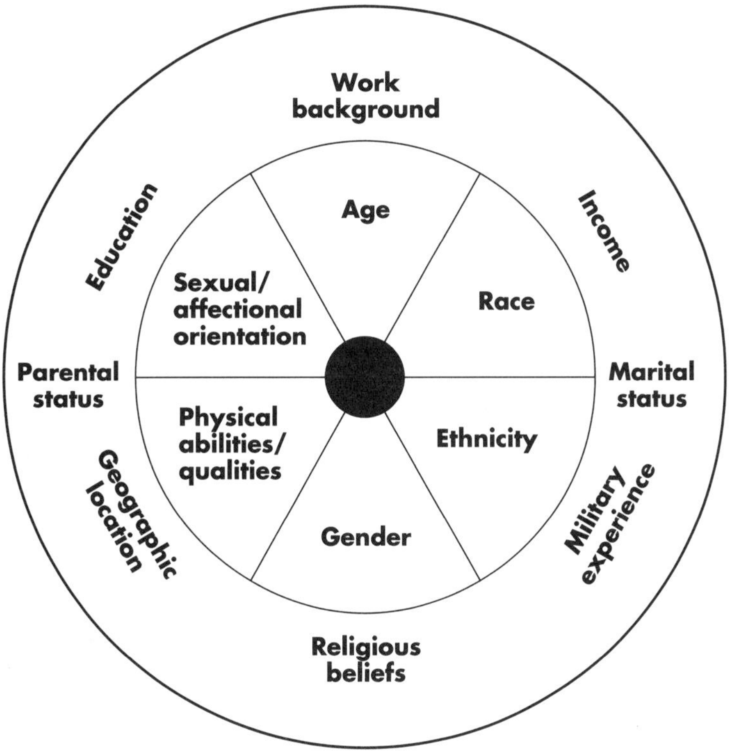

Source: Marilyn Loden and Judy Rosener. *Workforce America! Managing Employee Diversity as a Vital Resource.* Copyright © 1991 by Irwin: Business One. Reprinted with permission of The McGraw-Hill Companies.

▶ The average age of the U.S. population will increase, and more workers who retire from full-time jobs will work part time. The total number of individuals aged 16 to 24 available to enter the workforce will decrease.

▶ As a result of these shifts, employers in a variety of industries will face shortages of qualified workers.

Women in the Workforce

The influx of women into the workforce has major social and economic consequences. From 1970 to 1990, the percentage of women of working age in the workforce rose from 43% to 57%. It is projected that 63% of all women of working age, and over 80% of women from 25 to 40 years old, will be working or looking for work by 2000. This increase will mean that women will make up 47% of the total workforce by 2005. Employers increasingly are having to address such issues as child care and elder care, particularly in light of the Family and Medical Leave Act (FMLA) requirements. In summary, as more women enter the workforce, greater diversity will be found in organizations.

Racial/Ethnic Diversity in the Workforce

The fastest-growing segments of the U.S. population are minority racial and ethnic groups, especially Hispanics, African Americans, and Asian Americans. By 2000, about 30% of the U.S. population will be from such groups. Already, "minority" individuals make up a majority in many cities of at least 100,000 population in California, Texas, and Florida.

Aging of the Workforce

Most of the developed countries are experiencing an aging of their populations-including Australia, Japan, most European countries, and the United States. In the United States, the median age will increase from 31.5 in 1986 to 39 by 2000. This increase is due in part to people living longer and in part to a decrease in the number of children and young adults, particularly in the 16-24 age bracket. Little growth in this "teen" age group is projected until at least 2000.

Individuals with Disabilities in the Workforce

Another group adding diversity to the workforce is composed of individuals with disabilities. With the passage of the Americans with Disabilities Act (ADA) in 1990, employers were reminded of their responsibilities for employing individuals with disabilities. The number of individuals with disabilities is expected to continue growing as the workforce ages. Also, people with AIDS or other life-threatening illnesses are considered disabled, and their numbers are expected to increase.

Individuals with Differing Sexual Orientations

As if demographic diversity did not place enough pressure on managers and organizations, individuals in the workforce today have widely varying lifestyles that can have work-related consequences. A growing number of employers are facing legislative efforts to protect individuals with differing sexual orientations from employment discrimination, though at present only a few cities and states have passed such laws. In addition, there are growing concerns about balancing employee privacy rights with legitimate employer requirements.

Management of Diversity

All of these changes have led organizations and HR professionals to make management of diversity part of their change processes. **Diversity management** is concerned with developing organizational initiatives that value all people equally, regardless of their differences. With the management of diversity at the forefront of HR, organizations have taken various approaches to diversity.

According to Roosevelt Thomas of the American Institute for Managing Diversity, there are three approaches to diversity.[2]

▶ *Traditional.* The traditional approach requires that diverse individuals be assimilated into the workforce by use of affirmative action programs, so that an employee "melting pot" is achieved.

▶ *Understanding*. The objective of understanding diversity is to expand the abilities of employees to understand, accept, and value differences among co-workers.

▶ *Managing*. Management of diversity is a continuing process requiring a variety of proactive efforts by employers, managers, and employees.

By addressing diversity issues and managing them effectively, organizations benefit in various ways. Conflicts within the organization can be ameliorated, better productivity can result, and the organization can be more attractive to potential applicants and current employees.

Figure 3–2 shows that diversity management is the highest level at which organizations have addressed diversity issues. As the figure shows, organizations can also address diversity issues in more restricted ways: equal employment opportunity and affirmative action. These levels are discussed next.

▶ EQUAL EMPLOYMENT OPPORTUNITY

Equal employment opportunity (EEO) is a broad concept holding that individuals should have equal treatment in all employment-related actions. Individuals who are covered under equal employment laws are protected from illegal discrimination, which occurs when individuals having a common characteristic are discriminated against based on that characteristic. Various laws have been passed to protect individuals who share certain characteristics, such as race, age, or gender. Those having the designated characteristics are referred to as a protected class or as members of a protected group. A **protected class** is composed of individuals who fall within a group identified for protection under equal employment laws and regulations. Many of the protected classes historically have been subjected to illegal discrimination. The following bases for protection have been identified by various federal laws:

▶ *Race, ethnic origin, color* (African Americans, Hispanics, Native Americans, Asian Americans)

▶ *Gender* (women, including those who are pregnant)

▶**F I G U R E 3–2 Diversity Management, Equal Employment Opportunity, and Affirmative Action**

▶ *Age* (individuals over 40)
▶ *Individuals with disabilities* (physical or mental)
▶ *Military experience* (Vietnam-era veterans)
▶ *Religion* (special beliefs and practices)

Notice that what the firm is providing is equal employment opportunity for *qualified* individuals to be considered for employment. To remedy areas in which it appears that individuals in protected classes have not had equal employment opportunities, some employers have developed affirmative action policies.

▶ AFFIRMATIVE ACTION

Affirmative action occurs when employers identify problem areas, set goals, and take positive steps to guarantee equal employment opportunities for people in a protected class. Affirmative action focuses on hiring, training, and promoting of protected-class members where they are *underrepresented* in an organization in relation to their availability in the labor markets from which recruiting occurs. Sometimes employers have instituted affirmative action voluntarily, but many times employers have been required to do so because they are government contractors having over 50 employees and over $50,000 in government contracts annually.

When equal employment opportunity regulations are discussed, probably the most volatile issues concern the view that affirmative action leads to *quotas, preferential selection,* and *reverse discrimination.* At the heart of the conflict is the employer's role in selecting, training, and promoting protected-class members when they are underrepresented in various jobs in an organization. Those who are not members of any protected class have claimed that they are being discriminated against in reverse.

Along with the economic restructuring of many organizations has come a growing backlash against affirmative action. As noted, some see it as an unfair quota system rather than sound HR management. Proponents of affirmative action maintain that it is a proactive way for employers to ensure that protected-class members have equal opportunity in all aspects of employment and that it is indeed sound management.

Regardless of the ultimate outcome of the debate on affirmative action, it is critical that employers recognize the diversity of their workforces and that diversity issues be addressed. Many employers have stated that their employees truly are assets and represent human capital that has accumulated value for the organization. As a result, managing diversity effectively and providing equal employment opportunities are elements of good business, resulting in the full use of the talents present in the widely diverse workforce of today.

▶ INTERPRETATIONS OF EEO LAWS AND REGULATIONS

Laws establishing the legal basis for equal employment opportunity generally have been written broadly. Consequently, only through application to specific organizational situations can one see how the laws affect employers.

When Does Illegal Discrimination Occur?

Equal employment laws and regulations address concerns about discrimination in employment practices. The word *discrimination* simply means that differences among items or people are recognized. Thus, discrimination involves choosing among alternatives. For example, employers must discriminate (choose) among applicants for a job on the basis of job requirements and candidates' qualifications. However, discrimination can be illegal in employment-related situations in which either: (1) different standards are used to judge different individuals, or (2) the same standard is used, but it is not related to the individuals' jobs.

When deciding if and when illegal discrimination has occurred, courts and regulatory agencies have had to consider the following issues:

- ▶ Employer intentions
- ▶ Disparate treatment
- ▶ Disparate impact
- ▶ Business necessity and job-relatedness
- ▶ Bona fide occupational qualifications
- ▶ Burden of proof
- ▶ Retaliation

Disparate Treatment.   **Disparate treatment** occurs when protected-class members are treated differently from others. For example, if female applicants must take a special skills test not given to male applicants, then disparate treatment may be occurring. If disparate treatment has occurred, the courts generally have said that intentional discrimination exists.

Disparate Impact.   **Disparate impact** occurs when there is a substantial underrepresentation of protected-class members as a result of employment decisions that work to their disadvantage. The landmark case that established the importance of disparate impact as a legal foundation of EEO law is *Griggs v. Duke Power* (1971).[3]

Business Necessity and Job-Relatedness.   A **business necessity** is a practice necessary for safe and efficient organizational operations. Business necessity has been the subject of numerous court decisions. Educational requirements often are based on business necessity. However, an employer who requires a minimum level of education, such as a high school diploma, must be able to defend the requirement as essential to the performance of the job.

Bona Fide Occupational Qualification (BFOQ).   Title VII of the 1964 Civil Rights Act specifically states that employers may discriminate on the basis of sex, religion, or national origin if the characteristic can be justified as a "bona fide occupational qualification reasonably necessary to the normal operation of the particular business or enterprise."[4] Thus, a **bona fide occupational qualification (BFOQ)** is a legitimate reason why an employer can exclude persons on otherwise illegal bases of consideration. What constitutes a BFOQ has been subject to different interpretations in various courts across the country.

Burden of Proof.   Another legal issue that arises when discrimination is alleged is the determination of which party has the **burden of proof.** At issue is what individuals who are filing suit against employers must prove in order to establish that illegal discrimination has occurred.

Based on the evolution of court decisions, current laws and regulations state that the plaintiff charging discrimination (1) must be a protected-class member and (2) must prove that disparate impact or disparate treatment existed.

Retaliation.   Employers are prohibited by EEO laws from retaliating against individuals who file discrimination charges. **Retaliation** occurs when employers take punitive actions against individuals who exercise their legal rights.

▶ CIVIL RIGHTS ACTS OF 1964 AND 1991

Numerous federal, state, and local laws address equal employment opportunity concerns. This section discusses two major broad-based civil rights acts that encompass many areas. In later sections of this chapter, specific acts and priorities will be discussed.

Civil Rights Act of 1964, Title VII

The Civil Rights Act of 1964 was passed in part to bring about equality in all employment-related decisions. As is often the case, the law contains ambiguous provisions giving considerable leeway to agencies that enforce the law. The Equal Employment Opportunity Commission (EEOC) was established to enforce the provisions of Title VII, the portion of the act that deals with employment.

Title VII, as amended by the Equal Employment Opportunity Act of 1972, covers most employers in the United States. Any organization meeting one of the criteria listed below is subject to rules and regulations that specific government agencies set up to administer the act:

- ▶ All private employers of 15 or more persons who are employed 20 or more weeks per year
- ▶ All educational institutions, public and private
- ▶ State and local governments
- ▶ Public and private employment agencies
- ▶ Labor unions with 15 or more members
- ▶ Joint (labor/management) committees for apprenticeships and training

Civil Rights Act of 1991

The major purpose for the passage of the Civil Rights Act of 1991 was to overturn or modify seven U.S. Supreme Court decisions handed down during the 1988–1990 period. Those decisions made it more difficult for individuals filing discrimination charges to win their cases.

By overturning some U.S. Supreme Court decisions, the 1991 act negated many of the more "employer-friendly" decisions made by the Supreme Court from 1988 to 1990. Allowing jury trials and compensatory and punitive damages in cases involving allegations of intentional discrimination means that the costs of being found guilty of illegal discrimination have increased significantly. The number of EEO complaints filed likely will continue to increase because of some of the provisions of the 1991 act. Consequently, more than ever before, employers must make sure their actions are job related and based on business necessity.

► ENFORCEMENT AGENCIES

Government agencies at several levels have powers to investigate illegal discriminatory practices. At the state and local levels, various commissions have enforcement authority. At the federal level, the two most prominent agencies are the Equal Employment Opportunity Commission (EEOC) and the Office of Federal Contract Compliance Programs (OFCCP).

Equal Employment Opportunity Commission (EEOC)

The EEOC, created by the Civil Rights Act of 1964, is responsible for enforcing the employment-related provisions of the act. The agency initiates investigations, responds to complaints, and develops guidelines to enforce various laws.

Office of Federal Contract Compliance Programs (OFCCP)

While the EEOC is an independent agency, the OFCCP is part of the Department of Labor, established by executive order to ensure that federal contractors and subcontractors have nondiscriminatory practices. A major thrust of OFCCP efforts is to require that federal contractors and subcontractors take affirmative action to overcome the effects of prior discriminatory practices.

State and Local Enforcement Agencies

In addition to federal laws and orders, many states and municipalities have passed their own laws prohibiting discrimination on a variety of bases. Often, these laws are modeled after federal laws; however, state and local laws sometimes provide greater remedies, require different actions, or prohibit discrimination in areas beyond those addressed by federal law. As a result, state and local enforcement bodies have been established to enforce EEO compliance.

► UNIFORM GUIDELINES ON EMPLOYEE SELECTION PROCEDURES

The Uniform Guidelines on Employee Selection Procedures apply to the federal EEOC, the U.S. Department of Labor's OFCCP, the U.S. Department of Justice, and the federal Office of Personnel Management. The guidelines provide a framework used to determine if employers are adhering to federal laws on discrimination. These guidelines affect virtually all phases of HR management because they apply to employment procedures.

No Disparate Impact Approach

Generally, when courts have found discrimination in organizations, the most important issue has concerned the *effect* of employment policies and procedures, regardless of the *intent*. Remember, *disparate impact* occurs whenever there is a substantial underrepresentation of protected-class members in employment decisions. The Uniform Guidelines identify one approach in the following statement: "These guidelines do not require a user to conduct validity studies of selection procedures where no adverse impact results."[5]

Under the guidelines, disparate impact is determined with the **4/5ths rule.** If the selection rate for any protected group is less than 80% (4/5ths) of the selection rate for the majority group or less than 80% of the group's representation in the relevant labor market, discrimination exists. Thus, the guidelines have attempted to define discrimination in statistical terms. Disparate impact can be checked both internally and externally.

Internal.   Checking for disparate impact internally requires that employers compare the treatment received by protected-class members with that received by nonprotected-group members.

HR activities for which internal disparate impact can be checked internally include:

▶ Candidates selected for interviews of those recruited
▶ Performance appraisal ratings as they affect pay increases
▶ Promotions, demotions, and terminations
▶ Pass rates for various selection tests

External.   Employers can check for disparate impact externally by comparing the percentage of employed workers in a protected class in the organization with the percentage of protected-class members in the relevant labor market. The relevant labor market consists of the areas where the firm recruits workers, not just where those employed live. External comparisons can also consider the percentage of protected-class members who are recruited and who apply for jobs to ensure that the employer has drawn a "representative sample" from the relevant labor market. Although employers are not required to maintain exact proportionate equality, they must be "close." Courts have applied statistical analyses to determine if any disparities that exist are too high.

Effect of the No Disparate Impact Strategy.   The 4/5ths rule is a yardstick that employers can use to determine if there is disparate impact on protected-class members. However, to meet the 4/5ths compliance requirement, employers must have no disparate impact at any level or in any job for any protected class. Consequently, using this strategy is not really as easy or risk-free as it may appear. Instead, employers may want to turn to another compliance approach: validating that their employment decisions are based on job-related factors.

Job-Related Validation Approach

Under the job-related validation approach the employment practices that must be valid include such practices and tests as job descriptions, educational requirements, experience requirements, work skills, application forms, interviews, paper-and-pencil tests, and performance appraisals. Hence, the concept of validity affects many of the common tools used to make HR decisions.

Validity is simply the extent to which a test actually measures what it says it measures. The concept relates to inferences made from tests. As applied to employment settings, a test is any employment procedure used as the basis for making an employment-related decision. For a general intelligence test to be valid, it must actually measure intelligence, not just vocabulary. An employment test that is valid must measure the person's ability to perform the job for which he or she is being hired.

The ideal condition for employment-related tests is to be both valid and reliable. **Reliability** refers to the consistency with which a test measures an item. For a test to be reliable, an individual's score should be about the same every time the individual takes that test (allowing for the effects of practice). Unless a test measures a trait consistently (or reliably), it is of little value in predicting job performance.

▶ VALIDITY AND EQUAL EMPLOYMENT

If a charge of discrimination is brought against an employer on the basis of disparate impact, a *prima facie* case has been established. The employer then must be able to demonstrate that its employment procedures are valid, which means to demonstrate that they relate to the job and the requirements of the job. A key element in establishing job-relatedness is to conduct a *job analysis* to identify the *knowledge, skills,* and *abilities (KSAs)* and other characteristics needed to perform a job satisfactorily. A detailed examination of the job provides the foundation for linking the KSAs to job requirements and job performance.

The 1978 uniform selection guidelines recognize two validation strategies:

▶ Content validity
▶ Criterion-related validity (concurrent and predictive)

Content Validity

Content validity is measured when a logical, nonstatistical method is used to identify the KSAs and other characteristics necessary to perform a job. A test is content valid if it reflects an actual sample of the work done on the job in question. For example, an arithmetic test for a retail cashier should contain problems that typically would be faced by cashiers on the job. Content validity is especially useful if the workforce is not large enough to allow other, more statistical approaches.

Criterion-Related Validity

Employment tests of any kind attempt to predict how well an individual will perform on the job. In measuring **criterion-related validity,** a test is the *predictor* and the desired KSAs and measures of job performance are the *criterion variables.* Job analysis determines as exactly as possible what KSAs and behaviors are needed for each task in the job.

There are two different approaches to criterion-related validity. *Concurrent validity* represents an "at-the-same-time" approach, while *predictive validity* represents a "before-the-fact" approach.

When an employer measures **concurrent validity,** a test is given to current employees and the scores are correlated with their performance ratings, determined by such measures as accident rates, absenteeism records, and supervisory performance appraisals. A high correlation suggests that the test can differentiate between the better-performing employees and those with poor performance records.

To measure **predictive validity,** test results of applicants are compared with their subsequent job performance. In the past, predictive validity has been preferred by the EEOC because it is presumed to give the strongest tie to job performance. However, predictive validity requires: (1) a fairly large number of people (usually at least 30) and (2) a time gap between the test and the performance (usually one year). As a result, it is not useful in many situations. Because of these and other problems, other types of validity often are used.

▶ SEX DISCRIMINATION

One of the purposes of this chapter is to discuss the range of issues that have been addressed by EEO laws, regulations, and court decisions. The other purpose is to review what employers should do to comply with the regulations and requirements of various EEO enforcement agencies.

Title VII of the Civil Rights Act of 1964 prohibits discrimination in employment on the basis of sex. Other laws and regulations are aimed at eliminating sex discrimination in specific areas. This section begins with a discussion of sexual harassment and then discusses other forms of sex discrimination.

Sexual Harassment

The EEOC has issued guidelines designed to curtail sexual harassment. A variety of definitions of sexual harassment exist, but generally **sexual harassment** refers to actions that are sexually directed, are unwanted, and subject the worker to adverse employment conditions or create a hostile work environment. Sexual harassment can occur between a boss and a subordinate, among co-workers, and among nonemployees who have business contacts with employees.

Two types of sexual harassment are defined as follows.

▶ *Quid pro quo* harassment occurs when an employer or supervisor links specific employment outcomes to the individual's granting sexual favors.
▶ *Hostile environment* harassment occurs when the harassment has the effect of unreasonably interfering with work performance or psychological well-being or when intimidating or offensive working conditions are created.

Quid pro Quo.   Linking any condition of employment-including pay raises, promotions, assignments of work and work hours, performance appraisals, meetings, disciplinary actions, and many others-to the granting of sexual favors can be the basis for a charge of *quid pro quo* harassment. Certainly, harassment by supervisors and managers who expect sexual favors as a condition for a raise or promotion is inappropriate behavior in a work environment. This view has been supported in a wide variety of cases.

Hostile Environment.   The second type of sexual harassment involves the creation of a hostile work environment. In *Harris v. Forklift Systems,* the U.S. Supreme Court ruled that in determining if a hostile environment exists the following factors should be considered.[6]

▶ Whether the conduct was physically threatening or humiliating, rather than just offensive
▶ Whether the conduct interfered unreasonably with an employee's work performance
▶ Whether the conduct affected the employee's psychological well-being

Numerous cases in which sexual harassment has been found illustrate that what is harmless joking or teasing in the eyes of one person may be offensive and hostile behavior in the eyes of another.

Sexual Harassment Policy.   Every employer should have a policy on sexual harassment. Support for that policy must begin with strong support from top management. The policy should address such issues as the following:

▶ Instructions on how to report complaints, including how to bypass a supervisor if he or she is involved in the harassment
▶ Assurances of confidentiality and protection against retaliation by those against whom the complaint is filed
▶ A guarantee of prompt investigation
▶ A statement that disciplinary action will be taken against sexual harassers up to and including termination of employment

Pregnancy Discrimination

The Pregnancy Discrimination Act (PDA) of 1978 was passed as an amendment to the Civil Rights Act of 1964. Its major provision was that any employer with 15 or more employees had to treat maternity leave the same as other personal or medical leaves. Closely related to the PDA is the Family and Medical Leave Act (FMLA) of 1993, which requires that individuals be given up to 12 weeks of family leave without pay and also requires that those taking family leave be allowed to return to jobs. The FMLA applies to both men and women.

Compensation Issues and Sex Discrimination

A number of concerns have been raised about employer compensation practices that discriminate on the basis of sex. At issue in several compensation practices is the extent to which men and women are treated differently, with women most frequently receiving less compensation or benefits.

Equal Pay. The Equal Pay Act, enacted in 1963, requires employers to pay similar wage rates for similar work without regard to gender. Tasks performed only intermittently or infrequently do not make jobs different enough to justify significantly different wages. Differences in pay may be allowed because of: (1) differences in seniority, (2) differences in performance, (3) differences in quality and/or quantity of production, and (4) factors other than sex, such as skill, effort, and working conditions.

Pay Equity. According to the concept of **pay equity,** the pay for jobs requiring comparable levels of knowledge, skill, and ability should be similar even if actual duties differ significantly. The Equal Pay Act applies to jobs that are substantially the same, whereas pay equity applies to jobs that are *valued* similarly in the organization, whether or not they are the same. A major reason for the development of the pay equity idea is the continuing gap between the earnings of women and men.

Sex Discrimination in Jobs and Careers

The selection or promotion criteria that employers use can discriminate against women. Some cases have found that women were not allowed to enter certain jobs or job fields. Particularly problematic is the use of marital or family status as a basis for not selecting women.

Nepotism. Many employers have policies that restrict or prohibit **nepotism,** the practice of allowing relatives to work for the same employer. Other firms require only that relatives not work directly for or with each other or be placed in a position where potential collusion or conflicts could occur.

The "Glass Ceiling". For years, women's groups have alleged that women encounter a "glass ceiling" in the workplace. The **glass ceiling** refers to discriminatory practices that have prevented women and other protected-class members from advancing to executive-level jobs.

▶ AGE DISCRIMINATION

For many years, race and sex discrimination cases overshadowed age discrimination cases. Starting with passage of the 1978 amendments to the Age Discrimination in Employment Act (ADEA) of 1967, a dramatic increase in age discrimination suits occurred. However, in recent years, age discrimination still has followed race and sex discrimination as the basis for complaints filed with the EEOC.

Age Discrimination in Employment Act (ADEA)

The Age Discrimination in Employment Act (ADEA) of 1967, amended in 1978 and 1986, makes it illegal for an employer to discriminate in compensation, terms, conditions, or privileges of employment because of an individual's age.

The later amendments first raised the minimum mandatory retirement age to 70 and then eliminated it completely. The ADEA applies to all individuals above the age of 40 working for employers having 20 or more workers. However, the act does not apply if age is a job-related occupational qualification.

Prohibitions against age discrimination do not apply when an individual is disciplined or discharged for good cause, such as poor job performance. Older workers who are poor performers can be terminated just as anyone else can be. However, numerous suits under the ADEA have been filed involving workers over 40 who were forced to take "voluntary retirement" when organizational restructuring or workforce reduction programs were implemented.[7]

Older Workers Benefit Protection Act (OWBPA)

The Older Workers Benefit Protection Act (OWBPA) of 1990 was passed to amend the ADEA and to overturn a 1989 decision by the U.S. Supreme Court in *Public Employees Retirement System of Ohio v. Betts.*[8] This act requires equal treatment for older workers in early retirement or severance situations. It sets forth some very specific criteria that must be met when older workers sign waivers promising not to sue for age discrimination.

▶ AMERICANS WITH DISABILITIES ACT (ADA)

The passage of the Americans with Disabilities Act (ADA) in 1990 represented an expansion in the scope and impact of laws and regulations on discrimination against individuals with disabilities. All employers with 15 or more employees are covered by the provisions of the ADA, which are enforced by the EEOC. The ADA was built upon the Vocational Rehabilitation Act of 1973 and the Rehabilitation Act of 1974, both of which applied only to federal contractors.

The ADA affects more than just employment matters, as Figure 3–3 shows, and it applies to private employers, employment agencies, labor unions, and state and local governments. The ADA contains the following requirements regarding employment:

▶ Discrimination is prohibited against individuals with disabilities who can perform the *essential job functions,* a standard that is somewhat vague.
▶ A covered employer must make *reasonable accommodation* for persons with disabilities, so that they can function as employees, unless *undue hardship* would be placed on the employer.
▶ Preemployment medical examinations are prohibited except after an employment offer is made, conditional upon passing a physical examination.
▶ Federal contractors and subcontractors with contracts valued at more than $2,500 must take affirmative action to hire qualified disabled individuals.

As defined by the ADA,[9] a **disabled person** is someone who has a physical or mental impairment that substantially limits that person in some major life activities, who has a record of such an impairment, or who is regarded as having such an impairment.

► **FIGURE 3–3 Major Sections of the Americans with Disabilities Act**

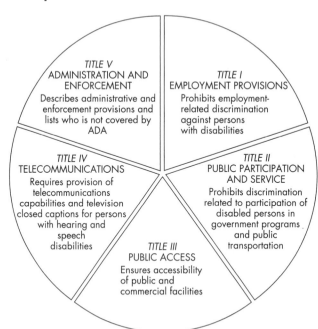

Essential Job Functions

The ADA requires that employers identify for all jobs the **essential job functions**—the fundamental job duties of the employment position that an individual with a disability holds or desires. These functions do not include marginal functions of the position.

Reasonable Accommodation

A **reasonable accommodation** is a modification or adjustment to a job or work environment that enables a qualified individual with a disability to enjoy equal employment opportunity. Employers are required to provide reasonable accommodation for individuals with disabilities to ensure that illegal discrimination does not occur.

Undue Hardship

Reasonable accommodation is restricted to actions that do not place an "undue hardship" on an employer. An action places **undue hardship** on an employer if it poses significant difficulty or expense. The ADA offers only general guidelines on when an accommodation becomes unreasonable and places undue hardship on an employer.

▶ OTHER BASES OF DISCRIMINATION

The original purpose of the Civil Rights Act of 1964 was to address race discrimination. This area continues to be important today, and employers must be aware of practices that may be discriminatory on the basis of race.

Discrimination Based on National Origin and Citizenship

What are the rights of people from other countries, especially those illegally in the United States, with regard to employment and equality? Illegal aliens often are called *undocumented workers* because they do not have the appropriate permits and documents from the Immigration and Naturalization Service. The passage of the Immigration Reform and Control Acts (IRCA) in 1986, 1990, and 1996 clarified issues regarding employment of immigrants that had confronted politicians, labor leaders, and employers for many years.

Immigration Reform and Control Acts (IRCA).   To deal with problems arising from the continued flow of immigrants to the United States, the Immigration Reform and Control Act (IRCA) was passed in 1986 and revised in 1990. The IRCA makes it illegal for an employer to discriminate in recruiting, hiring, or terminating based on an individual's national origin or citizenship.

Under the acts just described, employers are required to examine identification documents for new employees, who also must sign verification forms about their eligibility to work legally in the United States. Employers must ask for proof of identity.

Religious Discrimination

Title VII of the Civil Rights Act identifies discrimination on the basis of religion as illegal. However, religious schools and institutions can use religion as a BFOQ for employment practices on a limited scale.

A major guide in this area was established by the U.S. Supreme Court in *Trans World Airlines v. Hardison*.[10] In that case, the Supreme Court ruled that an employer is required to make *reasonable accommodation* of an employee's religious beliefs.

Sexual Orientation and Gay Rights

Recent battles over revising policies for nonheterosexuals in the U.S. military services illustrate the depth of emotions that accompany discussions of "gay rights." Some states and a number of cities have passed laws prohibiting discrimination based on sexual orientation or lifestyle. However, at the federal level no laws of a similar nature have been passed. Whether gay men and lesbians have rights under the equal protection amendment to the U.S. Constitution has not been decided by the U.S. Supreme Court.

Conviction and Arrest Records

Generally, courts have held that conviction records may be used in determining employability if the offense is job related. For example, a bank could use an applicant's conviction for embezzlement as a valid basis for rejection. Some courts have held that only job-related convictions occurring within the most recent five to seven years may be considered. Consequently, employers inquiring about convictions often add a phrase such as "indication of a conviction will not be an absolute bar to employment."

Veterans' Employment Rights

The employment rights of military veterans and reservists have been addressed several times. The two most important laws are highlighted next.

Vietnam-Era Veterans Readjustment Act of 1974.   Concern about the readjustment and absorption of Vietnam-era veterans into the workforce led to the passage of the Vietnam-Era Veterans Readjustment Act. The act requires that affirmative action in hiring and advancing Vietnam-era veterans be undertaken by federal contractors and subcontractors having contracts of $10,000 or more.

Uniformed Services Employment and Reemployment Rights Act of 1994.   Under the Uniformed Services Employment and Reemployment Rights Act of 1994, employees are required to notify their employers of military service obligations. Employees serving in the military must be provided leaves of absence and have reemployment rights for up to five years. Other provisions protect the right to benefits of employees called to military duty.

▶ EEO COMPLIANCE

Employers must comply with all EEO regulations and guidelines. To do so, managers should be aware of what specific administrative steps are required and how charges of discrimination are investigated.

EEO Records

All employers with 15 or more employees are required to keep certain records that can be requested by the Equal Employment Opportunity Commission (EEOC). If the organization meets certain criteria, then reports and investigations by the Office of Federal Contract Compliance Programs (OFCCP) also must be addressed. Under various laws, employers also are required to post an "officially approved notice" in a prominent place where employees can see it. This notice states that the employer is an equal opportunity employer and does not discriminate.

EEO Records Retention.   All employment records must be maintained as required by the EEOC, and employer information reports must be filed with the federal government. Further, any personnel or employment record made or kept by the employer must be maintained for review by the EEOC.

Preemployment vs. After-Hire Inquiries

Appendix C lists preemployment inquiries and identifies whether they may or may not be discriminatory. Once an employer tells an applicant he or she is hired (the "point of hire"), inquiries that were prohibited earlier may be made. After hiring, medical examination forms, group insurance cards, and other enrollment cards containing inquiries related directly or indirectly to sex, age, or other bases may be requested. Photographs or evidence of race, religion, or national origin also may be requested after hire for legal and necessary purposes, but not before. Such data should be maintained in a separate personnel records system in order to avoid their use in making appraisal, discipline, termination, or promotion decisions.

▶ AFFIRMATIVE ACTION PLANS (AAPS)

Even though affirmative action as a concept has been challenged in court, most federal government contractors still are required to have affirmative action plans (AAPs). Generally, an employer with at least 50 employees and over $50,000 in government contracts must have a formal, written affirmative action plan. A government contractor with fewer than 50 employees and contracts totaling more than $50,000 can be required to have an AAP if it has been found guilty of discrimination by the EEOC or other agencies. The contract size can vary depending on the protected group and the various laws on which the regulations rest.

The contents of an AAP and the policies flowing from it must be available for review by managers and supervisors within the organization. Plans vary in length; some are long and require extensive staff time to prepare.

One of the major sections of an AAP is the **utilization analysis,** which identifies the number of protected-class members employed and the types of jobs they hold. As part of the utilization analysis, an **availability analysis** also must be conducted, identifying the number of protected-class members available to work in the appropriate labor market in given jobs.

The implementation of an AAP must be built on a commitment to affirmative action. The commitment must begin at the top of the organization. A crucial factor is the appointment of an affirmative action officer to monitor the plan.

▶ SUGGESTED READINGS

1. Fried, Barbara. 1994. *Domestic Partner Benefits: A Case Study.* Washington, DC: College & University Personnel Association.
2. Graham, Lawrence Otis. 1997. *Proversity.* New York: John Wiley & Sons.
3. Loverde, Joy. 1997. *The Complete Eldercare Planner: Where to Start, Questions to Ask and How to Find Help.* New York: Hyperion.
4. Thomas, R. Roosevelt, Jr. 1996. *Redefining Diversity.* New York: American Management Association.

▶ NOTES

1. Throughout the following section, various statistics on workforce composition and trends are taken from U.S. Department of Labor, Bureau of Labor Statistics, and Census Bureau data widely reported in various reference and news media reports. For additional details, pertinent issues of the *Monthly Labor Review* can be consulted.

2. R. Roosevelt Thomas, *Beyond Race and Gender: Unleashing the Power of Your Total Workforce by Managing Diversity* (New York: AMACOM, 1991).

3. *Griggs v. Duke Power Co.,* 401 U.S. 424 (1971).

4. Civil Rights Act of 1964, Title VII, Sec. 703e.

5. "Adoption by Four Agencies of Uniform Guidelines on Employee Selection Procedures (1978)," *Federal Register,* August 15, 1978, Part IV, 38295-38309.

6. *Harris v. Forklift Systems, Inc.,* 114 S.Ct. 367 (1993).

7. Cathy Ventrell-Monsees, "The ADEA Backlash," *Textbook Authors Conference Presentation* (Washington, DC: American Association of Retired Persons, 1995), 49–58.

8. *Public Employees Retirement System of Ohio v. Betts,* 109 S.Ct. 256 (1989).

9. All of the definitions used in the discussion of the Americans with Disabilities Act are those contained in the act itself or in the *Technical Assistance Manual* issued by the EEOC.

10. *Trans World Airlines v. Hardison,* 432 U.S. 63 (1977).

4

Job Analysis

The most basic building block of HR management, **job analysis,** is a systematic way to gather and analyze information about the content and human requirements of jobs and the context in which jobs are performed. This information is essential to other HR management activities.

Job analysis identifies what the existing tasks, duties, and responsibilities of a job are. A **task** is a distinct, identifiable work activity composed of motions, whereas a **duty** is a larger work segment composed of several tasks that are performed by an individual. Because both tasks and duties describe activities, it is not always easy or necessary to distinguish between the two. For example, if one of the employment supervisor's duties is to "interview applicants," one task associated with that duty would be "asking questions." **Responsibilities** are obligations to perform certain tasks and duties. Because managerial jobs carry greater responsibilities, they are usually more highly paid.

▶ NATURE OF JOB ANALYSIS

Job analysis usually involves collecting information on the characteristics of a job that differentiate it from other jobs. Information that can be helpful in making the distinction includes the following:

- ▶ Work activities and behaviors
- ▶ Interactions with others
- ▶ Performance standards
- ▶ Machines and equipment used

- ▶ Working conditions
- ▶ Supervision given and received
- ▶ Knowledge, skills, and abilities needed

What Is a Job?

Although the terms *job* and *position* are often used interchangeably, there is a slight difference in emphasis. A **job** is a grouping of common tasks, duties, and responsibilities. A **position** is a job performed by one person. Thus, if there are two persons operating postage meters in a mail room, there are two positions (one for each person) but just one job (postage meter operator).

A **job family** is a grouping of jobs having similar characteristics. There are a variety of ways of identifying and grouping job families. At one insurance company, the HR director decided that jobs requiring specialized technical knowledge, skills, and abilities related to information systems (IS) should be viewed as a separate job family, regardless of the geographic locations of those jobs. Because of the nature of information systems jobs, attracting and retaining IS professionals was difficult, and special compensation programs were needed to match the compensation packages given by competing employers.

Job Analysis and Legal HR Practices

Much current interest in job analysis results from the importance assigned to the activity by federal and state courts. The legal defensibility of an employer's recruiting and selection procedures, performance appraisal system, employee disciplinary actions, and pay practices rests in part on the foundation of job analysis. In a number of court cases, employers have lost because their HR processes and practices were not viewed by judges or juries as sufficiently job related.

Components Developed by Job Analysis

Job analysis provides the information necessary to develop job descriptions and specifications. In most cases, the job description and job specifications are combined into one document that contains several different sections.

Job Descriptions.   A **job description** indicates the tasks, duties, and responsibilities of a job. It identifies what is done, why it is done, where it is done, and, briefly, how it is done. **Performance standards** should flow directly from a job description, telling what the job accomplishes and what performance is considered satisfactory in each area of the job description. Unfortunately, performance standards often are omitted from job descriptions. Even if performance standards have been identified and matched to job descriptions, they may not be known by employees if the job descriptions are not provided to employees but used only as tools by the HR department and managers. Such an approach limits the value of job descriptions.

Job Specifications.   While the job description describes activities to be done in the job, **job specifications** list the knowledge, skills, and abilities (KSAs) an individual needs to perform the job satisfactorily. **Knowledge, skills,**

and **abilities (KSAs)** include education, experience, work skill requirements, personal abilities, and mental and physical requirements. It is important to note that accurate job specifications identify what KSAs a person needs to do the job, not necessarily what qualifications the current employee possesses.

Job Analysis Responsibilities

Most methods of job analysis require that a knowledgeable person describe what goes on in the job or make a series of judgments about specific activities required to do the job. Such information can be provided by the employee doing the job, the supervisor, and/or a trained job analyst.

▶ LEGAL ASPECTS OF JOB ANALYSIS

Permeating the discussion of equal employment laws, regulations, and court cases in the previous chapters is the concept that legal compliance must focus on the jobs that individuals perform. The 1978 Uniform Guidelines on Employee Selection Procedures, discussed in Chapter 3, make it clear that HR requirements must be tied to specific job factors if employers are to defend their actions as job related and a business necessity.

Job Analysis and the Americans with Disabilities Act (ADA)

The passage of the Americans with Disabilities Act (ADA) dramatically increased the legal importance of job analysis, job descriptions, and job specifications. One result of the passage of the ADA is increased emphasis by employers on developing and maintaining current and accurate job descriptions. Also, many employers have had to revise their job specifications to reflect the essential prerequisite KSAs, rather than the "puffed up" ones favored by some managers and employees.

Identification of Essential Functions. The ADA requires that organizations identify the *essential functions* of jobs. Specifically, the ADA indicates that:

> **essential functions** means "the fundamental job duties of the employment position that an individual with the disability holds or desires." The term "essential functions" does not include the marginal functions of the positions.

Evidence that functions are essential may include, but is not limited to, the following:[1]

▶ Employer's judgment about which functions are essential
▶ Job descriptions prepared *before* advertising for or interviewing applicants
▶ Amount of time on the job spent performing the function
▶ Consequences of not requiring the employee to perform the function
▶ Terms of a collective bargaining agreement
▶ Work experience of past incumbents in the job and/or incumbents in similar jobs

Selection and Performance Appraisal. The ADA makes it even more important that selection criteria and performance appraisal standards be clearly job related. Identifying the essential job functions forms the base for:

▶ Developing selection interview questions
▶ Determining what competencies are needed to perform jobs
▶ Developing any selection tests to determine ability to perform essential functions
▶ Identifying performance standards for approving employee performance of the essential functions
▶ Identifying to what extent, if any, job accommodation can be made for a particular individual with a disability
▶ Evaluating whether making such accommodation would be an unreasonable hardship on the employer

Job Analysis and Wage/Hour Regulations

Typically, a job analysis identifies the percentage of time spent on each duty in a job. This information helps determine whether someone should be classified as exempt or nonexempt under the wage/hour laws.

The federal Fair Labor Standards Act (FLSA) and most state wage/hour laws indicate that the percentage of time employees spend on routine, manual, or clerical duties affects whether or not they must be paid overtime for hours over 40 per week. To be exempt from overtime, the employees must perform their *primary duties* as executive, administrative, or professional employees. *Primary* has been interpreted to mean occupying at least 50% of the time. Additionally, the exemption regulations state that no more than 20% (40% in retail settings) of the time can be spent on manual, routine, or clerical duties.

Other legal-compliance efforts, such as those involving workplace safety and health, can be aided through the data provided by job analysis, too. In summary, it is extremely difficult for an employer to have a legal staffing system without performing job analysis. Truly, job analysis is the most basic HR activity.

▶ JOB ANALYSIS AND OTHER HR ACTIVITIES

The completion of job descriptions and job specifications, based on a job analysis, is at the heart of many other HR activities, as Figure 4–1 indicates. But even if legal requirements did not force employers to do job analysis, effective HR management would demand it.

HR Planning

HR planning requires auditing of current jobs. Current job descriptions provide the basic details necessary for this internal assessment, including such items as what jobs, how many jobs and positions currently exist, and what are the reporting relationships of the jobs.

▶**FIGURE 4–1   Job Analysis and Other HR Activities**

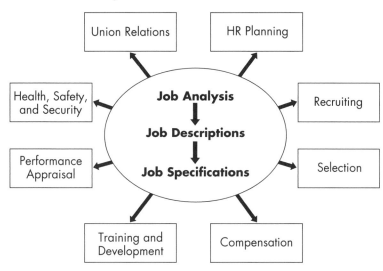

Recruiting and Selection

Organizations use job analysis to identify job specifications in order to plan how and where to obtain employees for anticipated job openings, whether recruited internally or externally. For example, a job analysis in a small manufacturer of electric equipment showed that the Accountant II job, which traditionally had required a college-trained person, really could be handled by someone with high school training in bookkeeping and several years of experience. As a result, the company could select from within and promote a current accounting clerk. In addition to saving on recruiting costs, promotion can have a positive impact on employee commitment and career-planning efforts.

Compensation

Job analysis information is very useful in determining compensation. People should be paid more for doing more difficult jobs. Information from job analysis can be used to give more weight, and therefore more pay, to jobs involving more difficult tasks, duties, and responsibilities. Employees' perceptions of fairness and equity are linked to how the extrinsic rewards they receive compare with those given to others, as well as those they expected for themselves.

Training and Development

By defining what activities a job comprises, a job analysis helps the supervisor explain that job to a new employee. In addition, information from job descriptions and job specifications can help in career planning by showing employees what is expected in jobs that they may choose to move to in the future. Job specification information can point out areas in which employees might need to develop in order to further their careers. Employee development efforts by organizations depend on the job descriptions and job specifications generated from job analyses.

Performance Appraisal

By comparing what an employee is supposed to be doing with what the person actually has done, a supervisor can determine the level of the employee's performance. Many organizations publicly embrace the ideal of "pay for performance," meaning that pay should reflect how well a person is performing a job, not just the level of the job.

Safety and Health

Job analysis information is useful in identifying possible job hazards and working conditions associated with jobs. From the information gathered, managers and HR specialists can work together to identify the health and safety equipment needed, specify work methods, and train workers.

Union Relations

Where workers are represented by a labor union, it is common for job descriptions to be very specific about what tasks are and are not covered in a job. Job analysis information may be needed to determine if the job should be covered by the union agreements. Specifically, management may be able to exclude a supervisory job and its incumbents from the bargaining unit.

▶ JOB ANALYSIS METHODS

Job analysis information can be gathered in a variety of ways. Common methods are observation, interviewing, questionnaires, and computerized methods of analysis. Combinations of these approaches frequently are used, depending on the situation and the organization. Each of these methods is discussed next.

Observation

When the observation method is used, a manager, job analyst, or industrial engineer observes the individual performing the job and takes notes to describe the tasks and duties performed. Observation may be continuous or based on sampling.

Use of the observation method is limited because many jobs do not have complete and easily observed job duties or complete job cycles. Thus, observation may be more useful for repetitive jobs and in conjunction with other methods.

Interviewing

The interview method of gathering information requires that a manager or HR specialist visit each job site and talk with the employees performing each job. A standardized interview form is used most often to record the information. Frequently, both the employee and the employee's supervisor must be interviewed to obtain a complete understanding of the job.

The interview method can be quite time consuming, especially if the interviewer talks with two or three employees doing each job. Professional and managerial jobs often are more complicated to analyze and usually require longer interviews. The interview frequently is used as a follow-up to the questionnaire method, in which the analyst may ask a supervisor or employee to clarify information on the questionnaire. Also, the analyst may be able to get clarification of special terminology used on the questionnaire.

Questionnaires

The typical job questionnaire often includes questions in the following areas:

▶ Duties and percentage of time spent on each
▶ Special duties performed less frequently
▶ External and internal contacts
▶ Work coordination and supervisory responsibilities
▶ Materials and equipment used
▶ Decisions made and discretion exercised
▶ Records and reports prepared
▶ Knowledge, skills, and abilities used
▶ Training needed
▶ Physical activities and characteristics
▶ Working conditions

The major advantage of the questionnaire method is that information on a large number of jobs can be collected inexpensively in a relatively short period of time. However, follow-up observations and discussions often are necessary.

Position Analysis Questionnaire (PAQ).   The PAQ is a specialized questionnaire method incorporating checklists. Each job is analyzed on 27 dimensions composed of 187 elements.

Computerized Job Analysis

A computerized job analysis system often can reduce the time and effort involved in writing job descriptions. These systems have banks of job duty statements that relate to each of the task and scope statements of the questionnaires, and the job questionnaire data is input into the computer using optical scan forms. Then the data from employees are used to generate behaviorally specific job descriptions. These descriptions categorize and identify the relative importance of various job tasks, duties, and responsibilities.

▶ THE JOB ANALYSIS PROCESS

The process of conducting a job analysis must be done in a logical manner that follows appropriate psychometric practices. Therefore, a multistep process usually is followed, regardless of the job analysis methods used. The steps for a typical job analysis are outlined here. The steps used may vary with the methods used and the number of jobs included. However, the basic process is that shown in Figure 4–2.

A. Identify Jobs and Review Existing Documentation

The first step is to identify the jobs under review. For example, are the jobs to be analyzed hourly jobs, clerical jobs, all jobs in one division, or all jobs in the entire organization? Part of the identification phase is to review existing documentation, such as existing job descriptions, organization charts, previous job analysis information, and other industry-related resources. In this phase, those who will be involved in conducting the job analysis and the methods to be used

---

▶FIGURE 4–2 Typical Job Analysis Process

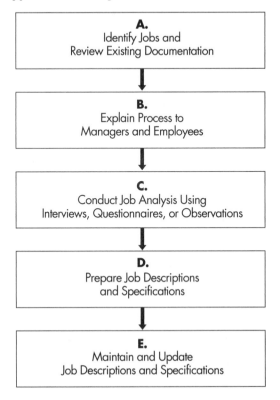

are identified. Also specified is how current incumbents and managers will participate in the process and how many employees' jobs will be considered.

B. *Explain the Process to Managers and Employees*

A crucial step is to explain the process to managers, affected employees, and other concerned people, such as union stewards. Explanations should address the natural concerns and anxieties people have when someone puts their jobs under close scrutiny. Items to be covered often include the purpose of the job analysis, the steps involved, the time schedule, how managers and employees will participate, who is doing the analysis, and whom to contact as questions arise.

C. *Conduct the Job Analysis*

The next step is actually gathering the job analysis information. Questionnaires might be distributed, interviews conducted, and/or observations made. Depending on the methods used, this phase often requires follow-up contacts to remind managers and employees to return questionnaires or to schedule interviews. As the job analysis information is received, analysts review it to ensure its completeness. Additional clarifying information can be gathered, usually through interviews.

D. *Prepare Job Descriptions and Specifications*

All job analysis information must be sorted, sifted, and used in drafting the descriptions and specifications for each job. Usually, the drafts are prepared by members of the HR department. Then they are sent to appropriate managers and employees for review. Following the review, all necessary changes are made, and the final job descriptions and specifications are prepared.

Once job descriptions and specifications have been prepared, managers should provide feedback to current jobholders, especially those who assisted in the job analysis. One feedback technique is to give employees draft copies of their own job descriptions and specifications for review. Giving current employees the opportunity to make corrections, ask for clarification, and discuss their job duties with the appropriate manager or supervisor enhances manager/employee communications. Questions may arise about how work is done, why it is done that way, and how it can be changed. When employees are represented by a union, it is essential that union representatives be included in reviewing the job descriptions and specifications to lessen the possibility of future conflicts.

E. *Maintain and Update Job Descriptions and Specifications*

Once job descriptions and specifications have been completed and reviewed by all appropriate individuals, a system must be developed for keeping them current. Otherwise, the entire process, beginning with job analysis, may have to be repeated in several years. Because organizations are dynamic and evolving entities, rarely do all jobs stay the same for years.

▶ JOB DESCRIPTIONS AND JOB SPECIFICATIONS

The output from analysis of a job is used to develop a job description and job specifications. Together, they summarize job analysis information in a readable fashion and provide the basis for defensible job-related actions. In addition, they serve the individual employees by providing documentation from management that identifies their jobs.

Job Description Components

A typical job description, such as the one in Figure 4–3, contains several major parts. Overviews of the most common ones are presented next.

Identification. The first part of the job description is the identification section, in which the job title, reporting relationships, department, location, and date of analysis may be given. Usually, it is advisable to note other information that is useful in tracking jobs and employees through human resource information systems (HRISs).

Common items noted in the identification section are:

▶ Job number
▶ Pay grade
▶ Fair Labor Standards Act (FLSA) status (exempt/nonexempt)
▶ EEOC Code (from EEO-1 form)

General Summary. The second part, the general summary, is a concise summation of the general responsibilities and components that make the job different from others. One HR specialist has characterized the general summary statement as follows: "In thirty words or less, describe the essence of the job."

Essential Functions and Duties. The third part of the typical job description lists the essential functions and duties. It contains clear and precise statements on the major tasks, duties, and responsibilities performed. Writing this section is the most time-consuming aspect of preparing job descriptions.

Job Specifications. The next portion of the job description gives the qualifications needed to perform the job satisfactorily. The job specifications typically are stated as: (1) knowledge, skills, and abilities (KSAs), (2) education and experience, and (3) physical requirements and/or working conditions. The components of the job specifications provide information necessary to determine what accommodations might and might not be possible under ADA regulations.

Disclaimer and Approvals. The final section on many job descriptions contains approval signatures by appropriate managers and a legal disclaimer. This disclaimer allows employers to change employees' job duties or request employees to perform duties not listed, so that the job description is not viewed as a "contract" between the employer and the employee.

▶**FIGURE 4–3   Job Description and Specifications**

POSITION TITLE: Human Resources Assistant   JOB CODE:
DEPARTMENT: Human Resources   EEOC CLASS: Office and Clerical
REPORTS TO: Human Resources Manager   FLSA STATUS: Nonexempt
PREPARED BY: Deann Mandel

GENERAL SUMMARY:
Assists the Human Resources Director with facilitation and administration of employee benefits, company safety program, governmental compliance, and health and wellness program. Assists the Director with hiring and orientation of new employees and maintains employee files.

ESSENTIAL JOB FUNCTIONS:
1. Assists with human resource functions, including preparing job postings, placing advertisements, conducting job interviews, giving company tours, checking references, and orienting new employees and interns. (25%)
2. Writes internal and external correspondence, including memos, employee notices, and letters, as directed by the Human Resources Director. (20%)
3. Coordinates Occupational Safety and Health Administration (OSHA) compliance and comprehensive safety program, including chairing regular safety committee meetings, performing on-site inspections for regulatory compliance, and conducting employee safety training. (20%)
4. Administers employee benefits, including 401(k) savings, retirement, AFLAC, workers' compensation, and health/dental benefits. Answers questions from employees and investigates claims problems. (20%)
5. Prepares paperwork for termination of employment, including retirement, 401(k) distribution, COBRA benefits, final work hours, and leave benefits due. (6%)
6. Reconciles employee's leaves, such as vacation and sick time, by adjusting information in employee's personnel file. (5%)
7. Coordinates pre-employment drug testing and random drug testing for designated employees. (4%)
8. Performs other related duties as assigned by management.

KNOWLEDGE, SKILLS, AND ABILITIES:
1. Knowledge of company policies, procedures, products, and services.
2. Knowledge of human resource practices and procedures.
3. Knowledge of employment laws, such as the Americans with Disabilities Act, Family Medical Leave Act, Occupational Safety and Health Act, and others.
4. Knowledge of workers' compensation claims administration.
5. Knowledge of health insurance claims administration.
6. Knowledge of basic requirements related to the job, such as RUS requirements, National Electric Code requirements, and OSHA requirements.
7. Skill in analytical thinking and problem solving.
8. Skill in conflict resolution techniques and practices.
9. Skill in written and oral communication.
10. Ability to communicate with co-workers and various business contacts in a courteous and professional manner.

continued on next page

EDUCATION AND EXPERIENCE:
Associate degree in business or related field or equivalent plus two years of experience in human resource management or equivalent experience.

PHYSICAL REQUIREMENTS:	0–24%	25–49%	50–74%	75–100%
Seeing: Must be able to see computer screens, data reports, and other documents.				X
Hearing: Must be able to hear well enough to communicate with co-workers, employees, and customers, attend meetings, and prepare company information.				X
Standing/Walking:	X			
Climbing/Stooping/Kneeling:	X			
Lifting/Pulling/Pushing:	X			
Fingering/Grasping/Feeling: Must be able to write, type, and use phone system.				X

WORKING CONDITIONS:
Normal working conditions with the absence of disagreeable conditions.

Note:
The statements herein are intended to describe the general nature and level of work being performed by employees, and are not to be construed as an exhaustive list of responsibilities, duties, and skills required of personnel so classified. Furthermore, they do not establish a contract for employment and are subject to change at the discretion of the employer.

Preparing Job Descriptions

The ADA focused attention on the importance of well-written job descriptions. Legal compliance requires that they accurately represent the actual jobs.

Writing the General Summary and Essential Function Statements.
Most experienced job analysts have found that it is easier to write the general summary *after* the essential function statements have been completed. Otherwise, there is a tendency for the general summary to be too long.

The general format for an essential function statement is as follows: (1) *action verb*, (2) *to what applied*, (3) *what/how/how often*. There is a real art to writing statements that are sufficiently descriptive without being overly detailed. It is important to use precise action verbs that accurately describe the employee's tasks, duties, and responsibilities.[2] For example, generally it is advisable to avoid the use of vague words such as *maintains, handles,* and *processes.*

The language of the ADA has highlighted the fact that the essential function statements should be organized in the order of importance or "essentiality." Therefore, it is important that job duties be arranged so that the most essential (in terms of criticality and amount of time spent) be listed first and the supportive or marginal ones listed later. The *miscellaneous clause* typically is included to assure some managerial flexibility.

Dictionary of Occupational Titles (DOT). The *Dictionary of Occupational Titles (DOT),*[3] a standardized data source provided by the federal government, is a valuable source of job information, regardless of the job analysis method used. The *DOT* describes a wide range of jobs. A manager of HR specialist confronted with preparing a large number of job descriptions can use the *DOT* as a starting point. The job description from the *DOT* then can be modified to fit the particular organizational situation.

Writing Job Specifications

Job specifications can be developed from a variety of information sources. Obviously, the job analysis process provides a primary starting point. But any KSA included must be based on what is needed to perform a job duty. Furthermore, the job specifications listed should reflect what is necessary for satisfactory job performance, not what the ideal candidate would have.

► SUGGESTED READINGS

1. Arthur, Diane. 1997. *The Complete Human Resources Writing Guide.* New York: AMACOM.
2. Bruce, Stephen D., ed. 1995. *Encyclopedia of Prewritten Job Descriptions.* Madison, CT: Business & Legal Reports, Inc.
3. Thomson, Sue Ellen. 1995. *Encyclopedia of Prewritten Personnel Policies.* Madison, CT: Business & Legal Reports, Inc.

► NOTES

1. "Equal Employment for Individuals with Disabilities," Federal Register 56 (144), 35735.
2. Herbert G. Heneman III and Robert L. Heneman, *Staffing Organizations* (Homewood, IL: Mendota Press, 1994), 148-153.
3. U. S. Department of Labor, *Dictionary of Occupational Titles,* 4th ed., revised (Washington, D.C.: U.S. Government Printing Office, 1991).

5

Staffing

Staffing includes attracting and choosing potential jobholders. First we will consider recruiting. **Recruiting** is the process of generating a pool of qualified applicants for organizational jobs. If the number of available candidates only equals the number of people to be hired, there is no selection-the choice has already been made. The organization must either leave some openings unfilled or take all the candidates. Many employers today are facing shortages of workers with the appropriate knowledge, skills, and abilities.

▶ STRATEGIC APPROACH TO RECRUITING

A strategic approach to recruiting has become more important as competitive pressures have shifted in many industries. Regardless of organizational size, the following decisions about recruiting must be made:

- ▶ How many people does the organization need?
- ▶ What labor markets will be tapped?
- ▶ Should the organization have its own staff or use other sources such as flexible staffing?
- ▶ To what extent should recruiting be focused internally vs. externally?
- ▶ What special skills and experience are *really* necessary?
- ▶ What legal considerations affect recruiting?
- ▶ How can diversity and affirmative action concerns be addressed when recruiting?
- ▶ How will the organization spread its message of openings?
- ▶ How effective are the recruiting efforts?

Recruiting and Labor Markets

Employers compete in a variety of labor markets for employees. **Labor markets** are the external sources from which organizations attract employees. If the organization does not position itself in these markets as a desirable place to work, then its ability to attract and retain employees will be reduced, and its ability to achieve organizational objectives and strategies will be hampered.

There are many ways to identify labor markets, including by geographical area, type of skill, and educational level. Some labor market segments might include managerial, clerical, professional and technical, and blue collar. Classified differently, some markets are local, others regional, others national; and there are international labor markets as well.

Recruiting vs. Flexible Staffing

Increasingly, organizations are examining whether to recruit "employees" or to utilize other staffing arrangements. A growing number of employers have found that the cost of keeping a full-time regular workforce has become excessive and is getting worse because of government-mandated costs. But it is not just the money that is at issue. It is also the number of rules that define the employment relationship, making many employers reluctant to hire new employees even when the economy turns up after a recession. The use of alternative staffing arrangements allows an employer to avoid such issues, as well as the cost of full-time benefits such as vacation pay and pension plans.

Flexible staffing makes use of recruiting sources and workers who are not employees. These arrangements use independent contractors, temporary workers, and employee leasing. A look at each of these kinds of workers and some of the important considerations associated with each type follows.

Independent Contractors. Some firms employ **independent contractors** to perform specific services on a contract basis. However, those contractors must be independent as determined by a 20-item test identified by the U.S. Internal Revenue Service and the U.S. Department of Labor, which is discussed in greater detail in Chapter 8. Independent contractors are used in a number of areas, including building maintenance, security, and advertising/public relations. Estimates are that employers can save up to 40% by using independent contractors because benefits do not have to be provided.

Temporary Workers. Employers who wish to use temporary employees can hire their own temporary staff or use a temporary-worker agency. Such agencies supply workers on a rate-per-day or per-week basis.

The use of temporary workers may make sense for an organization if its work is subject to seasonal or other fluctuations. Hiring regular employees to meet peak employment needs would require that the employer find some tasks to keep employees busy during less active periods or resort to layoffs.

Employee Leasing.   Employee leasing is a concept that has grown rapidly in recent years. The employee leasing process is simple: an employer signs an agreement with an employee leasing company, after which the existing staff is hired by the leasing firm and leased back to the company. For a small fee, a small business owner or operator turns his or her staff over to the leasing company, which then writes the paychecks, pays the taxes, prepares and implements HR policies, and keeps all the required records.

All this service comes at a cost. Leasing companies often charge between 4% and 6% of a monthly salary for their services.

Internal vs. External Recruiting

Both pros and cons are associated with promoting from within (internal source for recruitment) and hiring from outside the organization (external recruitment) to fill openings. Figure 5–1 summarizes some of the most commonly cited advantages and disadvantages of each type of source.

Most organizations combine the use of internal and external methods. Organizations that operate in rapidly changing environments and competitive conditions may need to place a heavier emphasis on external sources as well as developing internal sources. However, for those organizations existing in environments that change slowly, promotion from within may be more suitable.

▶**FIGURE 5–1   Advantages and Disadvantages of Internal and External Sources**

ADVANTAGES	DISADVANTAGES
Internal Sources for Recruiting	
• Morale of promotee • Better assessment of abilities • Lower cost for some jobs • Motivator for good performance • Causes a succession of promotions • Have to hire only at entry level	• Inbreeding • Possible morale problems of those not promoted • "Political" infighting for promotions • Need for management-development program
External Sources for Recruiting	
• "New blood" bringing new perspectives • Cheaper and faster than training professionals • No group of political supporters in organization already	• May bring industry insights • May not select someone who will "fit" the job or organization • May cause morale problems for internal candidates not selected • Longer "adjustment" or orientation time

▶ THE RECRUITING PROCESS

Based upon an *HR plan*, the organization maintains appropriate *recruiting visibility*. The steps in a typical recruitment process are identified in Figure 5–2.

Recruiting and Legal Considerations

Recruiting as a key employment-related activity is subject to a variety of legal considerations. The wide range of equal employment laws and regulations was discussed in previous chapters, but it is useful to highlight their impact on recruiting activities here.

Disparate Impact and Affirmative Action.   One facet of legal compliance in the recruiting process is to ensure that external disparate impact is not occurring. Remember that disparate impact occurs when there is underrepresentation of protected-class members in relation to the labor markets utilized by the employer.

▶ **F I G U R E 5–2   The Recruiting Process**

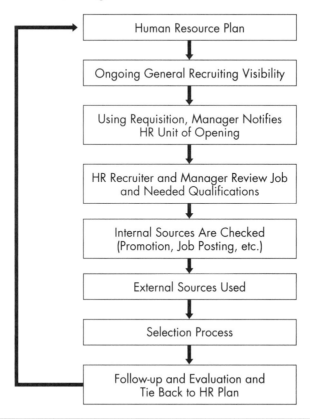

Employment Advertising.   Employers covered by equal employment regulations must take care when preparing the wording for employment advertisements. The Equal Employment Opportunity Commission has issued guidelines stating that no direct or indirect references that have gender or age connotations are permitted.

Additionally, employment advertisements should indicate that the employer has a policy of complying with equal employment regulations. Typically, advertisements should contain a general phrase such as *Equal Opportunity Employer* or more specific designations such as *EEO/M-F/AA/ADA*.

Internal Recruiting Sources

Among internal recruiting sources are present employees, friends of present employees, former employees, and previous applicants. Promotions, demotions, and transfers also can provide additional people for an organizational unit, if not for the entire organization.

Among the ways in which internal recruiting sources have an advantage over external sources is that they allow management to observe the candidate for promotion (or transfer) over a period of time and to evaluate that person's potential and specific job performance. Second, an organization that promotes its own employees to fill job openings may give those employees added motivation to do a good job. Employees may see little reason to do more than just what the current job requires if management's policy is usually to hire externally. This concern is indeed the main reason why an organization generally considers internal sources of qualified applicants first.

Job Posting and Bidding.   The major means for recruiting employees for other jobs within the organization is a job posting system. **Job posting and bidding** is a system in which the employer provides notices of job openings and employees respond by applying for specific openings. The organization can notify employees of all job vacancies by posting notices, circulating publications, or in some other way inviting employees to apply for jobs. In a unionized organization, job posting and bidding can be quite formal; the procedure often is spelled out in the labor agreement. Seniority lists may be used by organizations that make promotions based strictly on seniority, so candidates are considered for promotions in the order of seniority.

Job posting and bidding systems can be ineffective if handled improperly. Jobs generally are posted *before* any external recruiting is done. The organization must allow a reasonable period of time for present employees to check notices of available jobs before it considers external applicants. When employees' bids are turned down, they should have discussions with their supervisors or someone in the HR area regarding the knowledge, skills, and abilities they need in order to improve their opportunities in the future.

External Recruiting Sources

If internal sources do not produce an acceptable candidate, many external sources are available. These sources include schools, colleges and universities, employment agencies, temporary-help firms, labor unions, media sources, and trade and competitive sources.

School Recruiting.   High schools or vocational/technical schools may be a good source of new employees for many organizations. A successful recruiting program with these institutions is the result of careful analysis and continuous contact with the individual schools.

Many schools have a centralized guidance or placement office. Contact can be established and maintained with the supervisors of these offices. Promotional brochures that acquaint students with starting jobs and career opportunities can be distributed to counselors, librarians, or others. Participating in career days and giving tours of the company to school groups are other ways of maintaining good contact with school sources. Cooperative programs in which students work part time and receive some school credits also may be useful in generating qualified applicants for full-time positions.

College Recruiting.   At the college or university level, the recruitment of graduating students is a large-scale operation for many organizations. Most colleges and universities maintain placement offices in which employers and applicants can meet. However, college recruiting presents some interesting and unique problems.

College recruiting can be expensive; therefore, an organization should determine if the positions it is trying to fill really require persons with college degrees. A great many positions do not; yet many employers insist on filling them with college graduates. The result may be employees who must be paid more and who are likely to leave if the jobs are not sufficiently challenging.

Media Sources.   Media sources such as newspapers, magazines, television, radio, and billboards are widely used. When using recruitment advertisements in the media, employers should ask five key questions:

1. What do we want to accomplish?
2. Who are the people we want to reach?
3. What should the advertising message convey?
4. How should the message be presented?
5. In which medium should it run?

Recruiting Evaluation

Evaluating the success of recruiting efforts is important because that is the only way to find out whether the efforts are cost effective in terms of time and money spent. General areas for evaluating recruiting include the following:

▶ *Quantity of applicants.* Because the goal of a good recruiting program is to generate a large pool of applicants from which to choose, quantity is a natural place to begin evaluation. Is it sufficient to fill job vacancies?
▶ *EEO goals met.* The recruiting program is the key activity used to meet goals for hiring protected-class individuals. This is especially relevant when

a company is engaged in affirmative action to meet such goals. Is recruiting providing qualified applicants with an appropriate mix of protected-class individuals?

▶ *Quality of applicants.* In addition to quantity, there is the issue of whether the qualifications of the applicant pool are sufficient to fill the job openings. Do the applicants meet job specifications, and can they perform the jobs?

▶ *Cost per applicant hired.* Cost varies depending on the position being filled, but knowing how much it costs to fill an empty position puts turnover and salary in perspective. The greatest single expense in recruiting is the cost of having a recruiting staff. Is the cost for recruiting employees from any single source excessive?

▶ *Time required to fill openings.* The length of time it takes to fill openings is another means of evaluating recruiting efforts. Are openings filled quickly with qualified candidates, so the work and productivity of the organization are not delayed by vacancies?

HR managers correctly regard recruiting as an important activity. Inability to generate enough or the appropriate type of applicants for jobs can be costly.

In a cost/benefit analysis to evaluate recruiting efforts, costs may include both *direct costs* (advertising, recruiters' salaries, travel, agency fees, telephone) and *indirect costs* (involvement of operating managers, public relations, image). Benefits to consider include the following:

▶ Length of time from contact to hire
▶ Total size of applicant pool
▶ Proportion of acceptances to offers
▶ Percentage of qualified applicants in the pool

In summary, the effectiveness of various recruiting sources will vary depending on the nature of the job being filled and the time available to fill it. But unless calculated, the effectiveness may not be entirely obvious.

▶ NATURE OF SELECTION

Selection is the process of choosing individuals who have relevant qualifications to fill jobs in an organization. The selection process begins when a manager or supervisor needs to hire an individual to fill a certain vacancy. In large organizations, a requisition is sent to the in-house employment office or an HR staff member. A *job description,* based on *job analysis,* identifies the vacancy. A *job specifications* statement, which may also accompany the request, describes the knowledge, skills, and abilities (KSAs) a person needs to fill the vacancy. HR specialists use the job description and specifications to begin the recruiting process. From the pool of applicants generated by recruiting activities, one person is selected to fill the job. In small organizations, the manager often handles the whole process.

More than anything else, selection of human resources should be seen as a *matching process.* Gaps between employment skills and requirements of the job are common factors that lead to rejection of applicants. How well an employee is matched to a job affects the amount and quality of the employee's work. This matching also directly affects training and operating costs. Workers who are unable to produce the expected amount and quality of work can cost an organization a great deal of money and time.

Selection Criteria and Predictors

Because certain KSAs are so important in being able to perform a given job, they become the standards for selection. **Selection criteria** are those standards that are so important that in order to be hired people *must* meet them. They may be identified through a careful job analysis and job description as critical selection criteria. They are attempts to predict the likelihood of successful job behavior by each applicant. For example, in a bookkeeper, the ability to accurately transcribe numerical amounts from receipts and vouchers to a ledger or database is a selection criterion. The ability of applicants to transcribe accurately can be measured with a test of transcription ability before hiring.

▶ THE SELECTION PROCESS

Most organizations take certain common steps to process applicants for jobs. Variations on this basic process depend on organizational size, nature of jobs to be filled, number of people to be selected, and pressure of outside forces such as EEO considerations. Figure 5–3 shows the flow of this process.

Reception

The job applicant's attitudes about the organization, and even about the products or services it offers, will be influenced by the reception stage of the selection process. Whoever meets the applicant initially should be tactful and able to offer assistance in a courteous, friendly manner. If no jobs are available, applicants can be informed at this point. Any employment possibilities must be presented honestly and clearly.

Job Preview/Interest Screen

In some cases, it is appropriate to have a brief interview, called an *initial screening interview* or a *job preview/interest screen,* to see if the applicant is likely to match any jobs available in the organization before the applicant is allowed to fill out an application form. In most large organizations, this initial screening is done by someone in the employment office or in the HR department. In some situations, the applicant may complete an application form before the short interview.

Some employers oversell their jobs in recruiting advertisements, making them appear better than they really are. The purpose of a **realistic job preview (RJP)** is to inform job candidates of the "organizational realities" of a job so that they can more accurately evaluate their own job expectations. By presenting applicants with a clear picture of the job, the organization hopes to reduce unrealistic expectations and thereby reduce employee disenchantment and

---

▶ **FIGURE 5-3 Selection Process Flowchart**

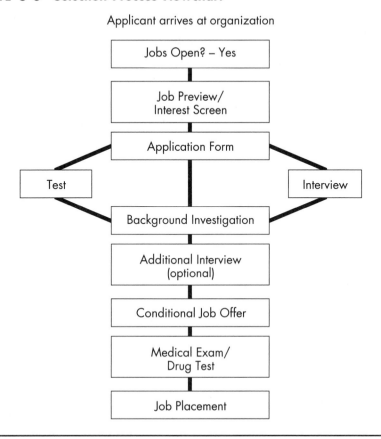

ultimately employee dissatisfaction and turnover. A review of research on RJPs found that they do tend to result in applicants having lower job expectations.[1]

Application Forms

Application forms are widely used. Properly prepared, the application form serves four purposes:

▶ It is a record of the applicant's desire to obtain a position.
▶ It provides the interviewer with a profile of the applicant that can be used in the interview.
▶ It is a basic employee record for applicants who are hired.
▶ It can be used for research on the effectiveness of the selection process.

It is increasing in importance that companies define more carefully exactly who is an *applicant,* given the legal issues involved. If there is no written policy defining conditions that make a person an applicant, any persons who call or send unsolicited resumes might later claim they were not hired because of illegal discrimination. A policy defining *applicant* might include the conditions shown in Figure 5–4.

It is wise for an organization to retain all applications for three years. Applicant flow data should be calculated if the organization has at least 50 employees.

EEO Considerations and Application Forms. Although application forms may not usually be thought of as "tests," the Uniform Guidelines of the EEOC and court decisions define them as employment tests. Consequently, the data requested on application forms must be job related. Illegal questions typically found on application forms ask for the following:

- Marital status
- Height/weight
- Number and ages of dependents

- Information on spouse
- Date of high school graduation
- Contact in case of emergency

Immigration Requirements. The Immigration Reform and Control Act (IRCA) of 1986, as revised in 1990, requires that within 72 hours of hiring, an employer must determine whether a job applicant is a U.S. citizen, registered alien, or illegal alien. Those not eligible to work in this country must not be hired.

Selection Testing

According to the Uniform Guidelines of the EEOC, any employment requirement is a "test." The focus in this section is on formal tests. As Figure 5–5 shows, a variety of types of tests are used. Notice that most of them focus on specific job-related aptitudes and skills. Some are paper-and-pencil tests (such as a math test), others are motor-skill tests, and still others use machines (polygraphs, for instance). Some employers purchase prepared tests, whereas others develop their own.

Many people claim that formal tests can be of great benefit in the selection process when properly used and administered. Considerable evidence supports this claim. Because of EEO concerns, many employers reduced or eliminated the use of tests beginning in the early 1970s, fearing that they might be judged discriminatory in some way. However, test usage appears to be increasing again.

▶**FIGURE 5–4 Employment Application Policies**

- Applications are accepted only when there is an opening.
- Only persons filling out application blanks are considered applicants.
- A person's application ceases to be effective after a certain date.
- Only a certain number of applications will be accepted.
- People must apply for a specific job, not "any job."

▶**FIGURE 5–5   Possible Tests Used for Selection**

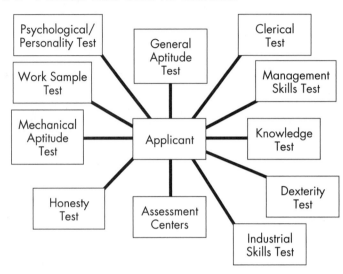

Selection Interviewing

A **selection interview** is designed to assess job-related knowledge, skills, and abilities (KSAs) and clarify information from other sources. This in-depth interview is designed to integrate all the information from application forms, tests, and reference checks so that a selection decision can be made. Because of the integration required and the desirability of face-to-face contact, the interview is the most important phase of the selection process in many situations.

The interview is not an especially valid predictor of job performance, but it has high "face validity"—that is, it *seems* valid to employers. Virtually no employers are likely to hire individuals without interviewing them.

Whether the interview is a valid selection tool depends on whether the interview results are related to the individual's job performance that follows the selection decision. Obviously, accuracy can affect the validity of the interview as a selection tool. The important point to remember is that the validity of the interview depends on the type of interview used and the capabilities of the individual interviewers.

Lawyers recommend the following to minimize EEO concerns with interviewing:

▶ Identify objective criteria related to the job to be looked for in the interview.
▶ Put criteria in writing.
▶ Provide multiple levels of review for difficult or controversial decisions.
▶ Use structured interviews, with the same questions asked of all those interviewed.

Structured Interview. The **structured interview** uses a set of standardized questions that are asked of all applicants. Every applicant is asked the same basic questions so comparisons among applicants can more easily be made. This type of interview allows an interviewer to prepare job-related questions in advance and then complete a standardized interviewee evaluation form.

Completion of such a form provides documentation if anyone, including an EEO enforcement body, should question why one applicant was selected over another.[2] Sample questions that might be asked of all applicants for a production maintenance management opening are:

▶ Tell me how you trained workers for their jobs.
▶ How do you decide the amount of work you and the maintenance crew will have to do during a day?
▶ How does the production schedule of the plant affect what a mechanic ought to repair first?
▶ How do you know what the needs of the plant are at any given time and what mechanics ought to be doing?
▶ How did you or would you go about planning a preventive maintenance program in the plant?

Even though a series of patterned questions is asked, the structured interview does not have to be rigid. The predetermined questions should be asked in a logical manner, but the interviewer can avoid reading the questions word for word down the list. The applicant should be allowed adequate opportunity to explain answers clearly. The interviewer should probe until he or she fully understands the applicant's responses.

Behavioral Description Interview. In a **behavioral description interview**, applicants are required to give specific examples of how they have performed a certain procedure or handled a problem in the past. For example, applicants might be asked the following:

▶ How did you handle a situation in which there were no rules or guidelines on employee discipline?
▶ Why did you choose that approach?
▶ How did your supervisor react?
▶ How was the issue finally resolved?

Like other structured methods, behavioral descriptions provide better validity than unstructured interviews.

Background Investigation

Background investigation may take place either before or after the in-depth interview. It costs the organization some time and money, but it is generally well worth the effort. Unfortunately, applicants frequently misrepresent their qualifications and backgrounds.

Background references can be obtained from several sources. Some of the following references may be more useful and relevant than others, depending on the jobs for which applicants are being considered:

▶ Academic references
▶ Prior work references
▶ Financial references
▶ Law enforcement records
▶ Personal references

Legal Constraints on Background Investigations

Various federal and state laws have been passed to protect the rights of individuals whose backgrounds may be investigated during preemployment screening. States vary in what they allow employers to investigate.

Of the laws passed to protect the privacy of personal information, the most important is the Federal Privacy Act of 1974, which applies primarily to government agencies and units. However, bills to extend the provisions of the Privacy Act to private-sector employers have been introduced in Congress at various times.

In a number of court cases, individuals have sued their former employers for slander, libel, or defamation of character as a result of what the employers said to other potential employers that prevented the individuals from obtaining jobs. Because of such problems, lawyers advise organizations who are asked about former employees to give out only name, employment dates, and title; and many organizations have adopted policies restricting the release of reference information.

The costs of a failure to check references may be high. A number of organizations have found themselves targets of lawsuits that charge them with negligence in hiring workers who committed violent acts on the job. Lawyers say that an employer's liability hinges on how well it investigates an applicant's fitness.

Medical Examinations

The Americans with Disabilities Act (ADA) prohibits a company from rejecting an individual because of a disability and from asking job applicants any question relative to current or past medical history until a conditional job offer is made.

Drug Testing. Drug testing may be a part of a medical exam, or it may be done separately. Using drug testing as a part of the selection process has increased in the past few years, not without controversy. Employers should remember that such tests are not infallible. The accuracy of drug tests varies according to the type of test used, the item tested, and the quality of the laboratory where the test samples are sent. If an individual tests positive for drug use, then a second, more detailed analysis should be administered by an independent medical laboratory. Because of the potential impact of prescription drugs on test results, applicants should complete a detailed questionnaire on this matter before the testing. Whether urine, blood, or hair samples are used, the process of obtaining, labeling, and transferring the samples to the testing lab should be outlined clearly and definite policies and procedures established.

Drug testing also has legal implications. In a number of cases, courts have ruled that individuals with previous substance-abuse problems who have received rehabilitation are disabled and thus covered by the Americans with Disabilities Act. Also, preemployment drug testing must be administered in a nondiscriminatory manner, not used selectively with certain groups. The results of drug tests also must be used consistently, so that all individuals testing positive are treated uniformly. An applicant for a production-worker position who tests positive should be rejected for employment, just as an applicant to be vice-president of marketing would be.

Challenges to drug testing are less likely to succeed in the private sector than in the government sector. The Fourth Amendment (relating to search and seizure) fails as an argument by employees because the government is not involved.[3]

▶ SUGGESTED READINGS

1. Allison, Loren K. 1996. *Employee Selection: A Legal Perspective.* Alexandria, VA: Society of Human Resource Management.

2. Betrus, Michael. 1997. *The Guide to Executive Recruiters.* New York: McGraw-Hill.

3. Hyatt, Carole. 1996. *Lifetime Employability: How to Become Indispensable.* New York: MasterMedia Limited.

4. Orey, Maureen C. 1996. *Successful Staffing in a Diverse Workplace.* Irvine, CA: Richard Chang Associates.

5. Weddle, Peter D. 1995. *Electronic Resumes for the New Job Market Resumes That Work for You 24 Hours A Day.* San Luis Obispo, CA: Impact Publishers.

▶ NOTES

1. Cheryl Adkins, "Previous Work Experience and Organizational Socialization," *Academy of Management Journal,* 20 (1995), 842.

2. S. Motowidlo and J. Burnett, "Sources of Validity in Structured Employment Interviews," *Organizational Behavior and Human Decision Processes,* March 1995, 239–249.

3. M. Harris and L. Heft, "Preemployment Urinalysis Drug Testing," *Human Resource Management Review* 3 (1993), 271–291.

Training and Development

Training is an *investment* in a person. The employer invests money, and the employee invests time (and sometimes money as well). The lower the likelihood of an employee's leaving the company, the higher the returns an employer receives on that investment. An organization can use training to try to overcome deficiencies in employees. Often effective training can produce productivity gains that more than offset the cost of the training. Training is especially important in industries with rapidly changing technologies.

Currently U.S. employers spend $55 billion on training, up from $44 billion in 1990.[1] That is about 1.5% of payroll for organizations with more than 100 employees. Traditionally, about two-thirds of the training expenses have been devoted to developing professional managers and one-third to front-line workers. But that proportion is changing. Organizations are realizing that they need to develop the skills of their front-line workers as much as those of their managers. Currently, in-house training is increasing because of a shortage of skilled workers.[2]

Training is a learning process whereby people acquire skills or knowledge to aid in the achievement of goals. Because learning processes are tied to a variety of organizational purposes, training can be viewed either narrowly or broadly. In a limited sense, training provides employees with specific, identifiable knowledge and skills for use on their present jobs. Sometimes a distinction is drawn between *training* and *development,* with development being broader in scope and focusing on individuals gaining *new* knowledge and skills useful for both present and future jobs.

▶ ORIENTATION: A SPECIAL KIND OF TRAINING

Orientation is the planned introduction of new employees to their jobs, co-workers, and the organization. However, orientation should not be a mechanical one-way process. Because all employees are different, orientation must incorporate a sensitive awareness to the anxieties, uncertainties, and needs of the individual.

Purposes of Orientation

The overall goal of orientation is to help new employees learn about their new work environments and get their performances to acceptable levels as soon as possible. Some benefits of good employee orientation include the following:

- ▶ Stronger loyalty to the organization
- ▶ Greater commitment to organizational values and goals
- ▶ Lower absenteeism
- ▶ Higher job satisfaction
- ▶ Reduction in turnover

Enhancing Interpersonal Acceptance.   Another purpose of orientation is to ease employee entry. New employees often are concerned about meeting the people in their work units. Furthermore, the expectations of the work group do not always parallel those presented at management's formal orientation. Also, if a well-planned formal orientation is lacking, the new employee may be oriented solely by the group, and thus possibly in ways not beneficial to the organization.

Providing New Employees with Needed Information.   The guiding question in the establishment of an orientation system is, "What does the new employee need to know *now*?" Often new employees receive a large amount of information they do not immediately need, and they fail to get the information they really need the first day of a new job.

Some organizations systematize this process by developing an orientation checklist. Figure 6–1 indicates the items to be covered by the HR department representative, the new employee's supervisor, or both. A checklist can ensure that all necessary items have been covered at some point, perhaps during the first week. Many employers have employees sign the checklist to verify that they have been told of pertinent rules and procedures.

Often, employees are asked to sign a form indicating that they have received the handbook and have read it. This requirement gives legal protection to employers who may have to enforce policies and rules later. Employees who have signed forms cannot deny later that they were informed about policies and rules.

▶**FIGURE 6–1** **Orientation Checklist**

Name of Employee _____
Starting Date _____
Department _____
Position _____

- -

HR DEPARTMENT	SUPERVISOR

HR DEPARTMENT

Prior to Orientation
__ Complete Form A and give or mail to new employee
__ Complete Form B
__ Attach Form B to "Orientation Checklist—Supervisor" and give to supervisor

Orientation
Organization and Employee
Policies and Procedures
__ History of XYZ Inc.
__ Organization Chart
__ Purpose of company
__ Employee classifications
Insurance Benefits
__ Group health plan
__ Disability insurance
__ Life insurance
__ Worker compensation
Other Benefits
__ Holidays
__ Vacation
__ Jury and election duty
__ Funeral leave
__ Health services
__ Professional discounts
__ Child care
End of Orientation—First Day
__ Make appointment for second day
__ Introduce supervisor
Other Items
__ Job posting
__ Bulletin board—location/use
__ Safety
__ Alcohol/drug use
__ Where to get supplies
__ Employee's records—updating

_____
Employee Signature

_____
Date

SUPERVISOR

Employee's First Day
__ Introduction to co-workers
__ Tour of department
__ Tour of company
Location of
__ Coat closet
__ Restroom
__ Telephone for personal use and rules concerning it
Working Hours
__ Starting and leaving
__ Lunch
__ Breaks
__ Overtime
__ Early departures
__ Time clock
Pay Policy
__ Pay period
__ Deposit system
Other Items
__ Parking
__ Dress

Employee's Second Day
__ Pension retirement plan
__ Sick leave
__ Personal leave
__ Job posting
__ Confidentiality
__ Complaints and concerns
__ Termination
__ Equal Employment Opportunity

During Employee's First Two Weeks
Emergencies
__ Medical
__ Power failure
__ Fire

At the end of the employee's first two weeks, the supervisor will ask if the employee has any questions concerning any items. After all questions have been discussed, both the employee and the supervisor will sign and date this form and return it to the HR Department.

_____
Orientation Conducted By

▶ NATURE OF TRAINING

Training is designed to help the organization accomplish its objectives. Determining organizational training needs is the diagnostic phase of setting training objectives. Just as a patient must be examined before a physician can prescribe medication to deal with an ailment, an organization or an individual employee must be studied before a course of action can be planned to make the "patient" function better. Managers can identify training needs through three types of analyses:

- ▶ Organizational analyses
- ▶ Task analyses
- ▶ Individual analyses

Setting Training Objectives

Objectives for training should relate to the training needs identified in the needs analysis. The success of the training should be measured in terms of the objectives set. Good objectives are measurable. For example, an objective for a new salesclerk might be to "demonstrate the ability to explain the function of each product in the department within two weeks." This objective serves as a check on internalization, or whether the person really learned.

Objectives for training can be set in any area by using one of the following four dimensions:

- ▶ *Quantity of work* resulting from training (for example, number of words per minute typed or number of applications processed per day)
- ▶ *Quality of work* after training (for example, dollar cost of rework, scrap loss, or errors)
- ▶ *Timeliness of work* after training (for example, schedules met or budget reports turned in on time)
- ▶ *Cost savings* as a result of training (for example, deviation from budget, sales expense, or cost of downtime)

On-the-Job Training

Objectives have been determined, and now actual training can begin. Regardless of whether the training is job specific or broader in nature, the appropriate training approach must be chosen. The most common type of training at all levels in an organization is *on-the-job training (OJT)*. Whether or not the training is planned, people do learn from their job experiences, particularly if these experiences change over time. On-the-job training usually is done by the manager, other employees, or both. A manager or supervisor who trains an employee must be able to teach, as well as to show, the employee what to do.

A special, guided form of OJT is *job instruction training (JIT)*. Developed during World War II, JIT was used to prepare civilians with little experience for jobs in the industrial sector producing military equipment. Because of its success, JIT is still used. In fact, its logical progression of steps is an excellent way to teach trainers to train. Figure 6–2 shows the steps in the JIT process.

▶ **FIGURE 6–2 Job Instruction Training (JIT) Process**

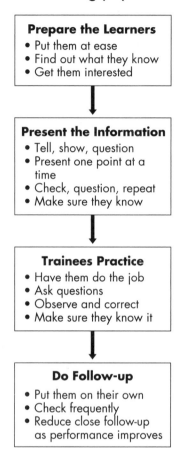

Prepare the Learners
- Put them at ease
- Find out what they know
- Get them interested

Present the Information
- Tell, show, question
- Present one point at a time
- Check, question, repeat
- Make sure they know

Trainees Practice
- Have them do the job
- Ask questions
- Observe and correct
- Make sure they know it

Do Follow-up
- Put them on their own
- Check frequently
- Reduce close follow-up as performance improves

Training Media

Several aids are available to trainers presenting information. Some aids can be used in many settings and with a variety of training methods. The most common ones are computer-assisted instruction and audiovisual aids. Another is distance training and learning using interactive two-way television or computer technology.

Computer-Assisted Instruction. *Computer-assisted instruction (CAI)* allows trainees to learn by interacting with a computer. Application of CAI technology is driven by the need to improve the efficiency or effectiveness of a training situation and to enhance the transfer of learning to improve job performance. Computers lend themselves well to instruction, testing, drill and practice, and application through simulation.

A major advantage of CAI is that it allows self-directed instruction, which many users prefer. Computers used as a training tool allow self-paced approaches and often can be used at the usual place of business. In contrast, instructor-led teaching in a campus-based setting requires employees to spend considerable time away from their jobs.

Audiovisual Aids.   Other technical training aids are audio and visual in nature, including audiotapes and videotapes, films, closed-circuit television, and interactive video teleconferencing. All but interactive video are one-way communications. They may allow the presentation of information that cannot be presented in a classroom. Demonstrations of machines, experiments, and examinations of behavior are examples. Interactive video capability adds audio and video capabilities to CAI, but it uses touch-screen input instead of a keyboard. Audio and visual aids also can be tied into satellite communications systems to convey the same information, such as new product details, to sales personnel in several states.

Distance Training/Learning.   Many colleges and universities are using interactive two-way television to present classes. The medium allows an instructor in one place to see and respond to a "class" in any number of other towns. If a system is fully configured, employees can take courses from anywhere in the world—at their job or home. Colleges are designing courses and even degrees for companies who pay for delivery to their employees using the Internet and other distance learning means.

Evaluation of Training

Evaluation of training compares the post-training results to the objectives expected by managers, trainers, and trainees. Too often, training is done without any thought of measuring and evaluating it later to see how well it worked. Because training is both time-consuming and costly, evaluation should be an integral part of the program.

▶ THE PSYCHOLOGY OF LEARNING

Whatever technology or approach to training is taken will have to fit the way people learn. The discipline of psychology has studied learning for a very long time. Some basic learning principles must be considered in the design of any training program.

Working in organizations is a continual learning process, and learning is at the heart of all training activities. People learn at different rates and are able to apply what they learn differently. *Ability* to learn must be accompanied by motivation, or *intention*, to learn. People are more willing to learn when the material is important to them.

Whole Learning

It is usually better to give trainees an overall view of what they will be doing than to deal immediately with the specifics. This concept is referred to as *whole learning* or *Gestalt learning*. As applied to job training, this means that instructions should be divided into small elements after employees have had an opportunity to see how all the elements fit together.

Reinforcement

The concept of **reinforcement** is based on the *law of effect,* which states that people tend to repeat responses that give them some type of positive reward and avoid actions associated with negative consequences. The rewards (reinforcements) an individual receives can be either external or internal. For example, a registered nurse receives an external reward for learning how to use a new electrocardiograph machine by receiving a certificate of completion. The internal reward may be a feeling of pride in having learned something new. Consider also a machinist who learns to use a new lathe in the machine shop. At first he makes many mistakes. With time and practice he begins to do better and better. One day he knows he has mastered the lathe. His feeling of accomplishment is a type of internal reward.

Immediate Confirmation

Another learning concept is **immediate confirmation:** people learn best if reinforcement is given as soon as possible after training. Feedback on whether a learner's response was right or wrong should be given as soon as possible.

Practice

Learning new skills requires practice. **Active practice** occurs when trainees perform job-related tasks and duties during training. It is more effective than simply reading or passively listening. Once some basic instructions have been given, active practice should be built into every learning situation.

Transfer of Training

Training must be transferred to the job. For effective transfer of training to occur, two conditions must be met:

1. The trainees must be able to take the material learned in training and apply it to the job context in which they work.
2. Use of the learned material must be maintained over time on the job.

Figure 6–3 contrasts development and training.

▶ HUMAN RESOURCE DEVELOPMENT

Development can be thought of as bringing about capacities that go beyond those required by the current job; it represents efforts to improve an employee's ability to handle a variety of assignments. As such, it can benefit both the organization and the individual's career. Employees and managers with appropriate experiences and abilities enhance the ability of an organiza-

▶ **FIGURE 6-3** **Comparison of Training and Development**

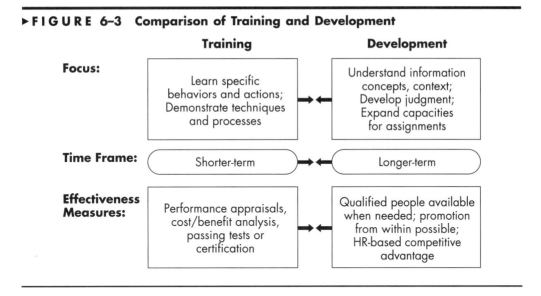

	Training	Development
Focus:	Learn specific behaviors and actions; Demonstrate techniques and processes	Understand information concepts, context; Develop judgment; Expand capacities for assignments
Time Frame:	Shorter-term	Longer-term
Effectiveness Measures:	Performance appraisals, cost/benefit analysis, passing tests or certification	Qualified people available when needed; promotion from within possible; HR-based competitive advantage

tion to compete and adapt to a changing competitive environment. In the development process, the individual's career also gains focus and evolves.

Developing human resources in an organization can help provide a **sustained competitive advantage** as long as three basic requirements are met:

1. The workforce adds positive economic benefits to the production of goods and services.
2. The abilities of the workforce provide an advantage over competitors.
3. Those abilities are not easily duplicated by a competitor.[3]

Employers to some extent face a "make or buy" choice: develop competitive human resources or "buy" them already developed from someone else. Current trends indicate that technical and professional people are hired according to the amount of skill development they have already achieved rather than their ability to learn or their behavioral traits.[4] There is an apparent preference to "buy" rather than "make" scarce employees in today's labor market. However, buying rather than developing human resource capacities does not contribute to the requirements for sustained competitive advantage through human resources noted earlier.

Development should begin with the HR plans of the firm. Such plans deal with analyzing, forecasting, and identifying the organizational HR needs. Development allows anticipation of the movement of people through the organization due to retirement, promotion, and transfers. It helps identify the kinds of abilities that will be needed and the development necessary to have people with those abilities on hand when needed.

Figure 6–4 diagrams the HR development process. As the figure shows, HR plans first identify necessary abilities and capacities. Such capacities can influence planning in return. The specific abilities needed also influence decisions as to who will be promoted and what the succession of leaders will be in the organization. Those decisions both influence and are influenced by an assessment of development needs in the organization. Various approaches to development follow from this needs assessment. Finally, the process must be evaluated and changes made as necessary over time.

Succession Planning

Succession planning can be an important part of development. For example, combined with skills training, management development, and promotion from within, it has been linked to "turning around" a plant acquired by another company. The general result for the plant was a large increase in capacity over four years with virtually no infusion of new managers or employees. Existing talent was developed instead.

▶ **F I G U R E 6–4**　**The HR Development Process**

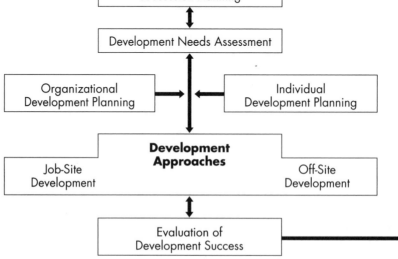
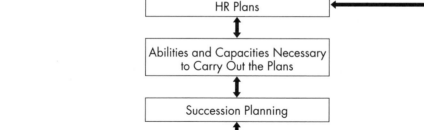

Development Needs Analysis

Either the company or the individual can analyze what a given person needs by way of development. The goal, of course, is to identify strengths and weaknesses. Methods used by organizations to assess development needs include assessment centers, psychological testing, performance appraisals, coaching, and self-assessment.

Assessment Centers. **Assessment centers** are not places as much as they are collections of instruments and exercises designed to diagnose a person's development needs. They are used both for developing and for selecting managers.

Typically, in an assessment-center experience, a potential manager spends two or three days away from the job performing many activities. These activities may include role playing, pencil-and-paper tests, case studies, leaderless group discussions, management games, peer evaluations, and in-basket exercises, in which the trainee handles typical problems coming across a manager's desk. For the most part, the exercises are samples of managerial situations that require the use of managerial skills and behaviors. During the exercises, participants are observed by several specially trained judges.

Psychological Testing. Psychological pencil-and-paper tests have been used for several years to determine employees' developmental potential and needs. Intelligence tests, verbal and mathematical reasoning tests, and personality tests are often used. Such testing can furnish useful information to employers about such factors as motivation, reasoning abilities, leadership styles, interpersonal response traits, and job preferences.

Performance Appraisals. Well-done performance appraisals can be a source of development information. Performance data on productivity, employee relations, job knowledge, and other relevant dimensions can be measured this way.

Coaching. The oldest on-the-job development technique is **coaching,** which is the daily training and feedback given to employees by immediate supervisors. Coaching involves a continual process of learning by doing. For effective coaching, a healthy and open relationship must exist between employees and their supervisors or managers. Many firms conduct formal training courses to improve the coaching skills of their managers.

Self-Assessment. In deciding which approaches to development hold most promise in a particular case, both an organizational plan for a person and the person's plans must receive consideration. Individuals may do some *self-assessment* as part of the process. Many tests, workshops, and books are available to assist in self-assessment.

Managerial Modeling

A common adage in management development says managers tend to manage as they were managed. Another way of saying this is that managers learn by

behavior modeling, or copying someone else's behavior. Management development efforts can take advantage of natural human behavior by matching young or developing managers with appropriate models and then reinforcing the desirable behaviors exhibited.

It is important to note that modeling is not a straightforward imitation, or copying, process; it is considerably more complex. For example, one can learn what *not* to do by observing a model. Thus, exposure to both positive and negative models can be beneficial to a new manager.

Mentoring

Mentoring is a relationship in which managers at the midpoints in their careers aid individuals in the first stages of their careers. Technical, interpersonal, and political skills can be conveyed in such a relationship from the more experienced to the less experienced person. Not only does the less experienced one benefit, but the more experienced one may enjoy the challenge of sharing his or her wisdom.

Problems with HR Development Efforts

Development efforts are subject to certain common mistakes and problems. Most of the problems result from inadequate planning and a lack of coordination of HR development efforts. Common problems include the following:

- ▶ Inadequate needs analysis
- ▶ Trying out fad programs or training methods
- ▶ Abdicating responsibility for development to staff
- ▶ Trying to substitute training for selection
- ▶ Lack of training among those who lead the development activities
- ▶ Using only "courses" as the road to development

▶ CAREERS

A **career** is the sequence of work-related positions a person occupies throughout life. While it is still possible to build a long career with a single organization, that certainly is not the norm today. People pursue careers to satisfy deeply individual needs. At one time, identity with one employer seemed to fulfill many of those needs. But now, the distinction between an individual's career as the organization sees it and the career as the individual sees it is important.

Organization-Centered vs. Individual-Centered Career Planning

The nature of career planning can be somewhat confusing because different perspectives exist. Career planning can be organization centered, individual centered, or both. The points of focus for organization- and individual-oriented career planning are compared in Figure 6–5.

▶**FIGURE 6–5** **Organizational and Individual Career-Planning Perspectives**

ORGANIZATIONAL CAREER PERSPECTIVE	INDIVIDUAL CAREER PERSPECTIVE
• Identify future organizational staffing needs • Plan career ladders • Assess individual potential and training needs • Match organizational needs with individual abilities • Audit and develop a career system for the organization	• Identify personal abilities and interests • Plan life and work goals • Assess alternative paths inside and outside the organization • Note changes in interests and goals as career and life stage change

Organization-centered career planning focuses on jobs and on constructing career paths that provide for the logical progression of people between jobs in an organization. These paths represent ladders that individuals can climb to advance in certain organizational units.

Individual-centered career planning focuses on individuals' careers rather than organizational needs. As done by employees themselves, individual goals and skills are the focus of the analysis. Such analyses might consider situations both within and outside the organization that could expand a person's career.

Dual-Career Paths for Technical and Professional Workers

Technical and professional workers, such as engineers and scientists, present a special challenge for organizations. Many of them want to stay in their labs or at their drawing boards rather than move into management; yet advancement frequently *requires* a move into management. Most of these people like the idea of the responsibility and opportunity associated with advancement, but they do not want to leave the technical puzzles and problems at which they excel.

The *dual-career ladder* is an attempt to solve this problem. A person can advance up either the management ladder or a corresponding ladder on the technical/professional side.

Dual-Career Couples

The increasing number of women in the workforce, particularly in professional careers, has greatly increased the number of dual-career couples. Marriages in which both mates are managers, professionals, or technicians have doubled since 1970. Problem areas involving dual-career couples include recruitment, transfer, and family issues.

It is important that the career-development problems of dual-career couples be recognized as early as possible, especially if they involve transfer, so that realistic alternatives can be explored.

Recruitment Problems with Dual-Career Couples. Recruiting a member of a dual-career couple increasingly means making an equally attractive job available for the candidate's partner at the new location. Dual-career couples have more to lose when relocating and, as a result, often exhibit higher expectations and request more help and money in such situations.

Relocation of Dual-Career Couples. Traditionally, transfers are part of the path upward in organizations. However, the dual-career couple is much less mobile, because one partner's transfer interferes with the other's career. Dual-career couples, besides having invested in two careers, have established support networks of friends and neighbors to cope with their transportation and dependent-care needs. These needs, in a single-career couple, would normally be met by the other partner. Relocating one partner in a dual-career couple means upsetting this carefully constructed network or creating a "commuting" relationship.

Careers, Work, and Family Issues

The pressures exerted by work and family issues affect individual careers, but they affect employers' strategic choices as well. Those strategic choices result in changes in the way employers are dealing with family/work issues.[5] Employers are concerned about balancing the needs of families and employee development because high-performing managers are difficult to recruit and to keep. Further, there is evidence that many job candidates are giving higher priority to the quality of family and personal life when choosing employers.

Moonlighting

Moonlighting traditionally has been defined as work outside a person's regular employment that takes 12 or more additional hours per week. More recently, the concept of moonlighting has been expanded to include such activities as self-employment, investments, hobbies, and other interests for which additional remuneration is received. The perception that moonlighting is a fixed outside commitment is no longer sufficiently broad, since the forms that it may take are varied and sometimes difficult to identify.

Moonlighting is not without its problems. The main argument against moonlighting has been that energy is being used on a second job that should be used on the primary job. This division of effort may lead to poor performance, absenteeism, and reduced job commitment. However, these arguments are less valid with ever-shorter average workweeks.

Key for employers in dealing with moonlighting employees is to devise and communicate a policy on the subject. Such a policy should focus on defining those areas in which the employer limits employee activities because of business reasons.

▶ SUGGESTED READINGS

1. Bell, Chip R. 1996. *Managers as Mentors: Building Partnerships for Learning.* San Francisco: Berrett-Koehler.
2. Crispin, Gary, and Mark Mehler. 1998. *Career X Roads.* Kendall Park, NJ: MMC Group.
3. Dempcy, Mary H., and Rene Tihista. 1996. *Dear Job Stressed: Answers for the Overworked, Overwrought and Overwhelmed.* Palo Alto, CA: Davies-Black Publishing.
4. Grote, Dick. 1995. *Discipline Without Punishment.* The Proven Strategy That Turns Problem Employees into Superior Performers. New York: AMACOM.
5. Holton, Elwood F., III, and Richard A, Swanson. 1997. *Human Resource Development Research Handbook Linking Research and Practice.* San Francisco: Berrett-Koehler.
6. Jones, Ken. 1997. *Icebreakers: A Sourcebook of Games, Exercises, and Simulations.* 2nd ed. Houston: Gulf Publishing.
7. Nelson, Bob. 1997. *1001 Ways to Energize Employees.* New York: Workman Publishing.
8. Rothwell, William J. 1996. *Beyond Training and Development.* New York: AMACOM.

▶ NOTES

1. William Tracey, "How to Weigh the Costs and Benefits of Training," *Benefits & Compensation Solutions,* December 1995, 52.
2. "In-House Training Increases," *The Wall Street Journal,* January 30, 1996, 1.
3. Wayne Cascio, "Whither Industrial and Organizational Psychology in a Changing World of Work?" *American Psychologist,* November 1995, 931.
4. P. Osterman, "Skill, Training and Work Organization in American Establishments," *Industrial Relations,* 34 (1995), 125–145.
5. J. Goodstein, "Institutional Pressures and Strategic Responsiveness: Employer Involvement in Work-Family Issues," *Academy of Management Journal,* 37 (1994), 350–382.

7

Appraising Performance

Human resource performance is an important issue in the strategy most organizations must follow to achieve their goals. **Performance management systems** are attempts to monitor, measure, report, improve, and reward employee performance. Performance management also should include some development planning designed to improve or expand employees' core capabilities. Performance management is the link between strategy and organizational results, as shown in Figure 7–1.

▶ **FIGURE 7-1 The Linkage between Strategy, Outcomes, and Organizational Results**

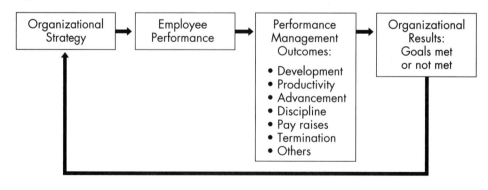

▶ MONITORING AND MEASURING PERFORMANCE

Employee performance is not controlled by management but ultimately by the employees themselves. A manager's job is to assist employees by making sure they understand how to do their jobs, what constitutes good performance, how they are doing, and how to improve if necessary. Understanding how to do the job and if employee performance is at an acceptable level requires identifying critical job dimensions and performance standards.

Critical Job Dimensions and Performance Standards

Job analysis helps identify the most important duties and tasks of jobs. From the job analysis, it is important to develop **critical job dimensions,** which are elements of a job on which performance is measured. If jobs have been properly designed, critical job dimensions will reflect what needs to be done to advance the strategy of the organization.

Each critical job dimension should be associated with a **performance standard,** which is the expected level of performance. But performance is almost never one-dimensional. The various dimensions for a given job also might be *weighted* to reflect the relative importance of the criteria. For example, in a word processing job, speed might be twice as important as accuracy, and accuracy might be as important as getting to work on time and being there every day.

Types of Performance Criteria

Performance criteria are standards commonly used for testing or measuring performances. Criteria for evaluating job performance can be classified as trait-based, behavior-based, or results-based. A *trait-based* criterion identifies a subjective character trait such as "pleasant personality," "initiative," or "creativity" and has little to do with the specific job. Such traits tend to be ambiguous, and courts have held that evaluations based on traits such as "adaptability" and "general demeanor" are too vague to use as the basis for performance-based HR decisions.

Behavior-based criteria focus on specific behaviors that lead to job success. Behavioral criteria are more difficult to develop but have the advantage of clearly specifying the behaviors management wants to see. A potential problem is that there may be several behaviors, all of which can be successful in a given situation.

Results-based criteria look at what the employee has done or accomplished. For some jobs where measurement is easy and appropriate, a results-based approach works very well. However, that which is measured tends to be emphasized, and equally important but nonmeasurable parts of the job may be left out. For example, a car salesman who gets paid only for sales may be unwilling to do any paperwork not directly necessary to sell cars. Further, when only results are emphasized and not *how the results were achieved,* ethical or even legal issues may arise.

Establishing Useful Performance Standards

Realistic, measurable, clearly understood performance standards benefit both the organization and the employees. In a sense, standards show the "right way" to do the job. It is important to establish standards *before* the work is performed so that all involved will understand the level of accomplishment expected.

Standards often are established for the following:

▶ Quantity of output
▶ Quality of output
▶ Timeliness of results
▶ Manner of performance
▶ Effectiveness in use of resources

Supervisory ratings of *quantity* of work produced have been found to be accurate, but measuring *quality* against standards is less precise, possibly because quality is more subjective in some cases.[1] Sales quotas and production output standards are familiar quantity performance standards.

Standards are often set by someone external to the job, but they can be written effectively by employees as well. Experienced employees know what constitutes satisfactory performance of tasks on their job descriptions. Their supervisors do as well. Therefore, these individuals often can collaborate with good effect. For example, two performance standards for difficult duties that were derived jointly are as follows:

Duty: Keep current on supplier technology.
Performance Standards: 1. Every six months, invite suppliers to make presentation of newest technology.
2. Visit supplier plants once per year.
3. Attend trade shows.

Duty: Do price or cost analysis as appropriate.
Performance Standard: Performance will be acceptable when all requirements of the procedure "Price and Cost Analysis" are followed.[2]

▶ PERFORMANCE APPRAISAL

Performance appraisal (PA) is the process of evaluating how well employees do their jobs compared with a set of standards and communicating that information to those employees. It also has been called *employee rating, employee evaluation, performance review, performance evaluation,* and *results appraisal.*

Performance appraisal sounds simple enough; research shows that it is widely used for wage/salary administration, performance feedback, and identification of individual employee strengths and weaknesses. Many U.S. companies have PA systems for office, professional, technical, supervisory, middle management, and nonunion production workers.

In situations in which an employer must deal with a strong union, performance appraisals may be conducted only on salaried, nonunion employees. Generally, unions emphasize seniority over merit, which precludes the use of performance appraisal. Unions view all members as equal in ability; therefore, the worker with the most experience is considered to be the most qualified. Thus, a performance appraisal is unnecessary.

Performance appraisal often is management's least favored activity. There may be good reasons for that feeling. Not all performance appraisals are positive, and for that reason, discussing ratings with the employee may not be pleasant.

In general terms, performance appraisal has two roles in organizations, and these roles often are seen as potentially conflicting. One role is to measure performance for the purpose of rewarding or otherwise making *administrative* decisions about employees. Promotions or layoffs might hinge on these ratings, making them difficult at times. Another role is *development* of individual potential. In this case, the manager is featured more as a counselor than as a judge, and the atmosphere is often different. Emphasis is on identifying potential and planning growth. Figure 7–2 shows the two potentially conflicting roles for performance appraisal.

Administrative Uses

A performance appraisal system is often the link between the reward employees hope to receive and their productivity. The linkage can be thought of as follows:

$$\text{productivity} \rightarrow \text{performance appraisal} \rightarrow \text{rewards}$$

This approach to compensation is at the heart of the idea that raises should be given for merit rather than for seniority. Under merit systems, employees receive raises based on performance. The manager's role historically has been as evaluator of a subordinate's performance, and the focus is usually on comparison of performance levels among individuals. If any part of the process fails, the most productive employees will not receive the larger rewards, resulting in all the problems that come from perceived inequity in compensation.

▶ **FIGURE 7–2   Conflicting Roles for Performance Appraisal?**

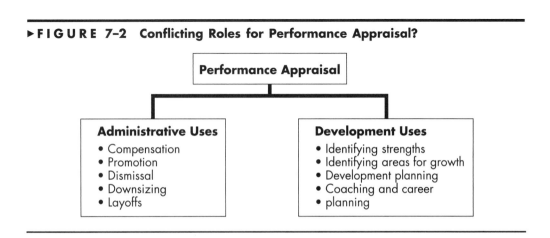

Administrative uses of performance appraisal, such as decisions on promotion, termination, layoff, and transfer assignments, are very important to employees. For example, the order of layoffs can be justified by performance appraisals. For this reason, if an employer claims that the decision was performance-based, the performance appraisals must document clearly the differences in employee performance. Similarly, promotion or demotion based on performance must be documented with performance appraisals.

Development Uses

Performance appraisal can be a primary source of information and feedback for employees, which is key for their future development. When supervisors identify the weaknesses, potentials, and training needs of employees through PA feedback, they can inform employees about their progress, discuss what skills they need to develop, and work out development plans.

The purpose of developmental feedback is to change or reinforce individual behavior, rather than to compare individuals as in the case of administrative uses of performance appraisal. Positive reinforcement for the behaviors the organization wants is an important part of development.

The use of teams provides a different set of circumstances for developmental appraisal. The manager may not see all of the employee's work, but team members do. Teams *can* provide developmental feedback, but it is still an open question whether teams can handle administrative appraisal.

Informal vs. Systematic Appraisal

Performance appraisal can occur in two ways, informally or systematically. An *informal appraisal* is conducted whenever the supervisor feels it is necessary. The day-to-day working relationship between a manager and an employee offers an opportunity for the employee's performance to be judged. Frequent informal feedback to employees can also avoid surprises (and therefore problems) later when the formal evaluation is communicated.

A *systematic appraisal* is used when the contact between manager and employee is formalized and a system is established to report managerial impressions and observations on employee performance. Although informal appraisal is useful, it should not take the place of formal appraisal.

▶ WHO CONDUCTS APPRAISALS?

Performance appraisal can be done by anyone familiar with the performance of individual employees. Possibilities include the following:

- ▶ Supervisors who rate their employees
- ▶ Employees who rate their superiors
- ▶ Team members who rate each other
- ▶ Outside sources
- ▶ Employee self-appraisal
- ▶ Multisource (360°) appraisal

Supervisory Rating of Subordinates

Traditional rating of employees by supervisors is based on the assumption that the immediate supervisor is the person most qualified to evaluate the employee's performance realistically, objectively, and fairly. As with any rating system, the supervisor's judgment should be objective and based on actual performance. Toward this end, some supervisors keep performance logs noting what their employees have done. A supervisor's appraisal typically is reviewed by the manager's boss to make sure that a proper job of appraisal has been done.

Employee Rating of Managers

The concept of having supervisors and managers rated by employees or group members is being used in a number of organizations today. A prime example of this type of rating takes place in colleges and universities where students evaluate the performance of professors in the classroom. Industry also uses employee ratings for developmental purposes.

Team/Peer Ratings

Peer ratings are especially useful when supervisors do not have the opportunity to observe each employee's performance but other work group members do. It may be that team/peer evaluations are best used for development purposes rather than for administrative purposes. However, some contend that any performance appraisal, including team/peer ratings, can affect teamwork and participative management efforts negatively.

Self-Ratings

Self-appraisal works in certain situations. Essentially, it is a self-development tool that forces employees to think about their strengths and weaknesses and set goals for improvement. If an employee is working in isolation or possesses a unique skill, the employee may be the only one qualified to rate his or her own behavior. However, employees may not rate themselves as supervisors would rate them; they may use quite different standards. Despite the difficulty in evaluating self-ratings, employee self-ratings can be a valuable and credible source of performance information.

Outside Raters

The customers or clients of an organization are obvious sources for outside appraisals. For salespeople and other service jobs, customers may provide the only really clear view of certain behaviors. One corporation uses measures of customer satisfaction with service as a way of helping to determine bonuses for top marketing executives.

Multisource Rating

The latest attempt to improve performance—multisource assessment, or 360° performance appraisal—increasingly has found favor with a growing number of organizations. Unlike traditional performance appraisals, which typically come from superiors to subordinates, 360° appraisal uses feedback from "all around" the appraisee. Superiors, subordinates, peers, customers—and perhaps a self-appraisal as well—provide input for the performance appraisal process.

Driving factors in 360° PA include the growing use of teams and an emphasis on customer satisfaction that comes from quality enhancement operations. Use of 360° PA with teams presents a problem, however. Should managers even do performance appraisals, should team leaders do them, or should team members evaluate each other? Further, after downsizing, many managers have seen their roles change, with more people reporting to them directly and a shift in accountability lower in the organization.

Multisource feedback obviously can be used for the development of managers, leaders, and others. Indeed, it is most often intended to serve a developmental role. But in some organizations, it is being used as input for evaluating performance in order to determine compensation adjustments and other more traditional administrative performance purposes.

Some potential problems clearly are present when 360° feedback is used for administrative purposes. Differences among raters can present a challenge, especially in the use of 360° ratings for discipline or pay decisions. Bias can just as easily be rooted in customers, subordinates, and peers as in a boss, and their lack of accountability can affect the ratings.[3] Multisource approaches to performance appraisal are possible solutions to the well-documented dissatisfaction with today's legally necessary administrative performance appraisal.

▶ METHODS FOR APPRAISING PERFORMANCE

Performance can be appraised by a number of methods. The simplest methods for appraising performance are methods that require a manager to mark an employee's level of performance on a specific form.

Graphic Rating Method

The **graphic rating** method allows the rater to mark an employee's performance on a continuum. Because of its simplicity, this method is the one most frequently used. The rater checks the appropriate place on a scale for each duty listed. More detail can be added in a space for comments following each factor rated.

There are some obvious drawbacks to the graphic rating method. Often, separate traits or factors are grouped together, and the rater is given only one box to check. Another drawback is that the descriptive words sometimes used in such scales may have different meanings to different raters. Terms such as *initiative* and *cooperation* are subject to many interpretations, especially in conjunction with words such as *outstanding, average,* and *poor.* Graphic rating scales in many forms are used widely because they are easy to develop; but for the same reason, they encourage errors on the part of the raters, who may depend too heavily on them.

Comparative Methods

Comparative methods require that managers directly compare the performances of their employees against one another. For example, a data-entry operator's performance would be compared with that of other data-entry operators by the computing supervisor.

Ranking.   The **ranking** method consists of listing all employees from highest to lowest in performance. The primary drawback of the ranking method is that the size of the differences among individuals is not well defined. Further, ranking becomes very unwieldy if the group to be ranked is very large.

Forced Distribution.   With the **forced distribution** method, the ratings of employees' performances are distributed along a bell-shaped curve. Using the forced distribution method, for example, a head nurse would rank nursing personnel along a scale, placing a certain percentage of employees at each performance level. Figure 7–3 shows a scale used with a forced distribution. This method assumes that the widely known bell-shaped curve of performance exists in a given group.

There are several drawbacks to the forced distribution method. One problem is that a supervisor may resist placing any individual in the lowest (or the highest) group. Difficulties may arise when the rater must explain to the employee why he or she was placed in one grouping and others were placed in higher groupings. Further, with small groups, there may be no reason to assume that a bell-shaped distribution of performance really exists. Finally, in some cases the manager may feel forced to make distinctions among employees that may not exist.

▶**F I G U R E 7–3   Forced Distribution on a Bell-Shaped Curve**

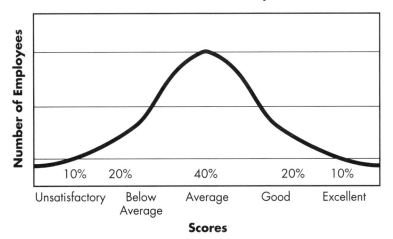

Narrative Methods

Some managers and HR specialists are required to provide written appraisal information. In one narrative method, the manager keeps a written record of both highly favorable and unfavorable actions in an employee's performance. When a "critical incident" involving an employee occurs, the manager writes it down. A list of critical incidents is kept during the entire rating period for each employee. The critical incident method can be used with other methods to document the reasons why an employee was rated in a certain way.

The critical incident method also has its unfavorable aspects. First, what constitutes a critical incident is not defined in the same way by all supervisors. Next, producing daily or weekly written remarks about each employee's performance can take considerable time. Further, employees may become overly concerned about what the superior writes and begin to fear the manager's "black book."

Behavioral Rating

One attempt to overcome some of the difficulties of the methods just described are several different behavioral approaches. Behavioral approaches hold promise for some situations in overcoming some of the problems with other methods. A **behavioral rating** assesses an employee's *behaviors* instead of other characteristics. Some of the different behavioral approaches are *behaviorally anchored rating scales* (BARS), *behavioral observation scales* (BOS), and *behavioral expectation scales* (BES). BARS match descriptions of possible behaviors with what the employee most commonly exhibits. BOS are used to count the number of times certain behaviors are exhibited. BES order behaviors on a continuum to define outstanding, average, and unacceptable performance.[4]

Management by Objectives (MBO)

Management by objectives (MBO) specifies the performance goals that an individual hopes to attain within an appropriate length of time. The objectives that each manager sets are derived from the overall goals and objectives of the organization, although MBO should not be a disguised means for a superior to dictate the objectives of individual managers or employees. Although not limited to the appraisal of managers, MBO is most often used for this purpose. Implementing a guided self-appraisal system using MBO is a four-stage process. These phases are shown in Figure 7–4.

Three key assumptions underlie an MBO appraisal system. First, if an employee is involved in planning and setting the objectives and determining the measure, a higher level of commitment and performance may result.

Second, if the objectives are identified clearly and precisely, the employee will do a better job of achieving the desired results.

Third, performance objectives should be measurable and should define results. Vague generalities, such as "initiative" and "cooperation," which are common in many superior-based appraisals, should be avoided. Objectives are

▶**FIGURE 7–4 MBO Process**

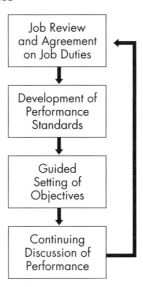

```
┌─────────────┐
│  Job Review │
│ and Agreement│←──┐
│ on Job Duties│   │
└──────┬──────┘    │
       ↓           │
┌─────────────┐    │
│Development of│    │
│ Performance │    │
│  Standards  │    │
└──────┬──────┘    │
       ↓           │
┌─────────────┐    │
│   Guided    │    │
│  Setting of │    │
│  Objectives │    │
└──────┬──────┘    │
       ↓           │
┌─────────────┐    │
│ Continuing  │    │
│Discussion of│────┘
│ Performance │
└─────────────┘
```

composed of specific actions to be taken or work to be accomplished. Sample objectives might include:

▶ Submit regional sales report by the fifth of every month
▶ Obtain orders from at least five new customers per month
▶ Maintain payroll costs at 10% of sales volume
▶ Have scrap loss less than 5%
▶ Fill all organizational vacancies within 30 days after openings occur

▶ **RATER ERRORS**

There are many possible sources of error in the performance appraisal process. One of the major sources is mistakes made by the rater. There is no simple way to eliminate these errors, but making raters aware of them is helpful. A variety of rater errors are discussed next.

Problems of Varying Standards

When appraising employees, a manager should avoid using different standards and expectations for employees performing similar jobs, which is certain to incur the anger of employees. Such problems are likely to exist when ambiguous criteria and subjective weightings by supervisors are used.

Recency Effect

The **recency effect** is present when a rater gives greater weight to recent occurrences when appraising an individual's performance. The recency effect is an understandable rater error. It may be difficult for a rater to remember performance that took place seven or eight months ago. Employees also become more concerned about performance as formal appraisal time approaches. The problem can be minimized by documenting both positive and negative performance.

Rating Patterns

Students are well aware that some professors tend to grade easier or harder than others. Likewise, a manager may develop a *rating pattern*. Appraisers who rate all employees within a narrow range (usually the middle or average) commit a **central tendency error.**

Rater Bias

Rater bias occurs when a rater's values or prejudices distort the rating. Rater bias may be unconscious or quite intentional. If a manager has a strong dislike of certain ethnic groups, this bias is likely to result in distorted appraisal information for some people. Age, religion, seniority, sex, appearance, or other arbitrary classifications may be reflected in appraisals if the appraisal process is not properly designed. Examination of ratings by higher-level managers may help correct this problem.

Halo Effect

The **halo effect** occurs when a manager rates an employee high or low on all items because of one characteristic. For example, if a worker has few absences, her supervisor might give her a high rating in all other areas of work, including quantity and quality of output, because of her dependability. The manager may not really think about the employee's other characteristics separately.

An appraisal that shows the same rating on all characteristics may be evidence of the halo effect. Clearly specifying the categories to be rated, rating all employees on one characteristic at a time, and training raters to recognize the problem are some means of reducing the halo effect.

▶ THE APPRAISAL FEEDBACK INTERVIEW

Once appraisals have been made, it is important to communicate them so that employees have a clear understanding of how they stand in the eyes of their immediate superiors and the organization. It is fairly common for organizations to require that managers discuss appraisals with employees.

The appraisal interview presents both an opportunity and a danger. It is an emotional experience for the manager and the employee because the manager must communicate both praise and constructive criticism. A major concern for managers is how to emphasize the positive aspects of the employee's performance while still discussing ways to make needed improvements. If the interview is handled poorly, the employee may feel resentment, and conflict may result, which could be reflected in future work. Figure 7–5 summarizes hints for an effective appraisal interview for supervisors and managers.

▶**FIGURE 7–5   Hints for Managers in the Appraisal Interview**

DO	DON'T
• Prepare in advance • Focus on performance and development • Be specific about reasons for ratings • Decide on specific steps to be taken for improvement • Consider the supervisor's role in the subordinate's performance • Reinforce desired behaviors • Focus on future performance	• Lecture the employee • Mix performance appraisal and salary or promotion issues • Concentrate only on the negative • Do all the talking • Be overly critical or "harp on" a failing • Feel it is necessary that both parties agree in all areas • Compare the employee with others

Reactions of Managers

Managers and supervisors who must complete appraisals of their employees often resist the appraisal process. As mentioned earlier, managers may feel they are put in the position of "playing God." A major part of the manager's role is to assist, encourage, coach, and counsel employees to improve their performance. However, being a judge on the one hand and a coach and counselor on the other may cause internal conflict and confusion for both the manager and the employee.

▶ PERFORMANCE APPRAISALS AND THE LAW

It may seem unnecessary to emphasize that performance appraisals must be job related, because appraisals are supposed to measure how well employees are doing their jobs. Yet in numerous cases, courts have ruled that performance appraisals were discriminatory and not job related.

The elements of a performance appraisal system that can survive court tests can be determined from existing case law. Various cases have provided guidance. The elements of a legally defensible performance appraisal are as follows:

▶ Performance appraisal criteria based on job analysis
▶ Absence of disparate impact and evidence of validity
▶ Formal evaluation criteria that limit managerial discretion
▶ Formal rating instrument
▶ Personal knowledge of and contact with appraised individual
▶ Training of supervisors in conducting appraisals
▶ Review process that prevents one manager acting alone from controlling an employee's career
▶ Counseling to help poor performers improve

It is clear that the courts are interested in fair and nondiscriminatory performance appraisals. Employers must decide how to design their appraisal systems to satisfy the courts, enforcement agencies, and their employees.

▶ SUGGESTED READINGS

1. Engelman, Curtis H., and Robert C. Roesch. 1996. *Managing Individual Performance: An Approach to Designing an Effective Performance Management System.* Scottsdale, AZ: American Compensation Association.
2. Hillgren, James S., and David W. Cheatham. 1996. *Understanding Performance Measures: An Approach to Linking Rewards to the Achievement of Organizational Objectives.* Scottsdale, AZ: American Compensation Association.
3. SHRM Information Center. 1996. *Performance Appraisals. A Collection of Samples.* Alexandria, VA: Society of Human Resource Management.
4. Singer, Marc, and Maureen Fleming. 1997. *Effective Human Resource Measurement Techniques.* Alexandria, VA: Society of Human Resource Management.

▶ NOTES

1. P. Bobko and A. Colella, "Employee Reactions to Performance Standards: A Review and Research Proposition," *Personnel Psychology* 47 (1994), 1–29.
2. Carolyn Pye, "Setting Employee Standards," *NAPM Insights,* May 1995, 18–21.
3. N. Merz and S. Motowidlo, "Effects of Rater Accountability on the Accuracy and Favorability of Performance Ratings," *Journal of Applied Psychology* 80 (1995), 517–524.
4. U. J. Wiersma, P. T. Van Den Berg, and G. P. Latham, "Dutch Reactions to Behavioral Observation, Behavioral Expectation, and Trait Scales," *Group and Organization Management,* September 1995, 297–309.

8

Compensation

Compensation is fundamentally about balancing human resource costs with the ability to attract and keep employees. By providing compensation, most employers attempt to provide fair remuneration for the knowledge, skills, and abilities of their employees. In addition, the compensation system should support organizational objectives and strategies.

▶ BASIC COMPENSATION CONSIDERATIONS

Compensation serves the function of allocating people among employers based on the attractiveness of jobs and compensation packages. Employers must be reasonably competitive with several types of compensation in order to hire and keep the people they need.

Compensation can be both tangible and intangible. As Figure 8–1 shows, tangible (financial) compensation is of two general types: direct and indirect. With the direct type of compensation, the actual tangible benefits are provided by the employer. The most common forms of direct compensation are *pay* and *incentives.*

Pay is the basic compensation an employee receives, usually as a wage or salary. An **incentive** is compensation that rewards an employee for efforts beyond normal performance expectations. Examples of incentives include bonuses, commissions, and profit-sharing plans.

With indirect compensation, employees receive the tangible value of the rewards without receiving the actual cash. A **benefit** is an indirect reward, such as health insurance, vacation pay, or retirement pensions, given to an employee or group of employees as a part of organizational membership.

▶FIGURE 8-1

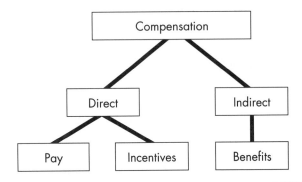

▶ STRATEGIC COMPENSATION

Because compensation is such a key activity, compensation philosophies and objectives must reflect the overall culture, philosophies, and strategic plans of the organization. The compensation practices that typically exist in a new organization may be different from those in a mature, bureaucratic organization. It is critical that organizations align their compensation practices with their organizational cultures, especially if efforts are made to change the cultures because of competitive pressures.

Compensation Philosophies

Compensation first must be seen strategically. Because so many organizational funds are spent on compensation-related activities, it is critical for top management and HR executives to view the "strategic" fit of compensation with the objectives of the organization as they identify the compensation philosophy to guide compensation planning.[1]

There are two basic compensation philosophies, which should be seen as opposite ends of a continuum. At one end of the continuum is the *entitlement* philosophy, at the other end the *performance-oriented* philosophy.

Entitlement Orientation. The entitlement philosophy can be seen in many organizations that traditionally have given automatic increases to their employees every year. Most of those employees receive the same or nearly the same percentage increase each year as well. Employees and managers who subscribe to the entitlement philosophy believe that individuals who have worked another year are *entitled* to a raise in base pay and that all incentives and benefit programs should continue unchanged, regardless of changing industry or economic conditions. Commonly, in organizations following an entitlement philosophy, pay increases are referred to as *cost-of-living* raises, whether or not they are tied specifically to economic indicators. Following an entitlement philosophy ultimately means that as employees continue their employment lives, employer costs increase, regardless of employee performance or other organizational competitive pressures.

Performance Orientation.   Where a *performance-oriented* philosophy is followed, no one is guaranteed compensation just for adding another year to organizational service. Instead, pay and incentives are based on performance differences among employees. Employees who perform well get larger compensation increases, and those who do not perform satisfactorily receive little or no increase in compensation. Few organizations are totally performance-oriented in all facets of their compensation practices, but breaking the entitlement mode increasingly is occurring in the organizational restructurings common throughout many industries.

Compensation Bases

Another strategic issue is how compensation philosophies and objectives are reflected in the design of compensation systems, particularly base pay programs. There are several bases that can be used, and different bases may be used in different parts of the organization.

Time vs. Productivity.   Employees of organizations can be paid for the amount of time spent on the job or on the amount of work produced. Many organizations use two pay categories, *hourly* and *salaried,* which are identified according to the way pay is distributed and the nature of the jobs. Hourly pay is the most common means of payment based on time; employees who are paid hourly are said to receive **wages,** which are payments directly calculated on the amount of time worked. In contrast, people who are paid a **salary** receive payment that is consistent from period to period despite the number of hours worked. Being salaried typically has carried higher status for employees than being paid wages.

Another general basis for compensation is performance or productivity. A direct productivity-based system, called a **piece-rate system,** is one in which an employee is paid for each unit of production. For example, an employee who works in a telemarketing firm may be paid an amount for every sale made.

Task-Based vs. Knowledge- and Skill-Based Pay.   Most base compensation programs are designed to reward employees for the tasks, duties, and responsibilities performed. It is the jobs done that determine, to a large extent, which employees have higher base rates than others. Employees are paid more for doing jobs that require more variety of tasks, more knowledge and skills, greater physical effort, or more demanding working conditions.

A growing number of organizations are paying employees, particularly hourly ones, for the skills or competencies they have rather than for the specific tasks being performed. Paying for skills rewards employees who are more versatile and have continued to develop their skills. In these *knowledge-based pay* (KBP) or *skill-based pay* (SBP) systems, employees start at a base level of pay and receive increases as they learn to do other jobs or gain other skills and therefore become more valuable to the employer.

▶ COMPENSATION STRATEGIES AND OBJECTIVES

The changes in many industries and organizations have led to forecasts that traditional compensation practices followed in the past are currently evolving and will be significantly different in the future. In virtually every organization, a compensation program should address three objectives:

▶ Legal compliance with all appropriate laws and regulations
▶ Cost effectiveness for the organization
▶ Internal, external, and individual equity for employees

Legal Compliance

First, the compensation program must comply with all *legal* constraints and regulations in all compensation areas in which the organization operates. Numerous laws and regulations affect pay, incentives, and benefits. The design and implementation of compensation programs must be built with the various legal restrictions in mind. The most important legal concerns are addressed later in the chapter.

Cost Effectiveness

Second, compensation must be *cost-effective* and affordable for the organization, given the competitive pressures it faces. A firm that provides compensation that is too high may have difficulty competing with lower-paying, more efficient competitors.

Equity

People want to be treated fairly in all facets of compensation, including base pay, incentives, and benefits. This is the concept of **equity,** which is the perceived fairness of the relation between what a person does (inputs) and what the person receives (outcomes). *Inputs* are what a person brings to the organization and include educational level, age, experience, productivity, and other skills or efforts. The items received by a person, or the *outcomes,* are the rewards obtained in exchange for inputs. Outcomes include pay, benefits, recognition, achievement, prestige, and any other rewards received. Note that an outcome can be either tangible (extrinsic rewards such as pay and economic benefits) or intangible (internal rewards such as recognition and achievement).

Procedural and Distributive Justice in Compensation. A growing equity issue in organizational research is organizational justice. Two major subareas are *procedural justice* and *distributive justice.* **Procedural justice** is the perceived fairness of the process and procedures used to make decisions about employees, including their pay. The process of determining the base pay for jobs, the allocation of pay increases, and the measurement of performance must be perceived as fair.[2] **Distributive justice,** which refers to the perceived fairness of the amounts given for performance, must be considered also.

Secret vs. Open Pay Systems. Another equity issue concerns the degree of openness or secrecy that organizations allow regarding their pay systems. Pay information kept secret in "closed" systems includes how much others make, what raises others have received, and even what pay grades and ranges exist in the organization.

Policies that prohibit discussion of individual pay are likely to be violated. Co-workers do share pay information, and explaining the pay system may prevent the spreading of misinformation through the grapevine. By having pay openness, organizations that truly base pay on performance can emphasize the importance of performance to higher pay. This approach is particularly useful when objective measures of individual performance exist, such as in some sales jobs.

▶ LEGAL CONSTRAINTS ON PAY SYSTEMS

Compensation systems must comply with a myriad of government constraints. Minimum wage standards and hours of work are two important areas that are addressed by the laws.

Fair Labor Standards Act (FLSA)

The major law affecting compensation is the Fair Labor Standards Act (FLSA). The act has three major objectives: (1) to establish a minimum wage floor, (2) to encourage limits on the number of weekly hours employees work through overtime provisions, and (3) to discourage oppressive use of child labor.

Employers Covered. Generally, private-sector employers engaged in inter-state commerce and retail service firms with two or more employees and gross sales of at least $500,000 per year are covered by the act. Very small, family-owned and -operated entities and family farms generally are excluded from coverage.

Exempt and Nonexempt Status. Under the FLSA, employees are classified as exempt or nonexempt. **Exempt employees** are those who hold positions classified as *executive, administrative, professional,* or *outside sales,* to whom employers are not required to pay overtime. **Nonexempt employees** are those who must be paid overtime under the Fair Labor Standards Act.

Three major factors are considered in determining whether an individual holds an exempt position:

▶ Discretionary authority for independent action
▶ Percentage of time spent performing routine, manual, or clerical work
▶ Earnings level

Under provisions of the FLSA, jobs can be categorized in three groupings:

▶ Hourly
▶ Salaried-nonexempt
▶ Salaried-exempt

Hourly jobs require employers to pay overtime and comply with the FLSA. Each salaried position must be identified as *salaried-exempt* or *salaried-nonexempt.* Employees in positions classified as salaried-nonexempt are covered by the overtime provisions of the FLSA and therefore must be paid overtime. Salaried-nonexempt positions sometimes include secretarial, clerical, and salaried blue-collar positions. Figure 8–2 shows the impact of these factors on each type of exemption.

Minimum Wage. The FLSA sets a minimum wage to be paid to the broad spectrum of covered employees. The actual minimum wage can be changed only by congressional action.

Overtime Provisions. The FLSA establishes overtime pay requirements. Its provisions set overtime pay at one and one-half times the regular pay rate for all hours in excess of 40 per week, except for employees who are not covered by the law.

Compensatory Time Off. Often called *comp time,* **compensatory time off** is given in lieu of payment for extra time worked. However, unless it is given at the rate of one and one-half times the hours worked over a 40-hour week, comp time is illegal in the private sector. Also, comp time cannot be carried over from one pay period to another. The only major exception to those provisions are for public-sector employees, such as fire and police employees, and a limited number of other workers.

Child-Labor Provisions. The child-labor provisions of the FLSA set the minimum age for employment with unlimited hours at 16 years. For hazardous occupations, the minimum is 18 years of age. Those aged 14 to 15 years old may work outside school hours with the following limitations:

1. No more than 3 hours on a school day, 18 hours in a school week, 8 hours on a nonschool day, or 40 hours in a nonschool week.
2. Work may not begin before 7 A.M. nor end after 7 P.M., except between June 1 and Labor Day, when 9 P.M. is the ending time.

Many employers require age certificates for employees because the FLSA places the responsibility on the employer to determine an individual's age.[3] The certificates may be issued by a representative of a state labor department, a state education department, or a local school district.

Independent Contractor Regulations

The growing use of contingent workers by many organizations has called attention to another group of legal regulations—those that identify the criteria that independent contractors must meet.

The criteria for deciding independent contractor status have been identified by the Internal Revenue Service (IRS), and most other federal and state entities rely on those criteria. The IRS has identified 20 factors that must be considered in making such a determination. Figure 8–3 shows some of the differences between employees and independent contractors.

▶ **FIGURE 8–2** Wage/Hour Status under Fair Labor Standards Act

EXEMPTION CATEGORY	A DISCRETIONARY AUTHORITY	B PERCENT OF TIME	C EARNINGS LEVELS
Executive	1. Primary duty is managing 2. Regularly directs work of at least two others 3. Authority to hire/fire or recommend these	1. Must spend 20% or less time doing clerical, manual, routine work (less than 40% in retail or service establishments)	1. Paid salary at $155/wk or $250/wk if meets A1–A2
Administrative	1. Responsible for nonmanual or office work related to management policies 2. Regularly exercises discretion and independent judgment and makes important decisions 3. Regularly assists executives and works under general supervision	1. Must spend 20% or less time doing clerical, manual, routine work (less than 40% in retail or service establishments)	1. Paid salary at $155/wk or $250/wk if meets A1–A2
Professional	1. Performs work requiring knowledge of an advanced field or creative and original artistic work or works as teacher in educational system 2. Must do work that is predominantly intellectual and varied	1. Must spend 20% or less time doing nonprofessional work	1. Paid salary at least $170/wk or $250/wk if meets A1
Outside Sales	1. Customarily works away from employer site and 2. Sells tangible or intangible items or 3. Obtains orders or contracts for services	1. Must spend 20% or less time doing work other than outside selling	1. No salary test

Note: For more details, see *Executive, Administrative, Professional, and Outside Sales Exemptions under the Fair Labor Standards Act,* WH Publication no. 1363 (Washington, DC: U.S. Department of Labor, Employment Standards Administration, Wage and Hour Division).

► **FIGURE 8-3   Employees vs. Independent Contractors**

AN EMPLOYEE
- Must comply with instructions about when, where, and how to work
- Renders services personally
- Has a continuing relationship with an employer
- Usually works on the premises of the employer
- Normally is furnished significant tools, materials, and other equipment by the employer
- Can be fired by an employer
- Can quit at any time without incurring liability

AN INDEPENDENT CONTRACTOR
- Can hire, supervise, and pay assistants
- Generally can set his or her own hours
- Usually is paid by the job or on straight commission
- Has a significant investment in facilities
- Can make a profit or suffer a loss
- Generally is free to provide services to two or more unrelated persons or firms at the same time
- Makes his or her services available to the public

Source: Internal Revenue Service.

Equal Pay Act of 1963

The Equal Pay Act was passed as a major amendment to the FLSA in 1963. The original act and subsequent amendments focus on wage discrimination on the basis of sex. The act applies to both men and women and prohibits paying different wage scales to men and women performing substantially the same jobs. Except for differences justifiable on the basis of merit (better performance), seniority (longer service), quantity or quality of work, or any factor other than sex, similar pay must be given for jobs requiring equal skills, equal effort, or equal responsibility or jobs done under similar working conditions.

Walsh-Healey and Service Contracts Acts

The Walsh-Healey Public Contracts Act and Service Contracts Act require companies with *federal supply or service contracts* exceeding $10,000 to pay a prevailing wage. Both acts apply only to those who are working directly on the contract or who substantially affect its performance. The *prevailing wage* is determined by a formula that considers the rate paid for a job by a majority of the employers in the appropriate geographic area.

Davis-Bacon Act of 1931

Still in force with many of the original dollar levels intact, the Davis-Bacon Act of 1931 affects compensation paid by firms engaged in federal construction projects valued in excess of $2,000. It deals only with federal construction projects and requires that the "prevailing wage" rate be paid on all federal construction projects.

Garnishment Laws

Garnishment of an employee's wages occurs when a creditor obtains a court order that directs an employer to submit a part of the employee's pay to the creditor for debts owed by the employee. Regulations passed as a part of the Consumer Credit Protection Act established limitations on the amount of wages that can be garnished and restricted the right of employers to discharge employees whose pay is subject to a single garnishment order. All 50 states have laws that apply to wage garnishments.

▶ WAGE AND SALARY ADMINISTRATION

The development, implementation, and ongoing maintenance of a base pay system usually is described as **wage and salary administration.** The purpose of wage and salary administration is to provide pay that is both competitive and equitable. Underlying the administered activities are pay policies that set the overall direction of pay within the organization.

Pay Policies

Organizations must develop policies as general guidelines to govern pay systems. Uniform policies are needed for coordination, consistency, and fairness in compensating employees.

A major policy decision must be made about the level of pay the organization wants to maintain relative to the market for employees. Specifically, an employer must identify how competitive it wishes to be in the market.

Some employers do not establish a formal wage and salary system. Smaller employers particularly may assume that the pay set by other employers is an accurate reflection of a job's worth, so they set their pay rates at **market price,** the prevailing wage paid for a job in the immediate job market.

Unions and Compensation

A major variable affecting an employer's pay policies is whether any employees are represented by a labor union. In nonunion organizations, employers have significantly more flexibility in determining pay levels and policies. Unionized employees usually have their pay set according to the terms of a collective bargaining contract between their employer and the union that represents them. Because pay is a visible issue, it is natural for unions to emphasize pay levels.

According to U.S. Bureau of Labor Statistics data, employers having unionized employees generally have higher wage levels than nonunion employers. The strength and extent of unionization in an industry and in an organization affect wage levels. The levels generally are higher in firms in heavily unionized industries with highly unionized workforces. As union strength in heavily unionized industries has declined, pay increases for nonunion employees have diminished somewhat in recent years.

▶ DEVELOPMENT OF A BASE PAY SYSTEM

As Figure 8–4 shows, the development of a wage and salary system assumes that accurate job descriptions and job specifications are available. The job descriptions then are used in two activities: *job evaluation* and *pay surveys*. These activities are designed to ensure that the pay system is both internally equitable and externally competitive. The data compiled in these two activities are used to design *pay structures*, including *pay grades* and minimum-to-maximum *pay ranges*. After the pay structures have been developed, individual jobs must be placed in the appropriate pay grades and employees' pay adjusted based on length of service and performance. Finally, the pay system must be monitored and updated.

▶ **FIGURE 8–4**   **Compensation Administration Process**

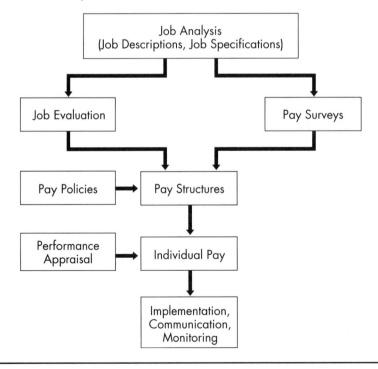

Job Evaluation

Job evaluation provides a systematic basis for determining the relative worth of jobs within an organization. It flows from the job analysis process and is based on job descriptions and job specifications. In a job evaluation, every job in an organization is examined and ultimately priced according to the following features:

► The relative importance of the job
► The skills needed to perform the job compared with other jobs
► The difficulty of the job compared with other jobs

It is important that employees perceive their pay as appropriate in relation to pay for jobs performed by others. Because jobs may vary widely in an organization, it is particularly important to identify **benchmark jobs**—jobs that are found in many other organizations and are performed by several individuals who have similar duties that are relatively stable and that require similar KSAs.

Ranking Method.   The ranking method is one of the simplest methods of job evaluation. It places jobs in order, ranging from highest to lowest in value to the organization. The entire job is considered rather than the individual components. Several different methods of ranking are available.

Classification Method.   The classification method puts the various jobs in the organization into grades according to common factors such as degree of responsibility, abilities or skills, knowledge, duties, volume of work, and experience needed. The grades are then ranked into an overall system.

Point Method.   The point method, the most widely used job evaluation method, is more sophisticated than the ranking and classification methods. It breaks down jobs into various compensable factors and places weights, or *points,* on them. A **compensable factor** is one used to identify a job value that is commonly present throughout a group of jobs. The factors are determined from the job analysis. For example, for jobs in warehouse and manufacturing settings, *physical demands, hazards encountered,* and *working environment* may be identified as factors and weighted heavily. However, in most office and clerical jobs, those factors are of little importance. Consequently, the compensable factors used and the weights assigned must reflect the nature of the job under study.

A special type of point method used by a consulting firm, Hay and Associates, has received widespread application, although it is most often used with exempt employees. The *Hay system* uses three factors and numerically measures the degree to which each of these factors is required in each job. The three factors and their subfactors are as follows:[4]

Know-How	Problem Solving	Accountability
► Functional expertise	► Environment	► Freedom to act
► Managerial skills	► Challenge	► Impact of end results
► Human relations		► Magnitude

Factor Comparison.   The factor-comparison method is a quantitative and complex combination of the ranking and point methods. Factor comparison not only tells which jobs are worth more but also indicates how much more, so factor values can be more easily converted to monetary wages.

Computerized Job Evaluation. The advent of computerized job analysis programs has led to computerized job evaluation programs. Generally, the computerized processes still must identify the prevalence of compensable factors in jobs.

Job Evaluation and Pay Equity. Many employers base their pay rates heavily on external equity comparisons in the labor market, which is their major defense for adopting the pay systems they use. **Pay equity** is the concept that the pay for all jobs requiring comparable knowledge, skills, and abilities should be similar even if actual duties and market rates differ significantly. Growing concerns about comparable worth have been translated into laws designed to address *pay equity*.

Pay Surveys

Another part of building a pay system is surveying the pay that other organizations provide for similar jobs. A **pay survey** is a collection of data on compensation rates for workers performing similar jobs in other organizations. An employer may use surveys conducted by other organizations or may decide to conduct its own survey.

Many different surveys are available from a variety of sources. National surveys on many jobs and industries are available through the U.S. Department of Labor, Bureau of Labor Statistics, and through national trade associations.

Pay Structure

Once survey data have been gathered, the pay structure for the organization can be developed by the process depicted in Figure 8–5. As indicated in that figure, one means of tying pay survey information to job evaluation data is to plot a *wage curve,* or *scattergram.* This plotting involves first making a graph that

▶**FIGURE 8-5   Establishing a Pay Structure**

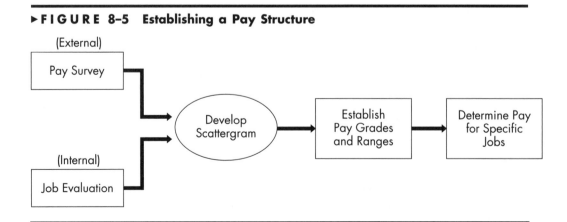

charts job evaluation points and pay survey rates for all surveyed jobs. In this way, the distribution of pay for surveyed jobs can be shown, and a linear trend line can be developed by use of the *least-squares regression method*. Also, a curvilinear line can be developed by use of multiple regression and other statistical techniques. The end result is the development of a *market line*. This line shows the relationship between job value as determined by job evaluation points, and wage/salary survey rates, as shown in Figure 8–6.

Establishing Pay Grades.   In the process of establishing a pay structure, organizations use **pay grades** to group together individual jobs having approximately the same job worth. While there are no set rules to be used in establishing pay grades, some overall suggestions have been made. Generally, 11 to 17 grades are used in small companies. However, a growing number of employers are reducing the number of grades by broadbanding. **Broadbanding** involves using fewer pay grades having broader ranges than traditional compensation systems.

By using pay grades, management can develop a coordinated pay system without having to determine a separate pay rate for each job in the organization. All the jobs within a grade have the same range of pay regardless of points. As discussed previously, the factor-comparison method of job evaluation uses monetary values, so an employer using that method can easily establish and price pay grades. A vital part of the classification method is developing grades. Organizations that use the ranking method can group several ranks together to create pay grades.

Pay Ranges.   The pay range for each pay grade also must be established. Using the market line as a starting point (see Figure 8–6), the employer can

▶**FIGURE 8–6   Pay Scattergram**

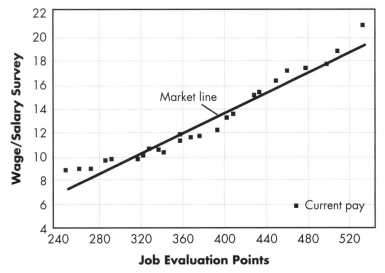

determine maximum and minimum pay levels for each pay grade by making the market line the midpoint line of the new pay structure. For example, in a particular pay grade, the maximum value may be 20% above the midpoint and the minimum value 20% below it.

▶ INDIVIDUAL PAY

Once managers have determined pay ranges, they can set the specific pay for individuals. Setting a range for each pay grade gives flexibility by allowing individuals to progress within a grade instead of having to be moved to a new grade each time they receive a raise.

Regardless of how well constructed a pay structure is, there usually are a few individuals whose pay is lower than the minimum or higher than the maximum. A **red-circled employee** is an incumbent who is paid above the range set for the job. An individual whose pay is below the range is a **green-circled employee.**

Pay Compression

One major problem many employers face is **pay compression,** which occurs when the range of pay differences among individuals with different levels of experience and performance becomes small. Pay compression occurs for a number of reasons, but the major one involves the situation in which labor market pay levels increase more rapidly than an employer's pay adjustments.

Occasionally, in response to competitive market shortages of particular job skills, managers may have to deviate from the priced grades to hire people with scarce skills. For example, suppose the worth of a welder's job is evaluated at $8 to $12 an hour in a company, but welders are in short supply and other employers are paying $14 an hour. The firm must pay the higher rate. But suppose several welders who have been with the firm for several years started at $8 an hour and have received 4% increases each year (these have been typical amounts in recent years). These welders may still be making less than the $14 an hour paid to new welders with lesser experience. One solution to pay compression is to have employees follow a step progression based on length of service, assuming performance is satisfactory or better.

Pay Increases

Once pay ranges have been developed and individuals' placements within the ranges identified, managers must look at adjustment to individual pay. There are several ways to determine pay increases.

Pay-for-Performance Systems. Many employers profess to have a pay system based on performance. Consequently, some system for integrating appraisals and pay changes must be developed and applied equally. Often, this integration is done through the use of a *pay adjustment matrix,* or *salary guide chart.* Pay adjustment matrices base adjustments in part on a person's **compa-ratio,** which is the pay level divided by the midpoint of the pay range.

Cost-of-Living Adjustments (COLA). A common pay-raise practice is the use of a *standard raise* or *cost-of-living adjustment* (COLA). Giving all employees a standard percentage increase enables them to maintain the same real wages in a period of economic inflation.

Seniority. Seniority, or time spent in the organization or on a particular job, also can be used as the basis for pay increases. Many employers have policies requiring that persons be employed for a certain length of time before they are eligible for pay increases. Pay adjustments based on seniority often are set as automatic steps once a person has been employed the required length of time, although performance must be at least satisfactory in many nonunion systems.

Lump-Sum Pay Increases (LSI). A **lump-sum increase (LSI),** sometimes called a *performance bonus,* is a one-time payment of all or part of a yearly pay increase. Some organizations place a limit on how much of a merit increase can be taken as a lump-sum payment. Other organizations split the lump sum into two checks, each representing one-half the year's pay raise.

▶ EXECUTIVE COMPENSATION

Many organizations, especially large ones, administer executive compensation somewhat differently than compensation for lower-level employees. An executive typically is someone in the top two levels of an organization, such as President or Senior Vice President. Executive compensation programs often include incentives, as well as other forms of compensation. Two objectives influence executive compensation: (1) tying the overall performance of the organization over a period of time to the compensation paid executives, and (2) ensuring that the total compensation packages for executives are competitive with the compensation packages in other firms that might employ them.

Compensation Committee

A **compensation committee** usually is a subgroup of the board of directors composed of directors who are not officers of the firm. Compensation committees generally make recommendations to the board of directors on overall pay policies, salaries for top officers, supplemental compensation such as stock options and bonuses, and additional perquisites ("perks") for executives.

Elements of Executive Compensation

Figure 8–7 shows the components of executive compensation, which are *salaries,* annual *bonuses, long-term incentives, benefits,* and *perquisites.*

Salaries of executives vary by type of job, size of organization, region of the country, and industry. On average, salaries make up about one-third of the typical top executive's annual compensation total.

Because executive performance may be difficult to determine, bonus compensation must reflect some kind of performance measure if it is to be

▶ **FIGURE 8-7** **Executive Compensation Components**

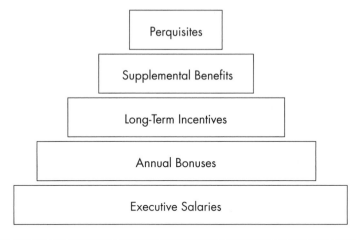

meaningful. *Bonuses* for executives can be determined in several ways. A discretionary system whereby bonuses are awarded based on the judgments of the chief executive officer and the board of directors is one way.

Performance-based incentives, often in the form of stock options, attempt to tie executive compensation to the long-term growth and success of the organization. A **stock option** gives an individual the right to buy stock in a company, usually at an advantageous price. Different types of stock options have been used depending on the tax laws in effect.

Where stock is closely held, firms may grant "stock equivalencies" in the form of *phantom stock* or *appreciation rights.* These plans pay recipients the cash value of increased value of the stock in the future, determined by a base valuation made at the time the phantom stock or share appreciation rights are given.

As with nonexecutive employees, *benefits* for executives may take several forms, including traditional retirement, health insurance, vacations, and so on. However, executive benefits may include some things that other employee benefits do not.

In addition to the regular benefits received by all employees, executives often receive benefits called perquisites. **Perquisites (perks)** are special executive benefits, usually noncash items. Perks are useful in tying executives to organizations and in demonstrating their importance to the companies. It is the status enhancement value of perks that is important to many executives.

A special perk available to some executives, a **golden parachute,** provides protection and security to executives in the event that they lose their jobs or their firms are acquired by other firms. Typically, employment contracts are written to give special compensation to executives if they are negatively affected in an acquisition or merger.

Criticisms of Executive Compensation

A number of criticisms have been directed at executive compensation. One is that it does not offer really long-term rewards. Instead, performance in a given year may lead to large rewards even though corporate performance over time may be mediocre. Another potential problem is that although supplements such as bonuses and stock options are supposed to be tied to the performance of the organization, research results conflict as to whether or not this linkage exists.

▶ SUGGESTED READINGS

1. Green, Ronald M., and John F. Buckley. 1997. *1997 State by State Guide to Human Resources Law.* New York: Panel Publishers.
2. Lough, David A, and Christopher J. Howe. 1996. *Business Basics for Compensation Professionals. Linking Pay to Financial Performance.* Scottsdale, AZ: American Compensation Association.

▶ NOTES

1. E. E. Lawler, III, *Strategic Pay: Aligning Organizational Strategies and Pay Systems* (Northbrook, IL: Brace-Park Press, 1995).
2. Blair H. Sheppard, Ray J. Lewichi, and John W. Minton, *Organizational Justice* (New York: Lexington Books, 1992), 122–129.
3. For more details, see J. E. Kalet, *Primer on FLSA and Other Wage & Hour Laws,* 3rd ed. (Washington, DC: Bureau of National Affairs, 1994).
4. For a detailed discussion of the Hay system, see Richard I. Henderson, *Compensation Management,* 6th ed. (Englewood Cliffs, NJ: Prentice-Hall, 1994), 288–305.

9

Incentives and Benefits

Employee incentives and benefits have become a major part of compensation in most American organizations. Incentives are attempts to tie employee reward to output. **Incentives** are compensation that rewards an employee for performance beyond normal expectations. Employee benefits are a smorgasbord of indirect compensations, such as pensions, health insurance, time off with pay, and others. A **benefit** is a form of indirect compensation.

Unlike employers in many other countries, in the United States employers have become a major provider of benefits for citizens. In many other nations, citizens and employers are taxed to pay for the government's provision of such benefits as health care and retirement. Although U.S. employers are required to provide some benefits, they voluntarily provide others.

▶ INCENTIVES

An incentive is compensation that rewards an employee for efforts beyond normal performance expectations. The need for new ways of paying people to increase their productivity has resulted in many different approaches, plans, and ideas. Generally, performance incentive systems are based on some simple assumptions:

▶ Some jobs contribute more to organizational success than others.
▶ Some people do better work than others.
▶ Employees who do more should receive more.

As Figure 9–1 shows, incentives can be focused on individual performance, team or group performance, or organization-wide performance. The three focuses have different impacts on cooperation among people.

▶**FIGURE 9-1   Incentive Plans: Focus and Cooperation Requirements**

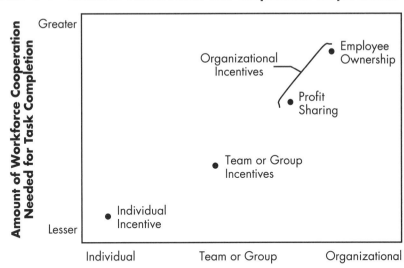

Individual incentives neither require nor foster much cooperation among individuals. In pursuit of individual rewards, an employee may withhold information from others, sabotage efforts of a competing employee, focus *only* on what is rewarded, or refuse to do anything that is not tied directly to the incentive reward. Despite such undesirable behaviors, individual incentives may be very successful if doing the job does not require a great deal of cooperation among employees.

When an entire work group or *team* is rewarded for its performance, more cooperation among the members is required and usually forthcoming. However, competition among different teams for rewards can lead to decline in overall performance under certain circumstances.

Organizational incentives reward people for the performance of the entire organization. This approach reduces individual and team competition and assumes that all employees working together can generate financial gain, which is then shared.

Guidelines for Incentive Systems

Incentive systems can be complex and can take many forms. However, certain general guidelines are useful in establishing and maintaining incentive systems.

Recognize Organizational Culture and Resources.   An important factor in the success of any incentive program is that it be consistent with both the culture and the financial resources of the organization.

Tie Incentives to Desired Performance.   Incentive systems should be tied as much as possible to desired performance. Employees must see a direct relationship between their efforts and their rewards. Further, both employees and managers must see the rewards as equitable and desirable.

Keep Incentive Plans Current.   An incentive system should consistently reflect current technological and organizational conditions. Incentive systems should be reviewed continually to determine whether they are operating as designed.

Recognize Individual Differences.   Incentive plans should provide for individual differences. People are complex, and a variety of incentive systems may have to be developed to appeal to various organizational groups and individuals. Not everybody will want the same type of incentive rewards. For this and other reasons, individual incentive systems must be designed carefully.

Separate Plan Payments from Base Pay.   Successful incentive plans separate the incentive payment from base salary. That separation makes a clear connection between performance and pay. It also reinforces the notion that one part of the employee's pay must be "re-earned" in the next performance period.

▶ INDIVIDUAL INCENTIVES

Individual incentive systems attempt to relate individual effort to pay. The most individual incentive system is the piece-rate system. Under the **straight piece-rate system,** wages are determined by multiplying the number of units produced by the piece rate for one unit. The rate per piece does not change regardless of the number of pieces produced.

Commissions

An individual incentive system widely used in sales jobs is the **commission,** which is compensation computed as a percentage of sales in units or dollars. Commissions are integrated into the pay given to sales workers in three common ways: straight commission, salary plus commission, and bonuses.

In the *straight commission* system, a sales representative receives a percentage of the value of the sales made. The most frequently used form of sales compensation is the *salary plus commission,* which combines the stability of a salary with the performance aspect of a commission. A common split is 80% salary to 20% commission, although the split varies by industry and with other factors.

Consultants criticize many sales commission plans as being too complex to motivate sales representatives. Others are too simple, focusing only on the salesperson's pay, not on organizational objectives. Although a majority of companies use overall sales growth as the only performance measure, performance would be much better if these organizations used a variety of criteria, including obtaining new accounts and selling high-value versus low-value items that reflect marketing plans.[1]

Bonuses

As mentioned, sales workers may receive commissions in the form of lump-sum payments, or **bonuses.** Other employees may receive bonuses as well. Bonuses are less costly than general wage increases, since they do not become part of employees' base wages, upon which future percentage increases are figured. Bonuses have gained in popularity recently. Individual incentive compensation in the form of bonuses often is used at the executive or upper-management levels of an organization, and it is increasingly used at lower levels, too.

▶ TEAM-BASED INCENTIVES

Figure 9–2 shows some reasons that companies establish group incentive programs. The size of the group is critical to the success of team-based incentives. If it becomes too large, employees may feel their individual efforts will have little or no effect on the total performance of the group and the resulting rewards. Incentive plans for small groups are a direct result of the growing number of complex jobs requiring interdependent effort. Team-based incentive plans may encourage teamwork in small groups where interdependence is high.

Team-based incentive plans can pose problems for the design and difficulties in the administration of team-based incentives. Furthermore, groups, like individuals, may restrict output, resist revision of standards, and seek to gain at the expense of other groups. Compensating different employee teams with different incentives may cause them to overemphasize certain efforts to the detriment of the overall organizational good.

▶ **FIGURE 9–2 Why Organizations Establish Team Incentives**

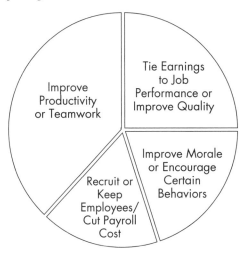

▶ ORGANIZATIONAL INCENTIVES

An organizational incentive system compensates all employees in the organization based on how well the organization as a whole performs during the year.

Gainsharing

Gainsharing is the sharing with employees of greater-than-expected gains in profits and/or productivity. Gainsharing attempts to increase "discretionary efforts"—that is, the difference between the maximum amount of effort a person can exert and the minimum amount of effort necessary to keep from being fired.

Payouts of the gains can be made monthly, quarterly, semiannually, or annually, depending on management philosophy and the performance measures used. The more frequent the payouts, the greater the visibility of the rewards to employees. Therefore, given a choice, most firms with gainsharing plans have chosen to make the payouts more frequently than annually. The rewards can be distributed in four ways:

- ▶ A flat amount for all employees
- ▶ Same percentage of base salary for all employees
- ▶ Percentage of the gains by category of employees
- ▶ Amount or percentage based on individual performance against measures

Profit Sharing

As the name implies, **profit sharing** distributes a portion of organizational profits to employees. Typically, the percentage of the profits distributed to employees is agreed on by the end of the year before distribution. In some profit-sharing plans, employees receive portions of the profits at the end of the year; in others, the profits are deferred, placed in a fund, and made available to employees on retirement or on their leaving the organization.

Employee Stock Ownership Plans (ESOPs)

A common type of profit sharing is the **employee stock ownership plan (ESOP)**. An ESOP is designed to give employees stock ownership of the organization for which they work, thereby increasing their commitment, loyalty, and effort.

Establishing an ESOP creates several advantages. The major one is that the firm can receive favorable tax treatment of the earnings earmarked for use in the ESOP. Second, an ESOP gives employees a "piece of the action" so that they can share in the growth and profitability of their firm.

A drawback is that ESOPs have been used as a management tool to fend off unfriendly takeover attempts. Holders of employee-owned stock often align with management to turn down bids that would benefit outside stockholders but would replace management and restructure operations. Surely, ESOPs were not created to entrench inefficient management. Despite these disadvantages, ESOPs have grown in popularity.

▶ BENEFITS

Why do employers provide benefits? Individuals could purchase their own health insurance and save for their own retirement. Certainly the money that employers spend on benefits could be given instead to employees in cash, and they could spend that cash for any benefits they might want. That amount is not insignificant.

Benefits must be viewed as part of total compensation, and total compensation is one of the key strategic decision areas in human resources. From management's perspective, benefits are thought to contribute to several strategic goals:

- ▶ Help attract employees
- ▶ Help retain employees
- ▶ Elevate the image of the organization with employees and other organizations
- ▶ Increase job satisfaction

Benefits generally are not taxed as income to employees. For this reason, they represent a somewhat more valuable reward to employees than an equivalent cash payment.

A classification of typical benefits is presented in Figure 9–3. Voluntary and mandated benefits are distinguished in the figure. **Mandated benefits** are those benefits which employers in the United States must provide to employees by law. Social Security and unemployment insurance are funded through a tax paid by the employer based on the employee's compensation. Workers' compensation laws exist in all states. In addition, employers must offer unpaid leave to employees during certain medical or family difficulties. The following sections detail many of the benefit types.

COBRA Provisions

Legal requirements in the Consolidated Omnibus Budget Reconciliation Act (COBRA) require that most employers (except churches and the federal government) with 20 or more employees offer *extended health-care coverage* to the following groups:

- ▶ Employees who voluntarily or involuntarily quit, except those terminated for "gross misconduct"
- ▶ Widowed or divorced spouses and dependent children of former or current employees
- ▶ Retirees and their spouses whose health-care coverage ends

Social Security

The Social Security Act of 1935, with its later amendments, established a system providing *old age, survivor's, disability,* and *retirement benefits.* Administered by the federal government through the Social Security Administration, this program provides benefits to previously employed individuals. Employees and employers share in the cost of Social Security through a tax on employees' wages or salaries.

► **FIGURE 9–3   Benefits Classified by Type**

▢ Government Mandated	▢ Employer Voluntary

SECURITY	HEALTH CARE	RETIREMENT
Workers' compensation	COBRA provisions	Social Security
Unemployment compensation	Medical	Early retirement
Social Security (retirement, old age, survivor's, and disability insurance)	Dental	Preretirement counseling
	Vision care	
Severance pay		Disability retirement benefits
Supplemental unemployment insurance	Prescription drugs	Health care for retirees
	Psychiatric counseling	
Family issues: child care, elder care		Pension plans
	Wellness programs	
FINANCIAL, INSURANCE, AND RELATED		IRA, 401(k), Keogh plans
Life insurance	HMO or PPO health-care plans	
Legal insurance	**SOCIAL AND RECREATIONAL**	**TIME OFF**
Disability insurance		
Stock plans	Tennis courts	Family and medical leaves
Financial counseling	Bowling leagues	Military reserve time off
Credit unions	Service awards	Election and jury leaves
Company-provided car and expense account	Sponsored events (athletic and social)	Lunch and rest breaks
	Cafeteria	
Educational assistance	Recreation programs	Holidays and vacations
Relocation and moving assistance		Funeral and bereavement leaves

Workers' Compensation

Workers' compensation provides benefits to persons injured on the job. Employers provide workers' compensation coverage by purchasing insurance from a private carrier or state insurance fund or by providing self-insurance.

Workers' compensation systems require employers to give cash benefits, medical care, and rehabilitation services to employees for injuries or illnesses occurring within the scope of their employment. Employees are entitled to quick and certain payment from the workers' compensation system without proving that the employer is at fault. In exchange, employees give up the right of legal actions and awards; so employers enjoy limited liability for occupational illnesses and injury.

Unemployment Compensation

Another benefit required by law is unemployment compensation, established as part of the Social Security Act of 1935. Each state operates its own unemployment compensation system, and provisions differ significantly from state to state.

Family Leave

In 1993, President Clinton signed into law the Family and Medical Leave Act (FMLA), which covers all employers with 50 or more employees who live within 75 miles of the workplace and includes federal, state, and private employers. Only employees who have worked at least 12 months and 1,250 hours in the previous year are eligible for leaves under FMLA. The law requires that employers allow eligible employees to take a total of 12 weeks' leave during any 12-month period for one or more of the following situations:

- ▶ Birth, adoption, or foster-care placement of a child
- ▶ Caring for a spouse, child, or parent with a serious health condition
- ▶ Serious health condition of the employee

A **serious health condition** is one requiring inpatient, hospital, hospice, or residential medical care or continuing physician care. An employer may require an employee to provide a certificate from a doctor verifying such an illness.

Severance Pay

Severance pay is a security benefit voluntarily offered by employers to employees who lose their jobs. Severed employees may receive lump-sum severance payments if their employment is terminated by the employer.

The Worker Adjustment and Retraining Notification Act (WARN) of 1988 requires that many employers give 60 days' notice if a mass layoff or facility closing is to occur. The act does not require employers to give severance pay.

▶ HEALTH-CARE BENEFITS

Employers provide a variety of health-care and medical benefits, usually through insurance coverage. The most common ones cover medical, dental, prescription-drug, and vision-care expenses for employees and their dependents.

The *Health Portability and Accountability Act* allows employees who switch from one company's health insurance plan to another's to get the new health coverage regardless of pre-existing conditions. The legislation also prohibits group insurance plans from dropping coverage from a sick employee and requires them to make individual coverage available to people who leave group plans.

In an effort to contain health-care costs, many employers are providing coverage through preferred provider organizations (PPOs) and health maintenance organizations (HMOs) that are often called **managed care** plans. Such approaches are designed to monitor and reduce medical costs using good management practices and the market system. Managed care plans have become an important health-care option.

As health insurance costs rose, employers also shifted some of those costs to employees. The **copayment** strategy requires employees to pay a portion of the cost of both insurance premiums and medical care. Many employers have raised the deductible per person from $50 to $250 or more.

Many employers have found that some of the health care provided by doctors and hospitals is unnecessary, incorrectly billed, or deliberately overcharged. Consequently, both employers and insurance firms are requiring that medical work and charges be audited and reviewed through a **utilization review.** This process may require a second opinion, review of procedures used, and review of charges for procedures done.

▶ RETIREMENT BENEFITS

Few people have financial reserves to use when they retire, so retirement benefits attempt to provide income for employees on retirement.

Early Retirement

Provisions for early retirement currently are included in many pension plans. Early retirement gives people an opportunity to get away from a long-term job; individuals who have spent 25 to 30 years working for the same employer may wish to use their talents in other areas. Phased-in and part-time retirements also are used by some individuals and firms.

Retirees and Health-Care Benefits

Some employers choose to offer health-care benefits to their retirees, paid by the retirees, the company, or both. These benefits are usually available until the retiree is eligible for Medicare.

Pension Plans

Pension plans are retirement benefits established and funded by employers and employees. Organizations are not required to offer pension plans to employees, and only 40% to 50% of U.S. workers are covered by them.

The Employee Retirement Income Security Act (ERISA) of 1974 essentially requires many companies to offer retirement plans to all employees if they are offered to any employees. Accrued benefits must be given to employees when they retire or leave. The act also sets minimum funding requirements. Plans that do not meet these requirements are subject to IRS financial penalties. Employers are required to pay plan termination insurance to ensure that employee pensions will be there even if the company goes out of business.

Pension Contributions.   Pension plans can be either contributory or non-contributory. In a **contributory plan,** money for pension benefits is paid in by both the employee and the employer. In a **noncontributory plan,** the employer provides all the funds. As would be expected, the noncontributory plan is preferred by employees and labor unions.

Pension Benefits.   Payment of benefits can follow one of two plans. In a **defined-contribution plan,** the employer makes an annual payment to an employee's pension account. The key to this plan is the *contribution rate;* employee retirement benefits depend on fixed contributions and employee earnings levels.

In a **defined-benefit plan,** an employee is promised a pension amount based on age and service. The employer's contributions are based on actuarial calculations that focus on the *benefits* to be received by employees after retirement and the *methods* used to determine such benefits.

Portability.   Another feature of some employee pensions is **portability.** In a portable plan, employees can move their pension benefits from one employer to another. If they leave before retirement, individuals who are not in a portable system must take a *lump-sum settlement* made up of the money that they contributed to the plan plus accumulated interest on their contribution.

Vesting Rights.   The right of employees to receive benefits from their pension plans is called **vesting.** Typically, vesting assures employees of a certain pension, provided they have worked a minimum number of years.

401(k) Plans.   The **401(k) plan** gets its name from Section 401(k) of the federal tax code and is an agreement in which a percentage of an employee's pay is withheld and invested in a tax-deferred account. It allows employees to choose whether to receive cash or have employer contributions from profit-sharing and stock-bonus plans placed into tax-deferred accounts. Employees can elect to have their current pay reduced by a certain percentage and that amount paid into a 401(k) plan.

▶ OTHER BENEFITS

Many employers offer a variety of other benefits to attract and retain employees. Two of the most popular are additional insurance benefits and educational benefits.

Other Insurance Benefits

In addition to health-related insurance, some employers provide other types of insurance. These benefits offer major advantages for employees because many employers pay some or all of the costs. Even when employers do not pay any of the costs, employees still benefit because of the lower rates available through group programs.

Educational Benefits

Another benefit used by employees comes in the form of *educational assistance* to pay for some or all costs associated with formal education courses and degree programs, including the costs of books and laboratory materials.

▶ TIME-OFF BENEFITS

Employers give employees paid time off in a variety of circumstances. Paid lunch breaks and rest periods, holidays, and vacations are the most well known. But leaves are given for a number of other purposes as well. Time-off benefits are estimated to represent from about 5% to 13% of total compensation. Some of the more common time-off benefits include holiday pay, vacation pay, and leaves of absence. Most, if not all, employers provide pay for a variety of holidays, as Figure 9–4 shows.

Paid vacations are a common benefit. Employers often use graduated vacation-time scales based on employees' length of service. Some organizations allow employees to accumulate unused vacation. As with holidays, employees often are required to work the day before and the day after a vacation to prevent abuse.

Leaves of Absence

Leaves of absence, taken as time off with or without pay, are given for a variety of reasons. All of the leaves discussed here add to employer costs even when they are unpaid, because usually the missing employee's work must be covered, either by other employees working overtime or by temporary employees working under contract.

Family Leave.   As mentioned earlier in the chapter, the passage of the Family and Medical Leave Act helped clarify the rights of employees and the responsibilities of most employers.

▶ **FIGURE 9–4   Most Common Paid Holidays in the United States**

1. Christmas
2. New Year's Day
3. Thanksgiving
4. Independence Day
5. Labor Day
6. Memorial Day
7. Day after Thanksgiving
8. Presidents' Day
9. Good Friday
10. Christmas Eve
11. New Year's Eve
12. Veterans Day
13. Columbus Day
14. Martin Luther King, Jr., Day
15. Employee's Birthday

Medical and Sick Leave.   Medical and sick leave are closely related. Many employers allow their employees to miss a limited number of days because of illness without losing pay. Some employers allow employees to accumulate unused sick leave, which may be used in case of catastrophic illnesses. Others pay employees for unused sick leave.

Some organizations have shifted emphasis to reward people who do not use sick leave by giving them **well-pay**—extra pay for not taking sick leave. Other employers have made use of the **earned-time plan,** which combines sick leave, vacations, and holidays into a total number of hours or days that employees can take off with pay. One organization found that when it stopped designating a specific number of sick-leave days and an earned-time plan was implemented, absenteeism dropped, time off was scheduled better, and employee acceptance of the leave policy improved.

Paid Time Off (PTO) Plans.   Still other firms are using *time-off banks,* which lump the various time-off-with-pay days together in one package to be used at the employee's discretion. The new programs provide more flexibility in using time off, and some say they add dignity to the process of taking time off.

Other types of leaves are given for a variety of purposes. Some, such as *military leave, election leave,* and *jury leave,* are required by various state and federal laws.

▶ BENEFITS ADMINISTRATION

With the myriad of benefits and regulations, it is easy to see why many organizations must make coordinated efforts to administer benefits programs. One of the greatest advances in administering benefits has been the development of computer software to help employers track benefits.

Benefits Communication

Employees generally do not know much about the values and costs associated with the benefits they receive from employers. Yet benefits communication and benefits satisfaction are linked. Many employers have instituted special benefits communication systems to inform employees about the value of the benefits provided. Explaining benefits during new employee orientation programs, holding periodic meetings, preparing special literature, and using in-house employee publications to heighten awareness of benefits are among the methods used.

Many employers also give employees annual "personal statements of benefits" that translate benefits into dollar amounts. Federal regulations under ERISA require that employees receive an annual pension-reporting statement, which also can be included in the personal statements. By having a personalized statement, each employee can see how much his or her own benefits are worth. Employers hope that by educating employees on benefits costs, they can manage expenditures better and can give employees a better appreciation for the employers' payments.[2]

Flexible Benefits

A **flexible benefits plan,** sometimes called a *flex* or *cafeteria* plan, allows employees to select the benefits they prefer from groups of benefits established by the employer. By making a variety of "dishes," or benefits, available, the organization allows each employee to select an individual combination of benefits within some overall limits. As a result of the changing composition of the workforce, flexible benefits plans have grown in popularity.

Flexible Spending Accounts. Under current tax laws (Section 125 of the Tax Code administered by the Internal Revenue Service), employees can divert some income before taxes into accounts to fund certain benefits. These **flexible spending accounts** allow employees to contribute pretax dollars to buy additional benefits. An example illustrates the advantage of these accounts to employees. Assume an employee earns $3,000 per month and has $100 per month deducted to put into a flexible spending account. That $100 does not count as gross income for tax purposes, so the taxable income is reduced. The employee uses the money in the account to purchase additional benefits.

Under tax law at the time of this writing, the funds in the account can be used only to purchase the following: (1) *additional health care* (including offsetting deductibles), (2) *life insurance,* (3) *disability insurance,* and (4) *dependent-care benefits.* Furthermore, tax regulations require that if employees do not spend all of the money in their accounts by the end of the year, they forfeit it. Therefore, it is important that employees estimate very closely the additional benefits they will use.[3]

▶ SUGGESTED READINGS

1. Barton, G. Michael. 1997. *Self-Insuring Benefits Programs: An Approach to Controlling Costs and Maintaining Quality.* Scottsdale, AZ: American Compensation Association.

2. Benna, R. Theodore. 1996. *Helping Employees Achieve Retirement Security.* Investors Press.

3. Graham-Moore, Brian, and Timothy L. Ross. 1995. *Gainsharing and Employee Involvement Plans for Improving Performance.* Washington, DC: Bureau of National Affairs.

4. Sanes, Richard, and Joseph L. Lineberry, Jr. 1995. *Implementing Flexible Benefits: An Approach to Facilitating Employee Choice.* Scottsdale, AZ: American Compensation Association.

5. SHRM Issues Management Survey Program. 1997. *SHRM® 1997 Benefits Survey.* Alexandria, VA: Society of Human Resource Management.

6. Sugar, David S., and Robert A. Romancheck. 1995. *Securing Nonqualified Arrangements. An Approach to Choosing a Funding Mechanism for Executive Deferral and Retirement Plans.* Scottsdale, AZ: American Compensation Association.

7. Wilson, Thomas B., and Carol C. Phalen. 1996. *Rewarding Group Performance: An Approach to Designing and Implementing Incentive Pay Programs.* Scottsdale, AZ: American Compensation Association.

▶ NOTES

1. T. M. Welbourne and D. M. Cable, "Group Incentives and Pay Satisfaction: Understanding the Relationship through an Identity Theory Perspective," *Human Relations* 48 (1995), 711–725.

2. M. L. Williams, "Antecedents of Employee Benefit Level Satisfaction: A Test of a Model," *Journal of Management* 21 (1995), 1097–1128.

3. J. F. Levy and A. Z. Krebs, "Flexible Spending Accounts: Medreal IRA's and Partner's Reimbursement Accounts," *Paytech*, July/August 1994, 38–42.

10

Employee Relations

This chapter examines several important aspects of employee relations. One set of issues focuses on health, safety, and security. Another set is composed of employee rights, HR policies, and discipline.

The terms *health, safety,* and *security* are closely related. The broader and somewhat more nebulous term is **health,** which refers to a general state of physical, mental, and emotional well-being.

Typically, **safety** refers to protection of the physical well-being of people. The main purpose of effective safety programs in organizations is to prevent work-related injuries and accidents.

The purpose of **security** is to protect employer facilities and equipment from unauthorized access and to protect employees while they are on work premises or work assignments.

▶ OCCUPATIONAL SAFETY AND HEALTH

The Occupational Safety and Health Act of 1970 was passed "to assure so far as possible every working man or woman in the Nation safe and healthful working conditions and to preserve our human resources." Every employer engaged in commerce who has one or more employees is covered by the act. Farmers having fewer than 10 employees are exempt. Covered under other health and safety acts are employers in specific industries such as coal mining. Federal, state, and local government employees are covered by separate provisions or statutes.

Basic Provisions

The act established the Occupational Safety and Health Administration, known as OSHA, to administer its provisions. Section 5a(1) of the act is known as the "general duty" clause. This section requires that in areas in which no standards have been adopted, the employer has a *general duty* to provide safe and healthy working conditions. Employers who know of, or who should reasonably know of, unsafe or unhealthy conditions can be cited for violating this clause. The existence of standard practices or of a trade association code not included in OSHA standards often is used as the basis for citations under the general duty clause.

Employers are responsible for knowing about and informing their employees of safety and health standards established by OSHA and for displaying OSHA posters in prominent places. In addition, they are required to enforce the use of personal protective equipment and to provide communications to make employees aware of safety considerations. The act also states that employees who report safety violations to OSHA cannot be punished or discharged by their employers.

Refusing Unsafe Work.   Both union and nonunion workers have refused to work when they considered the work unsafe. Current legal conditions for refusing work because of safety concerns are:

▶ The employee's fear is objectively reasonable.
▶ The employee has tried to get the dangerous condition corrected.
▶ Using normal procedures to solve the problem has not worked.

Work Assignments and Reproductive Health.   Related to unsafe work is the issue of assigning employees to work in areas where their ability to have children may be affected by exposure to chemical hazards. Women who are able to bear children or who are pregnant have presented the primary concerns, but in some situations, the possibility that men might become sterile also has been a concern.

In a court case involving reproductive health, the Supreme Court held that Johnson Controls' policy of keeping women of childbearing capacity out of jobs that might lead to lead exposure violated the Civil Rights Act and the Pregnancy Discrimination Act.[1]

Enforcement Standards.   To implement OSHA, specific standards were established regulating equipment and working environments. National standards developed by engineering and quality control groups are often used.

Hazard Communication.   OSHA also has enforcement responsibilities for the federal Hazard Communication Standard, which requires manufacturers, importers, distributors, and users of hazardous chemicals to evaluate, classify, and label these substances. Employers also must make available to employees, their representatives, and health professionals information about hazardous substances. This information is contained in *Material Safety Data Sheets* (MSDSs), which must be kept readily accessible to those who work with chemicals and other substances. The MSDSs also indicate antidotes or actions to be taken should someone contact the substances.

Inspection Requirements

The act provides for on-the-spot inspection by OSHA representatives called *compliance officers* or *inspectors*. Under the original act, an employer could not refuse entry to an OSHA inspector. Further, the original act prohibited a compliance officer from notifying an organization before an inspection. In 1978, the U.S. Supreme Court ruled on this *no-knock provision,* holding that safety inspectors must produce a search warrant if an employer refuses to allow an inspector into the plant voluntarily. However, the Court ruled that an inspector does not have to prove probable cause to obtain a search warrant.

In conjunction with state and local governments, OSHA has established a safety consultation service. An employer can contact the state agency and have an authorized safety consultant conduct an advisory inspection.

Citations and Violations

As noted, OSHA inspectors can issue citations for violations of the provisions of the act. Whether a citation is issued depends on the severity and extent of the problems and on the employer's knowledge of them. In addition, depending on the nature and number of violations, penalties can be assessed against employers. The nature and extent of the penalties depends upon the type and severity of the violations as determined by OSHA officials.

There are basically five types of violations, ranging from severe to minimal and including a special category for repeated violations:

▶ Imminent danger   ▶ *De minimis*
▶ Serious   ▶ Willful and repeated
▶ Other than serious

Imminent Danger.   When there is reasonable certainty that the condition will cause death or serious physical harm if it is not corrected immediately, an imminent-danger citation is issued and a notice posted by an inspector. Imminent-danger situations are handled on the highest-priority basis.

Serious.   When a condition could probably cause death or serious physical harm, and the employer should know of the condition, a serious-violation citation is issued. Examples are the absence of a protective screen on a lathe or the lack of a blade guard on an electric saw.

Other Than Serious.   Other-than-serious violations could have an impact on employees' health or safety but probably would not cause death or serious harm. Having loose ropes in a work area might be classified as an other-than-serious violation.

De Minimis.   A *de minimis* condition is one that is not directly and immediately related to employees' safety or health. No citation is issued, but the condition is mentioned to the employer.

Willful and Repeated. Citations for willful and repeated violations are issued to employers who have been previously cited for violations. If an employer knows about a safety violation or has been warned of a violation and does not correct the problem, a second citation is issued. The penalty for a willful and repeated violation can be very high. If death results from an accident that involves a safety violation, a jail term of six months can be imposed on responsible executives or managers.

Record-Keeping Requirements

OSHA has established a standard national system for recording occupational injuries, accidents, and fatalities. Employers are generally required to maintain a detailed annual record of the various types of accidents for inspection by OSHA representatives and for submission to the agency. Employers that have had good safety records in previous years and that have fewer than 10 employees are not required to keep detailed records. However, many organizations must complete OSHA form 200.

Reporting Injuries and Illnesses. Four types of injuries or illnesses are defined by the act:

1. *Injury- or illness-related deaths.*
2. *Lost-time or disability injuries.* These include job-related injuries or disabling occurrences that cause an employee to miss his or her regularly scheduled work on the day following the accident.
3. *Medical care injuries.* These injuries require treatment by a physician but do not cause an employee to miss a regularly scheduled work turn.
4. *Minor injuries.* These injuries require first-aid treatment and do not cause an employee to miss the next regularly scheduled work turn.

The record-keeping requirements for these injuries and illnesses are summarized in Figure 10–1. Notice that only minor injuries do not have to be recorded for OSHA. Managers may attempt to avoid reporting lost-time or medical care injuries. For example, if several managers are trained in first aid, some minor injuries can be treated at the worksite.

▶ SAFETY MANAGEMENT

Effective safety management begins with organizational commitment to a comprehensive safety effort. This effort should be coordinated from the top level of management to include all members of the organization. Once the organization has made a commitment to safety, different approaches can be used, as Figure 10–2 illustrates. With all facets of safety addressed, then safety management becomes integrated with effective HR management throughout the organization.

Organizational Safety Management

Once a commitment is made to safety, planning efforts must be coordinated, with duties assigned to supervisors, managers, safety specialists, and HR specialists.

▶ **FIGURE 10–1** **Guide to Recordability of Cases under the Occupational Safety and Health Act**

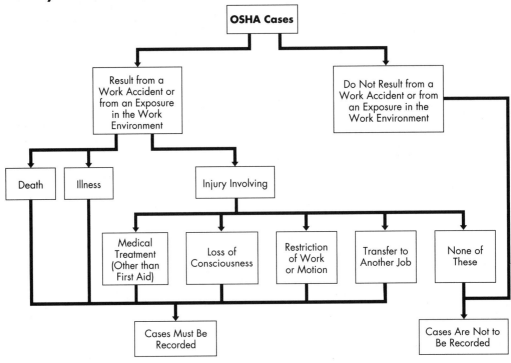

Source: U.S. Department of Labor Statistics, *What Every Employee Needs to Know About OSHA Record Keeping* (Washington, DC: U.S. Government Printing Office).

Naturally, duties vary according to the size of the organization and the industry. For this reason, it is impossible to suggest a single proper mixture of responsibilities. The focus of any systematic approach to safety is the continued diligence of workers, managers, and other personnel. Employees who are not reminded of safety violations, who are not encouraged to be safety conscious, or who violate company safety rules and policies are not likely to be safe.

Safety Policies and Discipline.   Enforcing safety policies and rules and disciplining violators are important components of safety efforts. Frequent reinforcement of the need for safe behavior and feedback on positive safety practices are extremely effective in improving worker safety.

Safety Training and Communications.   One way to encourage employee safety is to involve all employees at various times in safety training sessions and committee meetings and to have these meetings frequently. In addition to safety training, continuous communication to develop safety consciousness is necessary.

Safety Committees.   Workers frequently are involved in safety planning through safety committees, often composed of workers from a variety of levels

▶ **F I G U R E 10–2**   **Approaches to Effective Safety Management**

APPROACHES TO EFFECTIVE SAFETY MANAGEMENT

Organizational Approach
• Design of jobs
• Development/implementation of safety policies
• Use of safety committees
• Coordinating accident investigations

Engineering Approach
• Design of work environment
• Review of equipment
• Ergonomics

Individual Approach
• Reinforcing safety motivation and attitudes
• Providing employee safety training
• Rewarding safety through incentive programs

and departments. A safety committee generally has regularly scheduled meetings, has specific responsibilities for conducting safety reviews, and makes recommendations for changes necessary to avoid future accidents.

In approximately 32 states, all but the smallest employers may be required to establish safety committees. From time to time, legislation has been introduced at the federal level to require joint management-employee safety committees. But as yet, no federal provisions have been enacted.[2]

Safety Inspection and Accident Investigation.   It is not necessary to wait for an OSHA inspector to inspect the work area for safety hazards. Such inspections may be done by a safety committee or by the safety coordinator. They should be done on a regular basis because OSHA may inspect organizations with above-average lost workday rates more frequently.

In addition, when accidents occur, they should be investigated. In investigating the *scene* of an accident, it is important to determine the physical and environmental conditions that contributed to the accident.

Evaluation of Safety Efforts.   Organizations need to monitor their safety efforts. Just as organizational accounting records are audited, a firm's safety efforts should be periodically audited as well. Accident and injury statistics should be compared with previous accident patterns to determine if any significant changes have occurred.

Engineering Approach to Safety and Health

Logic and reason suggest that both work design and human work behaviors contribute to safety. Yet some approaches to reducing accidents focus on one or the other exclusively. Both approaches are valuable, so they tend to be most effective when considered together. The engineering approach to safety and health is one such approach.

Ergonomic Approach to Safety.   **Ergonomics** is the proper design of the work environment to address the physical demands experienced by people. An ergonomist studies physiological, psychological, and engineering design aspects of a job, including such factors as fatigue, lighting, tools, equipment layout, and placement of controls. Human factors engineering is a related field.

Most recently, attention has focused on the application of ergonomic principles to the design of workstations where computer operators work with personal computers and video display terminals (VDTs) for long periods of time.

Cumulative Trauma and Repetitive Stress.   Repetitive stress injuries, repetitive motion injuries, cumulative trauma disorders, carpal tunnel syndrome, ergonomic hazards—this listing of serious-sounding problems applies to many workplaces. **Cumulative trauma disorders (CTDs)** occur when workers repetitively use the same muscles to perform tasks, resulting in muscle and skeletal injuries.

Individual Factors and Safety Management

Engineers approach safety from the perspective of redesigning the machinery or the work area. Industrial psychologists see safety differently. They are concerned with the proper match of people to jobs and emphasize employee training in safety methods, fatigue reduction, and health awareness.

Behavioral Approach to Safety.   Industrial psychologists have conducted numerous field studies with thousands of employees looking at the "human factors" in accidents. The results show a definite relationship between emotional factors, such as stress, and accidents. Other studies point to the importance of individual differences, motivation, attitudes, and learning as key factors in controlling the human element in safety.

▶ HEALTH

Employee health problems are varied—and somewhat inevitable. They can range from minor illnesses such as colds to serious illnesses related to the jobs performed. Some employees have emotional problems; others have alcohol or drug problems. Some problems are chronic; others are transitory. But all may affect organizational operations and individual employee productivity.

Employers are increasingly confronted by the problems associated with employees who have AIDS or other life-threatening illnesses such as cancer. Some firms have policies to deal with AIDS and other life-threatening illnesses. Firms that have lost an employee to one of these diseases are more likely to have a policy than those that have not. But estimates are that only 25% of the larger employers in the United States have a policy on life-threatening illness.[3]

Smoking at Work

Arguments and rebuttals characterize the smoking-at-work controversy, and statistics are rampant. A multitude of state and local laws have been passed that deal with smoking in the workplace and public places. Passage of these laws has been viewed by many employers positively, as they relieve employers of the responsibility for making decisions on smoking issues.

Substance Abuse

Substance abuse is defined as the use of illicit substances or the misuse of controlled substances, alcohol, or other drugs. There are millions of substance abusers in the workforce, and they cost the United States billions of dollars annually.

Employers are concerned about substance abuse because it alters work behaviors. The effects may be subtle, such as tardiness, increased absenteeism, slower work pace, higher rate of mistakes, and less time spent at the workstation.

Substance Abuse and the ADA.   The Americans with Disabilities Act (ADA) determines how management can handle substance-abuse cases. The practicing illegal drug abuser specifically is excluded from the definition of *disabled* under the act. However, addiction to legal substances (alcohol, for example) is *not* excluded.

Drug Free Workplace Act.   The Drug Free Workplace Act of 1988 states that any employer who has contracts with the U.S. government must maintain a drug-free environment for its workers. Failure to do so can lead to contract termination. Tobacco and alcohol are not considered controlled substances under the act, and off-the-job drug use is not included.

Employer Responses to Health Issues

Employers who are concerned about maintaining a healthy workforce must move beyond simply providing safe working conditions and must address employee health and wellness in other ways. Two of the major ways employers address employee health issues are wellness programs and employee assistance programs.

Wellness Programs.   Employers' desires to improve productivity, decrease absenteeism, and control health-care costs have come together in the "wellness" movement. **Wellness programs** are designed to maintain or improve employee health before problems arise.

Employee Assistance Programs (EAPs).   One method that organizations are using to respond broadly to employee health issues is the **employee assistance program (EAP),** which provides counseling and other help to employees having emotional, physical, or other personal problems. Figure 10–3 identifies typical areas addressed by EAPs. In such a program, an employer establishes a liaison relationship with a social service counseling agency. Employees who have problems may then contact the agency, either voluntarily or by employer

▶**FIGURE 10–3** **Typical Areas Addressed by Employee Assistance Programs (EAPs)**

Career Counseling	Alcohol/Drug Abuse Programs
24-Hour Crisis Hot Line	Counseling for Marital/ Family Problems
AIDS Education/Support Groups	Counseling for Mental Disorders/ Emotional Stress
Health Risk Screening	
Financial Counseling	Health Education (Smoking, Weight)
Retirement Counseling	Termination/Outplacement Assistance
Legal Counseling	

referral, for assistance with a broad range of problems. Counseling costs are paid for by the employer in total or up to a preestablished limit.

▶ SECURITY

Security activities provide protection to employees and organizational premises, equipment, and systems. Many examples can be cited of security concerns at work. Security in workplaces is increasing as an HR issue. Vandalism against organizational property, theft of company equipment and employees' personal property, and unauthorized "hacking" on organizational computers are all examples of major security concerns today. Another growing concern is workplace violence, which may be seen in attacks by outsiders or co-workers on employees.

Workplace Violence

Workplace violence is a growing concern. During the last few years, workplace homicide has been the number one cause of job deaths in several states. In one year, approximately one thousand individuals were killed at work, and an additional two million people were attacked at work. About 70% of the workplace fatalities involved armed robberies.

The violence committed at work against employees by coworkers and former coworkers is a growing concern for employers. Also, employers have faced legal action by employees or their survivors for failure to protect workers from violence at work caused by disgruntled spouses or boyfriends/girlfriends.

These concerns have led a number of employers to conduct training for supervisors and managers on how to recognize the signs of a potentially violent employee and what steps should be taken. During the training at many firms, supervisors learn the typical profile of potentially violent employees. They are trained to notify the HR department and to refer employees to outside counseling professions, whose services are covered by employee assistance programs offered by the employers.

▶ EMPLOYEE RIGHTS

Some rights have applications both on and off the job. Health and safety rights, the right to free speech, and the right to due process are three examples. Other rights might apply in the workplace but not the home, and vice versa. For example, an employer may have restrictions on employees' right to smoke at work but not on their right to smoke at home off the job. Sometimes, management and employees do not have a clear agreement as to which rights exist in the workplace. Unions have tried over the years to define workplace rights, often through confrontation. Although unionism has declined, increased legal restrictions on employers' HR practices through state legislation and court decisions have increased employee rights.

Statutory Rights and Contractual Rights

Employees' **statutory rights** are the result of specific laws passed by federal, state, or local governments. The legal right to form or join unions is one such right.

An employee's **contractual rights** are based on an agreement or contract with an employer. Unions and management may agree on contracts that specify certain rights. Those contracts are legally enforceable in court. **Employment contracts** spell out details of an employment agreement. These contracts are usually written and very detailed. However, courts are enforcing "unwritten" promises and finding such items as an employee handbook to be part of an employment contract.[4]

Current employee rights, as widely defined under various laws, are divided here into three major categories:

1. Rights affecting the employment agreement, involving:
   ▶ Employment-at-will
   ▶ Implied employment contracts (employee handbooks)
   ▶ Due process
   ▶ Dismissal for just cause
2. Employee privacy rights, involving:
   ▶ Employee review of records
   ▶ Substance abuse and drug testing
3. Workplace investigations

Rights Affecting the Employment Agreement

Although it can be argued that all employee-rights issues affect the employment relationship, four basic issues predominate: employment-at-will, implied contracts, due process, and dismissal for just cause.

Employment-at-Will (EAW). Employment-at-will (EAW) is a common-law doctrine stating that employers have the right to hire, fire, demote, or promote whomever they choose, unless there is a law or contract to the contrary.

Implied Contracts and Employee Handbooks. The idea that a contract (even an implied, unwritten one) exists between workers and their employers affects the employment relationship. Several courts have held that if an employer hires someone for an indefinite period and promises job security or gives specific procedures for discharge, the employer has lost the right to terminate at will. These actions establish employee expectations. When the employer fails to follow up on them, the employee has recourse in court. In essence, the courts have held that such promises, especially when contained in an employee handbook, constitute a contract between an employer and its employees, even though there is no signed document.

Due Process. Due process is the opportunity to defend oneself against charges. For unionized employees, due process usually refers to the right to use the grievance procedure specified in the union contract. Due process may include specific steps in the grievance process, time limits, arbitration procedures, and providing knowledge of disciplinary penalties.

Dismissal for Just Cause. As with due process, what constitutes **just cause** as sufficient justification for dismissal usually is spelled out in union contracts but often is not as clear in at-will situations. While the definition of *just cause* varies, the criteria used by courts have become well defined.

Related to just cause is the concept of **constructive discharge,** which occurs when an employer deliberately makes conditions intolerable in an attempt to get an employee to quit. Under normal circumstances, an employee who resigns rather than being dismissed cannot later collect damages for violation of legal rights. An exception to this rule occurs when the courts find that the working conditions are so intolerable as to *force* a reasonable employee to resign. Then, the resignation is considered a discharge.

Employee Privacy Rights and Employee Records

Three categories of employee privacy rights are considered here: (1) employee rights to review records, (2) rights involving substance abuse and drug testing, and (3) rights involving polygraph and honesty testing.

Employee Right to Review Records. The following legal issues are involved in employee rights to privacy and HR records:

- ▶ Right to access personal information
- ▶ Opportunity to respond to unfavorable information
- ▶ Right to correct erroneous information
- ▶ Right to be notified when information is given to a third party
- ▶ Right to know how information is being used internally
- ▶ Right to reasonable precautions, assuring the individual that the information will not be misused

Substance Abuse and Drug Testing.   The issue of substance abuse and drug testing at work has received a great deal of attention. The importance of the problem to HR management is clear. At best, workers on drugs operate at about 75% of their capacity.[5] In addition, the accident rate, illness rate, workers' compensation rate, absenteeism rate, and voluntary turnover rate range from 3 to 16 times higher for drug users. It is easy to see why management is in favor of drug testing. However, the trade-off between employers' need to test for drugs and employees' right to privacy involves difficult issues.

Drug testing can be done before and/or after hiring. If done afterwards, three different methods may be used: (1) random testing of everyone at periodic intervals; (2) testing only when there is probable cause; or (3) after accidents. Each method raises its own set of problems.

Polygraph and Honesty Testing.   The theory behind a polygraph is that the act of lying produces stress, which in turn causes observable physical changes. An examiner can thus interpret the physical responses to specific questions and make a judgment as to whether the person being tested is practicing deception. However, the Polygraph Protection Act prohibits the use of polygraphs for most preemployment screening and for judging a person's honesty while employed.

"Pencil-and-paper" honesty tests have gained popularity recently. They are not restricted by the Polygraph Protection Act or by the laws of most states. Many organizations are using this alternative to polygraph testing, and over two dozen variations of such tests are being sold.

Workplace Investigations

Another area of concern regarding employee rights involves workplace investigations. Public-sector employees are protected by the Constitution in the areas of due process, search and seizure, and privacy. But employees in the private sector are not protected. Figure 10–4 shows typical methods of workplace investigations.

▶ HR POLICIES, PROCEDURES, AND RULES

It is useful at this point to consider some guidelines for HR policies, procedures, and rules. They greatly affect employee rights and discipline.

Guidelines for HR Policies and Rules

Well-designed HR policies and rules should be consistent, necessary, applicable, understandable, reasonable, and distributed and communicated. A discussion of each characteristic follows.

- ▶ **Consistent**   Rules should be consistent with organizational policies, and policies should be consistent with organizational goals. The principal intent of policies is to provide written guidelines and to specify actions. If some policies and rules are enforced and others are not, then all tend to lose their effectiveness.

▶ **FIGURE 10–4   Methods of Workplace Investigations**

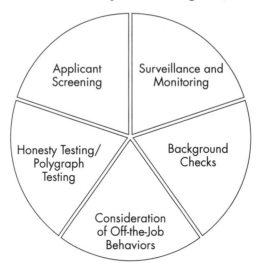

▶ **Necessary**   HR policies and rules should reflect current organizational philosophy and directions. To this end, managers should confirm the intent and necessity of proposed rules and eliminate obsolete ones.

▶ **Applicable**   Because HR policies are general guidelines for action, they should be applicable to a large group of employees. For policies that are not general, the appropriate areas or people must be identified.

▶ **Understandable**   HR policies and rules should be written so employees can clearly understand them.

▶ **Reasonable**   Ideally, employees should see policies as fair and reasonable. Policies and rules that are perceived as being inflexible or as penalizing individuals unfairly should be reevaluated.

▶ **Distributed and Communicated**   In order to be effective, HR policies must be distributed and communicated to employees. Employee handbooks can be creatively designed to explain detailed policies and rules so that people can refer to them at times when no one is available to answer a question.

Employee Handbooks

An employee handbook gives employees a reference source for company policies and rules and can be a positive tool for effective management of human resources. As mentioned, there is a current legal trend to use employee handbooks against employers in lawsuits charging a broken "implied" contract. But that is no reason to abandon employee handbooks as a way to communicate policies to employees. *Not* having an employee handbook with HR policies spelled out can also leave an organization open to costly litigation and out-of-court settlements.

A more sensible approach is first to develop sound HR policies and employee handbooks to communicate them and then have legal counsel review the language contained in them.

▶ EMPLOYEE DISCIPLINE

Employee rights have been an appropriate introduction to employee discipline because employee rights are often an issue in disciplinary cases. **Discipline** is a form of training that enforces organizational rules. The goal of preventive discipline is to heighten employee awareness of organizational policies and rules. Knowledge of disciplinary actions may prevent violations. The emphasis on preventive discipline is similar to the emphasis on preventing accidents. Counseling by a supervisor in the work unit can have positive effects. Many times people simply need to be made aware of rules.

Progressive Discipline

Progressive discipline incorporates a sequence of steps into the shaping of employee behaviors. Figure 10–5 shows a typical progressive discipline system. Like the procedures in the figure, most progressive discipline procedures use verbal and written reprimands and suspension before resorting to dismissal. Thus, progressive discipline suggests that actions to modify behavior become progressively more severe as the employee continues to show improper behavior.

▶ **FIGURE 10–5   Progressive Discipline Procedures**

First Offense	Verbal Caution
Second Offense	Written Reprimand
Third Offense	Suspension
Fourth Offense	Demotion
	Dismissal

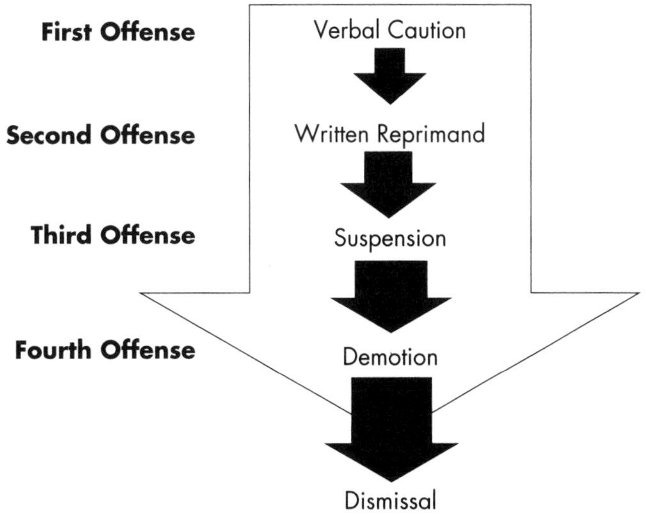

Effective Discipline

Because of legal aspects, managers must understand discipline and know how to administer it properly. Effective discipline should be aimed at the behavior, not at the employee personally, because the reason for discipline is to improve performance.

The manager administering discipline must consider the effect of actions taken by other managers and of other actions taken in the past. *Consistent* discipline helps to set limits and informs people about what they can and cannot do. Inconsistent discipline leads to confusion and uncertainty.

Effective discipline requires *accurate written record keeping* and written notification to the employee. In many cases, the lack of written notification has been evidence for an employee's argument that he or she "did not know." Also, effective discipline requires that *people know the rules*. When people perceive discipline as unfair, it is often on the basis that they did not realize they had broken a rule.

Additionally, effective discipline is *immediate*. The longer the time that transpires between the offense and the disciplinary action, the less effective the discipline will be. Finally, effective discipline is handled *impersonally*. Managers cannot make discipline an enjoyable experience, but they can minimize the unpleasant effects somewhat by presenting it impersonally and by focusing on behaviors, not on the person.

Discharge: The Final Alternative

The final stage in the discipline process is termination. A manager may feel guilty when dismissing an employee, and sometimes guilt is justified. If an employee fails, it may be because the manager was not able to create an appropriate working environment. Perhaps the employee was not adequately trained, or perhaps management failed to establish effective policies. Managers are responsible for their employees, and to an extent, they share the blame for failures.

Alternative Dispute Resolution

Alternatives to lawsuits in cases involving employee rights are being used with increasing frequency.[6] The most common of these alternative dispute resolution (ADR) methods are arbitration, peer review panels, and mediation.

▶ SUGGESTED READINGS

1. SHRM Congressional Affairs Department. 1996. *Compendium of Newly-Enacted Employment Laws.* Alexandria, VA: Society of Human Resource Management.

2. SHRM Issues Management Survey Program. 1996. *SHRM® Workplace Violence Survey.* Alexandria, VA: Society of Human Resource Management.

▶ **NOTES**

1. *United Autoworkers v. Johnson Controls, Inc.* 111 S.Ct. 1196 (1991).

2. J. W. Vigen and Timothy S. Brady, "Safety and Health Teams," *NBDC Report,* March 1995, 1–4.

3. Romuald A. Stone, "AIDS in the Workplace: An Executive Update," *Academy of Management Executive,* August 1994, 52–61.

4. "Attorney Suggests Employment Contracts for Workers at All Levels," *BNAC Communicator,* Fall 1994, 19.

5. Z. Kahn, et al., "Ethics of Drug Testing: What Are Worker's Attitudes?" *Business Forum,* Summer/Fall 1995, 17.

6. "Alternative Dispute Resolution Gaining in Popularity," *CCH Ideas and Trends,* March 29, 1995, 1.

11

Union-Management Relations

When employees choose a union to represent them, management and union representatives enter into formal collective bargaining over certain issues such as pay scales, benefits, and working conditions. Once these issues have been resolved in a labor contract, management and union representatives must work together to manage the contract and deal with grievances, which are formal complaints filed by workers with management. Collective bargaining and grievance procedures, then, are two important interfaces between management and labor unions.

▶ NATURE OF UNION-MANAGEMENT RELATIONS

Whether a union targets a group of employees or the employees themselves request union assistance, the union still must win sufficient support from the employees if it is to become their legal representative. Research consistently reveals that employees join unions for one primary reason: They are dissatisfied with their employers and how they are treated by their employers and feel the union can improve the situation. If the employees do not get organizational justice from their employers, they turn to the unions to assist them in getting what they believe is equitable. Important factors seem to be wages and benefits, job security, and supervisory treatment.

Over the past several decades, the statistics on union membership have told a disheartening story for organized labor in the United States. Unions represented over 30% of the workforce from 1945 through 1960. But by the mid-

1990s, unions represented less than 16% of all private-sector workers. The decline has continued, such that unions now represent less than 15% of civilian workers in the United States.

Economists speculate that several issues have sparked union decline: deregulation, foreign competition, a larger number of people looking for jobs, and a general perception by firms that dealing with unions is expensive compared with the nonunion alternative. Also, management has taken a much more activist stance against unions than during the previous years of union growth.

Many of the workforce changes discussed earlier have contributed to the decline in union representation of the labor force. The primary growth in jobs in the United States has been in service industries having large numbers of white-collar jobs. Also, the influx of women into the workforce and the growth in part-time workers indicate the changing mix of jobs. But unions traditionally have had the greatest difficulty convincing white-collar workers and women to join.

An area where unions have had some measure of success is with public-sector employees. Particularly with state and local government workers have unions been successful.

American labor is represented by many different kinds of unions. But regardless of size and geographic scope, there are two basic types of unions that have developed over time. A **craft union** is one whose members do one type of work, often using specialized skills and training. Examples include the International Association of Bridge, Structural, and Ornamental Iron Workers and the American Federation of Television and Radio Artists. An **industrial union** is one that includes many persons working in the same industry or company, regardless of jobs held. Examples are the United Food and Commercial Workers, the United Auto Workers, and the American Federation of State, County, and Municipal Employees.

Labor organizations have developed complex organizational structures with multiple levels. The broadest level is a **federation,** which is a group of autonomous national and international unions. The federation allows individual unions to work together and present a more unified front to the public, legislators, and members. The most prominent federation in the United States is the AFL-CIO, which is a confederation of national and international unions.

Local unions may be centered around a particular employer organization or around a particular geographic location. Officers in local unions are elected by the membership and are subject to removal if they do not perform satisfactorily.

Local unions typically have business agents and union stewards. A **business agent** is a full-time union official employed by the union to operate the union office and assist union members. The agent runs the local headquarters, helps negotiate contracts with management, and becomes involved in attempts to unionize employees in other organizations. A **union steward** is an employee of a firm or organization who is elected to serve as the first-line representative of unionized workers. Stewards negotiate grievances with supervisors and generally represent employees at the worksite.

► THE "NATIONAL LABOR CODE"

Together, three acts passed over a period of almost 25 years compose what has been labeled the "National Labor Code": (1) the Wagner Act, (2) the Taft-Hartley Act, and (3) the Landrum-Griffin Act. Each of the acts was passed to focus on some facet of the relationships between unions and management. Figure 11–1 shows each segment of the code and describes the primary focus of each act.

Wagner Act (National Labor Relations Act)

The *National Labor Relations Act*, more commonly referred to as the Wagner Act, has been called the Magna Carta of labor and is, by anyone's standards, *pro-union*. The Wagner Act declared, in effect, that the official policy of the U.S. government was to encourage collective bargaining. It helped union growth in three ways:

1. It established workers' right to organize, unhampered by management interference.
2. It defined unfair labor practices on the part of management.
3. It established the National Labor Relations Board (NLRB) as an independent entity to enforce the provisions of the Wagner Act.

Taft-Hartley Act (Labor-Management Relations Act)

The passage of the *Labor-Management Relations Act*, better known as the Taft-Hartley Act, in 1947 answered the concerns of many who felt that union power had become too strong. This act was an attempt to balance the collective bargaining equation. It was designed to offset the pro-union Wagner Act by limiting union actions; therefore, it was considered to be *pro-management*. It became

► **FIGURE 11–1** The National Labor Code

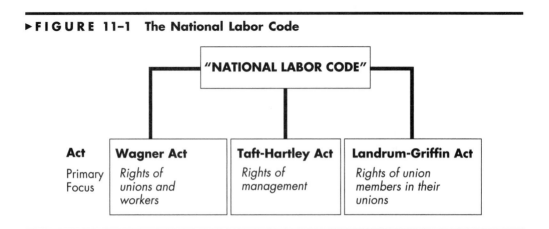

the second part of the "National Labor Code." The new law amended or qualified in some respect all of the major provisions of the Wagner Act and established an entirely new code of conduct for unions.

National Emergency Strikes.   The Taft-Hartley Act also allows the president of the United States to declare that a strike presents a national emergency. A **national emergency strike** is one that would affect an industry or a major part of it such that the national health or safety would be impeded.

The Right to Work.   One specific provision of the Taft-Hartley Act, Section 14(b), deserves special explanation. This so-called right-to-work provision affects the **closed shop,** which requires individuals to join a union before they can be hired. Because of concerns that a closed shop allows a union to "control" who may be considered for employment and who must be hired by an employer, Section 14(b) prohibits the closed shop except in construction-related occupations. The act does allow the **union shop,** which requires that an employee join the union, usually 30 to 60 days after being hired. The act also allows the **agency shop,** which requires employees who refuse to join the union to pay amounts equal to union dues and fees in return for the union's representative services.

The Taft-Hartley Act allows states to pass laws that restrict compulsory union membership. Accordingly, some states have passed **right-to-work laws,** which prohibit both the closed shop and the union shop. The laws were so named because they allow a person the "right to work" without having to join a union.

Landrum-Griffin Act (Labor-Management Reporting and Disclosure Act)

In 1959, the third segment of the "National Labor Code," the *Landrum-Griffin Act,* was passed. A union is a democratic institution in which union members vote on and elect officers and approve labor contracts. The Landrum-Griffin Act was passed in part to ensure that the federal government protects those democratic rights. Some important rights guaranteed to individual union members are as follows:

▶ Right to nominate and vote on officers
▶ Right to attend and participate in union meetings
▶ Right to have pension funds properly managed

Civil Service Reform Act of 1978

Passed as Title VII of the Civil Service Reform Act of 1978, the Federal Service Labor-Management Relations statute made major changes in how the federal government deals with unions. The act also identified areas that are and are not subject to bargaining. For example, as a result of the law, wages and benefits are not subject to bargaining. Instead, they are set by Congressional actions.

▶ THE UNIONIZATION PROCESS

The process of unionization may begin in one of two primary ways: (1) union targeting of an industry or company or (2) employee requests. Once the unionization efforts begin, all activities must conform to the requirements established by labor laws and the National Labor Relations Board for private-sector employees or the appropriate federal or state governmental agency for public-sector employees. Both management and the unions must adhere to those requirements, or the results of the effort can be appealed to the NLRB and overturned. With those requirements in mind, the union can embark on the typical union organizing process, shown in Figure 11–2.

Organizing Campaign

Like other entities seeking members, a union usually mounts an organized campaign to persuade individuals to support its efforts. This persuasion takes many forms, including personally contacting employees outside of work, mailing materials to employees' homes, inviting employees to attend special meetings away from the company, and publicizing the advantages of union membership. **Handbilling** is a practice in which unions give written publicity to employees to convince them to sign authorization cards. Brochures, leaflets, and circulars are all handbills. These items can be passed out to employees as they leave work, mailed to their homes, or even attached to their vehicles, as long as they comply with the rules established by laws and the NLRB.

Authorization

A **union authorization card** is signed by an employee to designate a union as his or her collective bargaining agent. At least 30% of the employees in the targeted group must sign authorization cards before an election can be called. If at least 50% of the targeted employees sign authorization cards, the union can request that the employer recognize the union as the official bargaining agent for all of the employees, meaning that no election need be held. However, as would be expected, most employers refuse this request. Consequently, the union must petition the NLRB to hold a representation election.

▶ **FIGURE 11-2 Typical Unionization Process**

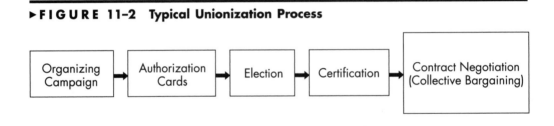

Representation Election

An election to determine if a union will represent the employees is supervised by the NLRB for private-sector organizations and by other legal bodies for public-sector organizations. Before the election is held, the appropriate bargaining unit must be determined. A **bargaining unit** is composed of all employees eligible to select a single union to represent and bargain collectively for them.

Unfair Labor Practices.   Employers and unions engage in a number of activities as authorization cards are being solicited and after an election has been requested. Both the Wagner Act and the Taft-Hartley Act place restrictions on these activities.

Election Process.   Assuming an election is held, the union need receive only the votes of a *majority of those voting* in the election. For example, if a group of 200 employees is the identified unit, and only 50 people vote, only 50% of the employees voting plus one (26) would need to vote "yes" in order for the union to be named as the representative of all 200.

If either side believes that unfair labor practices have been used by the other side, the election results can be appealed to the NLRB. If the NLRB finds that unfair practices were used, it can order a new election. Assuming that no unfair practices have been used and the union obtains a majority in the election, the union then petitions the NLRB for certification.

Certification and Decertification

Official certification of a union as the legal representative for employees is given by the NLRB (or by the relevant body for public-sector organizations). Once certified, the union attempts to negotiate a contract with the employer. The employer *must* bargain, as it is an unfair labor practice to refuse to bargain with a certified union.

Employees who have a union and no longer wish to be represented by it can use the election process called **decertification.** The decertification process is similar to the unionization process. Employees attempting to oust a union must obtain decertification authorization cards signed by at least 30% of the employees in the bargaining unit before an election may be called. If a majority of those voting in the election want to remove the union, the decertification effort succeeds. One caution: Management may not assist the decertification effort in any way by providing assistance or funding.

▶ NATURE OF COLLECTIVE BARGAINING

Collective bargaining is the process whereby representatives of management and workers negotiate over wages, hours, and other terms and conditions of employment. It is a give-and-take process between representatives of two organizations for the benefit of both.

Types of Bargaining Relationships

The attitude of management toward unions is one major factor in determining the collective bargaining relationship. This attitude plays a crucial role in management's strategic approach to collective bargaining.

Management-union relationships in collective bargaining can follow one of several patterns. Figure 11–3 shows the relationship as a continuum, ranging from conflict to collusion.

The Wagner Act clearly expects management and the union to bargain over "wages, hours, and other terms and conditions of employment." What specifically is included in those categories has been defined over the years by the National Labor Relations Board (NLRB) and Supreme Court rulings.

Mandatory Issues.   Those issues that are identified specifically by labor laws or court decisions as being subject to bargaining are **mandatory issues.** If either party demands that issues in this category be bargained over, then bargaining must occur. Generally, mandatory issues relate to wages, benefits, nature of jobs, and other work-related subjects.

Management Rights.   Virtually all labor contracts include **management rights,** which are those rights reserved to the employer to manage, direct, and control its business. Such a provision often reads as follows:

> The employer retains all rights to manage, direct, and control its business in all particulars, except as such rights are expressly and specifically modified by the terms of this or any subsequent agreement.[1]

By including such a provision, management is attempting to preserve its unilateral right to decide or make changes in any areas not identified in a labor contract. Some labor contracts spell out in more detail the issues that fall under management rights, while others use the general language just quoted. As would be expected, management representatives want to have as many issues defined as "management rights" as they can.

▶**FIGURE 11–3 Collective Bargaining Relationship Continuum**

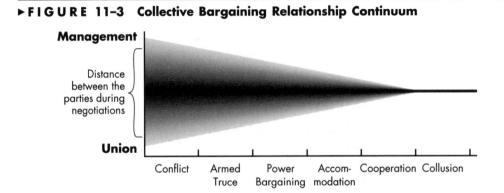

Union Security.   A major concern of union representatives when bargaining is to negotiate **union security provisions** to aid the union in obtaining and retaining members. One union security provision is the **dues checkoff,** which provides that union dues will be deducted automatically from the payroll checks of members. This provision makes it much easier for the union to collect its funds, which otherwise it must collect by billing each individual member.

▶ PROCESS OF COLLECTIVE BARGAINING

The collective bargaining process is made up of a number of stages. Over time, each situation develops slight modifications, which are necessary for effective bargaining. The process shown in Figure 11–4 is typical.

Preparation

Both labor and management representatives spend much time preparing for negotiations. If a previous contract is expiring, the grievances filed under the old contract will be reviewed to identify contract language changes to be negotiated. Employer and industry data concerning wages, benefits, working conditions, management and union rights, productivity, and absenteeism are gathered. Once the data are analyzed, each side identifies what its priorities are and what strategies and tactics it will use to obtain what it wants. Each tries to allow itself some flexibility in order to trade off less important demands for more critical ones.

▶ **F I G U R E 11–4 Typical Collective Bargaining Process**

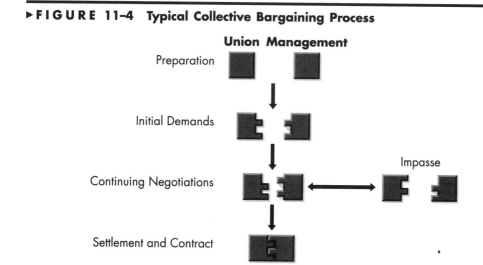

Initial Demands

Typical bargaining includes initial proposals of expectations by both sides. The amount of rancor or calmness exhibited sets the tone for future negotiations between the parties.

Continuing Negotiations

After opening positions have been taken, each side attempts to determine what the other values highly so the best bargain can be struck. During negotiations, both management and union must evaluate cost proposals concerning changes in wages, benefits, and other economic items quickly and accurately.

Good Faith. Provisions in federal labor law require that both employer and employee bargaining representatives negotiate in *good faith*. In good faith negotiations, the parties agree to send negotiators who can bargain and make decisions, rather than people who do not have the authority to commit either group to a decision.

Settlement and Contract Agreement

After an initial agreement has been made, the two sides usually return to their respective constituencies to determine if what they have informally agreed on is acceptable. A particularly crucial stage is **ratification** of the labor agreement, which occurs when union members vote to accept the terms of a negotiated agreement. Prior to the ratification vote, the union negotiating team explains the agreement to the union members and presents it for a vote. If approval is voted, the agreement is then formalized into a contract. The agreement also contains language on the duration of the contract.[2] If a contract does not match the perceptions and interests of those it covers, then the likelihood of ratification decreases.[3]

Bargaining Impasse

Regardless of the structure of the bargaining process, labor and management do not always reach agreement on the issues. If impasse occurs, then the disputes can be taken to conciliation, mediation, or arbitration.

Conciliation and Mediation. In conciliation or mediation, an outside party attempts to help two deadlocked parties continue negotiations and arrive at a solution. In **conciliation,** the third party attempts to keep union and management negotiators talking so that they can reach a voluntary settlement but makes no proposals for solutions. In **mediation,** the third party assists the negotiators in their discussions and also suggests settlement proposals. In neither conciliation nor mediation does the third party attempt to impose a solution.

Arbitration. The process of **arbitration** is a means of deciding a dispute in which negotiating parties submit the dispute to a third party to make a decision. It can be conducted by either an individual or a panel of individuals. Arbitration is used to solve bargaining impasses primarily in the public sector.

Strikes and Lockouts

If deadlocks cannot be resolved, then an employer may revert to a lockout or a union may revert to a strike. During a **strike,** union members refuse to work in order to put pressure on an employer. Often, the striking union members picket or demonstrate against the employer outside the place of business by carrying placards and signs. In a **lockout,** management shuts down company operations to prevent union members from working.

Union-Management Cooperation

The adversarial relationship that naturally exists between unions and management may lead to the impasses and conflicts discussed previously. But there is also a growing recognition by many union leaders and employer representatives that cooperation between management and labor unions is essential if organizations are going to compete in a global economy.

▶ GRIEVANCE MANAGEMENT

A **grievance** is an alleged misinterpretation, misapplication, or violation of a provision in a union-management agreement. Management should be concerned with both complaints and grievances, because complaints are good indicators of potential problems within the workforce. Also, unresolved complaints may turn into grievances in a union environment.

Union vs. Nonunion Grievance Management

Union and nonunion firms handle grievances differently. In an organization with a union, grievances might occur over interpretation of the contract, disputes not covered in the contract, and problems of individual employees. In nonunion organizations, complaints cover a variety of concerns that for a unionized organization would be covered in the contract: wages, benefits, working conditions, and equity.

A crucial measure of the performance of a grievance system is the rate of grievance resolution. Grievances that have been resolved become feedback to help resolve future grievances at an earlier stage. One study found that as management and union representatives work together to resolve grievances, the process of handling grievances becomes more efficient and effective.[4]

Approaches to Grievances

A formal grievance procedure sometimes leads management to conclude that the proper way to handle grievances is to abide by the "letter of the law." Therefore, management does no more nor less than what is called for in the contract. Such an approach can be labeled the *legalistic approach* to the resolution of grievances. A much more realistic approach, the *behavioral approach,* recognizes that a grievance may be a symptom of an underlying problem that management should investigate and rectify.

It is important to consider the behavioral aspects of grievances in order to understand why grievances are filed and how employees perceive them. Regarding why grievances have been filed, research has found that union stewards rather than employees tend to initiate grievances over job descriptions. Also, grievances over work rules are the least likely ones to be settled informally without resort to the use of grievance procedures.[5]

Management should recognize that a grievance is a behavioral expression of some underlying problem. This statement does not mean that every grievance is symptomatic of something radically wrong. Employees do file grievances over petty matters as well as over important concerns, and management must be able to differentiate between the two. However, to ignore a repeated problem by taking a legalistic approach to grievance resolution is to miss much of what the grievance procedure can do for management.

▶ GRIEVANCE PROCEDURES

Grievance procedures are formal communications channels designed to settle a grievance as soon as possible after the problem arises. First-line supervisors are usually closest to a problem; however, the supervisor is concerned with many other matters besides one employee's grievance and may even be the subject of an employee's grievance. Grievance procedures can vary in the number of steps they include. Figure 11–5 shows a typical one.

Grievance arbitration is a means by which disputes arising from different interpretations of a labor contract are settled by a third party. This should not

---

▶FIGURE 11–5 Steps in a Grievance Procedure

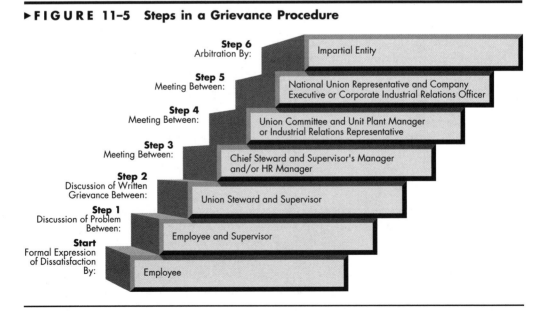

Step 6 Arbitration By:	Impartial Entity
Step 5 Meeting Between:	National Union Representative and Company Executive or Corporate Industrial Relations Officer
Step 4 Meeting Between:	Union Committee and Unit Plant Manager or Industrial Relations Representative
Step 3 Meeting Between:	Chief Steward and Supervisor's Manager and/or HR Manager
Step 2 Discussion of Written Grievance Between:	Union Steward and Supervisor
Step 1 Discussion of Problem Between:	Employee and Supervisor
Start Formal Expression of Dissatisfaction By:	Employee

be confused with contract arbitration, discussed earlier, which is arbitration to determine how a contract will be written. Grievance arbitration is a deeply ingrained part of the collective bargaining system.

▶ SUGGESTED READINGS

1. Cohen-Rosenthal, Edward. 1995. *Unions, Management, and Quality Opportunities for Innovation and Excellence.* Burr Ridge, IL: McGraw-Hill/Irwin Professional Publishing.
2. Hunt, James W., and Patricia K. Strongin. 1997. *The Law of the Workplace: Rights of Employers & Employees.* Washington, DC: Bureau of National Affairs.
3. SHRM Foundation. 1995. *Conducting Lawful Terminations.* Alexandria, VA: Society of Human Resource Management.

▶ NOTES

1. Adapted from William H. Holley and Kenneth M. Jennings, *The Labor Relations Process,* 3rd ed. (Chicago, Dryden Press, 1988), 395.
2. K. Murphy, "Determinants of Contract Duration in Collective Bargaining Agreements," *Industrial and Labor Relations Review* 45 (1992), 352.
3. James E. Martin and Ruth D. Berthiaume, "Predicting the Outcome of a Contract Ratification Vote," *Academy of Management Journal,* 38 (1995), 916–928.
4. David Meyer, "The Political Effects of Grievance Handling by Stewards in a Local Union," *Journal of Labor Research* 15 (1994), 33–52.
5. Brian Bemmels, "The Determinants of Grievance Initiation," *Industrial and Labor Relations Review* 47 (1994), 285–301.

12

Global HR Management

Unprecedented political realignments and a changing world economic order have guaranteed a new era for international business. Global competition is driving changes in organizations throughout the world. As a result, the number and types of jobs in firms have changed. The impact of global competition can be seen in many U.S. industries. At the same time, foreign-owned firms have been investing in plants and creating jobs in the United States. The growth in employment resulting from foreign investments has helped to replace some of the jobs lost at U.S. firms.

▶ GLOBAL FACTORS INFLUENCING HR MANAGEMENT

Doing business globally requires that adaptations be made to reflect cultural and other factors that differ from country to country and continent to continent. It is crucial that the various factors be seen as interrelated by managers and professionals as they do business and establish operations globally. Figure 12–1 depicts some of the more important factors to be considered by HR managers with global responsibilities. Each of those factors will be examined briefly.

Legal and Political Factors

The nature and stability of political systems vary from country to country. U.S. firms are accustomed to a relatively stable political system. Also, legal systems vary in character and stability, with contracts suddenly becoming unenforceable because of internal political factors.

▶ **F I G U R E 12–1   Some Factors Affecting Global HR Management**

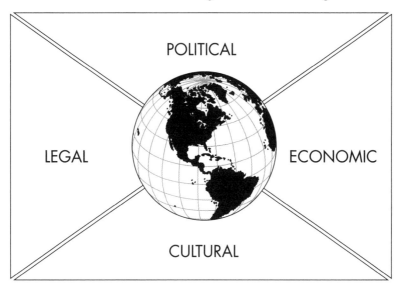

HR regulations and laws vary among countries in character and detail. In many countries in Western Europe, laws on labor unions and employment make it difficult to reduce the number of workers because required payments to ex-employees can be very high. Equal employment legislation exists to varying degrees. In some countries, laws address issues such as employment discrimination and sexual harassment. In others, because of religious or ethical differences, employment discrimination may be an accepted practice.

It is crucial for HR professionals to conduct a comprehensive review of the political environment and employment-related laws before beginning operations in a country. The role and nature of labor unions also should be investigated.

Cultural Factors

Cultural forces represent another important concern affecting international HR management. The culture of organizations was discussed earlier in the text, and of course, national cultures exist also. **Culture** is composed of the societal forces affecting the values, beliefs, and actions of a distinct group of people. Cultural differences certainly exist between nations, but significant cultural differences exist within countries also. One only has to look at the conflicts caused by religion or ethnicity in Central Europe and other parts of the world to see the importance of culture on international organizations. Even getting individuals from different ethnic or tribal backgrounds to work together may be difficult in some parts of the world.

Economic Factors

Economic conditions vary from country to country. Many lesser-developed nations are receptive to foreign investment in order to create jobs for their growing populations. Global firms often obtain significantly cheaper labor rates in these countries than they do in Europe and the United States. However, whether firms can realize significant profits may be determined by currency fluctuations and restrictions on transfer of earnings.

In many developed countries, especially in Europe, unemployment has grown, but employment restrictions and wage levels remain high. In addition, both personal and corporate tax rates are quite high. These factors all must be evaluated by HR professionals as part of the process of deciding whether to begin or purchase operations in foreign countries.

▶ TYPES OF GLOBAL ORGANIZATIONS

A growing number of organizations that operate only within one country are recognizing that they must change and develop a more international perspective. Organizations may pass through three stages as they broaden out into the world.[1]

Importing and Exporting

The first phase of international interaction consists of **importing and exporting.** Here, an organization begins selling and buying goods and services with organizations in other countries. Most of the international contacts are made by the sales and marketing staff and a limited number of other executives who negotiate contracts. Generally, HR activities are not affected except for travel policies for those going abroad.

Multinational Enterprises

As firms develop and expand, they identify opportunities to begin operating in other countries. A **multinational enterprise (MNE)** is one in which organizational units are located in foreign countries. Typically these units provide goods and services for the geographic areas surrounding the countries where operations exist. Key management positions in the foreign operations are filled with employees from the home country of the corporation. As the MNE expands, it hires workers from the countries in which it has operations. HR practices for employees sent from corporate headquarters must be developed so that these employees and their dependents may continue their economic lifestyles while stationed outside the home country.

Global Organizations

The MNE can be thought of as an *international* firm, in that it operates in various countries but each foreign business unit is operated separately. In contrast, a **global organization** has corporate units in a number of countries that are integrated to operate as one organization worldwide. An MNE may evolve into a global organization as operations in various countries become more integrated.

▶ INTERNATIONAL STAFFING AND SELECTION

When organizations expand to other countries, they often must develop operations and staff the operations in those countries. Large MNEs and global organizations typically employ individuals from throughout the world. Thus, staffing and selection activities must be tailored to obtaining individuals specifically suited for international responsibilities.

Types of International Employees

International employees can be placed in three different classifications:

▶ An **expatriate** is an employee working in a unit or plant who is not a citizen of the country in which the unit or plant is located but is a citizen of the country in which the organization is headquartered.
▶ A **host-country national** is an employee working in a unit or plant who is a citizen of the country in which the unit or plant is located but where the unit or plant is operated by an organization headquartered in another country.
▶ A **third-country national** is a citizen of one country, working in a second country, and employed by an organization headquartered in a third country.

Each of these individuals presents some unique HR management challenges. Because in a given situation each is a citizen of a different country, different tax laws and other factors apply. HR professionals have to be knowledgeable about the laws and customs of each country. They must establish appropriate payroll and record-keeping procedures, among other activities, to ensure compliance with varying regulations and requirements.

Use of Expatriates.   Many MNEs use expatriates to ensure that foreign operations are linked effectively with the parent corporations. Generally, expatriates also are used to develop international capabilities within an organization. Experienced expatriates can provide a pool of talent that can be tapped as the organization expands its operations more broadly into even more countries.

Use of Host-Country Nationals.   Using host-country nationals is important for several reasons. It is important if the organization wants to establish clearly that it is making a commitment to the host country and not just setting up a foreign operation. Host-country nationals often know the culture, the politics, the laws, and how business is done better than an outsider would.[2] Also, tapping into the informal "power" network may be important.

Use of Third-Country Nationals.   The use of third-country nationals is a way to emphasize that a global approach is being taken. Often, these individuals are used to handle responsibilities throughout a continent or region.

Selection for International Assignments

The selection process for an international assignment should provide a realistic picture of the life, work, and culture to which the employee may be sent. HR managers should prepare a comprehensive description of the job to be done. The description especially should note responsibilities that would be unusual in the home nation. Those responsibilities might include negotiating with public officials; interpreting local work codes; and responding to ethical, moral, and personal issues such as religious prohibitions and personal freedoms.

Cultural Adaptability.   Most staffing "failures" for those selected for foreign assignments occur because of cultural adjustment problems, not because of difficulties with the jobs or inadequate technical skills. Organizational support for the employees is particularly important in this area. Once employees have been selected for international assignments, continuing organizational support for the employees is crucial. One study found that the intention of expatriates to quit and their commitment to their organizations are affected significantly by how they view the support given to them by their employers.[3] Throughout the selection process, especially in the selection interviews, it is crucial to assess the potential employee's ability to accept and adapt to different customs, management practices, laws, religious values, and infrastructure conditions.

Communication Skills.   One of the most basic skills needed by expatriate employees is the ability to communicate orally and in writing in the host-country language. Inability to communicate adequately in the language may significantly inhibit the success of an expatriate. Numerous firms with international operations select individuals based on their technical and managerial capabilities and then have the selected individuals take foreign language training.

Family Factors.   The preferences and attitudes of spouses and other family members also are major staffing considerations. With the growth in dual-career couples, the difficulty of transferring international employees is likely to increase, particularly given work-permit restrictions common in many countries. Some international firms have begun career services to assist spouses in getting jobs with other international firms.[4]

Women Employees Overseas.   For years in many U.S. firms, women were not considered for overseas jobs. Because of cultural values and historical traditions in some foreign countries, women who worked as professionals were a rarity, if such employment was allowed at all. Unaccompanied women still have difficulty obtaining visas to enter some countries, particularly those in the Middle East and Far East. Also, the male-dominated cultures of some countries have continued to pose significant problems for women who attempt to represent U.S. firms to top-level host-country executives.

An HR management issue is that the assignment of women and members of racial/ethnic minorities to international posts can involve legal issues, as these individuals may be protected by Equal Employment Opportunity (EEO) regulations.

▶ INTERNATIONAL TRAINING AND DEVELOPMENT

Employees working internationally face special situations and pressures, and training and development activities must be tailored to address them. As illustrated in Figure 12–2, these activities are of three types:

1. Orientation and training of the expatriate employee and the employee's family before the international assignment begins
2. Continuing employee development in which the employee's broadened skills can be fitted into career planning and corporate development programs
3. Readjustment training and development to prepare the employee for a return to the home-country culture and to prepare the expatriate's new subordinates and supervisor for the return

Predeparture Orientation and Training

The orientation and training that expatriates and their families receive before departure have a major impact on the success of the overseas assignment. Three areas affect the cross-cultural adjustment process: (a) work adjustment, (b) interaction adjustment, and (c) general adjustment.[5] Permeating all of those areas is the need for training in foreign language and culture familiarization. Many firms have formal training programs for expatriates and their families, and this training has been found to have a positive effect on cross-cultural adjustment.

Continuing Employee Development

Career planning and continued involvement of expatriates in corporate employee development activities are essential. One of the greatest deterrents to accepting foreign assignments is employees' concern that they will be "out of sight, out of mind." If they do not have direct and regular contact with others

▶ **F I G U R E 12–2   International Training and Development**

at the corporate headquarters, many expatriates experience anxiety. Therefore, the international experiences of expatriates must be seen as beneficial to the employer and to the expatriate's career.

Readjustment Training and Development

The process of bringing expatriates home is called **repatriation.** Some major difficulties can arise when it is time to bring expatriates home. For example, the special compensation packages often available to expatriates are dropped, which means that the expatriates experience a net decrease in total income, even if they receive promotions and pay increases. In addition to concerns about personal finances, repatriated employees must readjust to a closer working and reporting relationship with other corporate employees.

▶ INTERNATIONAL COMPENSATION

Organizations with employees in many different countries face some special compensation pressures. Variations in laws, living costs, tax policies, and other factors all must be considered in establishing the compensation for expatriate managers and professionals. Even fluctuations in the value of the U.S. dollar must be tracked and adjustments made as the dollar rises or falls in relation to currency rates in other countries. Add to all of these concerns the need to compensate employees for the costs of housing, schooling of children, and yearly transportation home for themselves and their family members. When all these different issues are considered, it is evident that international compensation is extremely complex. Typical components of an international compensation package for expatriates are shown in Figure 12–3. Several approaches to international compensation are discussed next.

Balance-Sheet Approach

Many multinational firms have compensation programs that use the balance-sheet approach. The **balance-sheet approach** provides international employees with a compensation package that equalizes cost differences between the international assignment and the same assignment in the home country.

Global Market Approach

Unlike the balance-sheet approach, a **global market approach** to compensation requires that the international assignment be viewed as continual, not just temporary, though the assignment may take the employee to different countries for differing lengths of time. This approach is much more comprehensive in that the core components, such as insurance benefits and relocation expenses, are present regardless of the country to which the employee is assigned.

▶**FIGURE 12-3 Typical Expatriate Compensation Components**

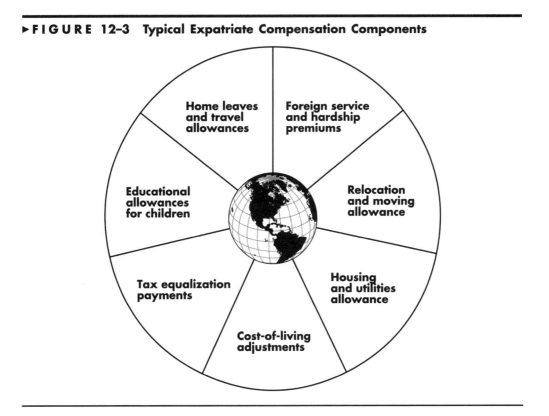

Tax Equalization Plan

Many international compensation plans attempt to protect expatriates from negative tax consequences by using a **tax equalization plan.** Under this plan, the company adjusts an employee's base income downward by the amount of estimated U.S. tax to be paid for the year. Thus, the employee pays only the foreign-country tax. The intent of the tax equalization plan is to ensure that expatriates will not pay any more or less in taxes than if they had stayed in the United States if they are U.S. citizens.

▶ GLOBAL EMPLOYEE AND LABOR RELATIONS

The nature of employee and labor relations varies from country to country. When international operations are considered, concerns related to health, safety, and security must be evaluated. Also, it is important to understand the applicable labor-management laws, regulations, and practices before commencing operations in foreign countries.

With more and more expatriates working internationally, especially in some of the less-developed countries, significant health and safety issues are arising, and addressing these issues is part of the HR role. Another consideration is provision of emergency evacuation services. Many global firms purchase coverage for their international employees from an organization that provides emergency services, such as International SOS, Global Assistance Network, or U.S. Assist.

International Security and Terrorism

As more U.S. firms operate internationally, the threat of terrorist actions against those firms and the employees working for them increases. U.S. citizens are especially vulnerable to extortions, kidnapping, bombing, physical harassment, and other terrorist activities. Many firms provide bodyguards who escort executives everywhere. Different routes of travel are used, so that "normal" patterns of movement are difficult for terrorists to identify. Family members of employees also receive training in security.

Global Labor-Management Relations

The strength and nature of unions differ from country to country. In some countries, unions either do not exist at all or are relatively weak. Some countries require that firms have union or worker representatives on their boards of directors. This practice is very common in European countries, where it is called **co-determination.**

▶ SUGGESTED READINGS

1. Adler, Nancy J. 1997. *International Dimensions of Organizational Behavior.* Boston: PWS-Kent.
2. *How to Write an Affirmative Action Plan.* 1995. Madison, CT: Business and Legal Reports, Inc.
3. *International Human Resource Management Reference Guide.* 1997. Alexandria, VA: Society of Human Resource Management.
4. Moran, Robert T., and Philip R. Harris. 1996. *Managing Cultural Differences: Leadership Strategies for a New World of Business.* 4th ed. Houston: Gulf Publishing.
5. Odenwald, Sylvia B., and William G. Matheny. 1996. *Global Impact Award-Winning Performance Programs from Around the World.* Burr Ridge, IL: McGraw-Hill/Irwin Professional Publishing.
6. Poole, Phebe-Jane. 1997. *Diversity: A Business Advantage.* Poole Publishing.
7. Rhinesmith, Stephen H. 1996. *A Manager's Guide to Globalization. Six Keys to Success in a Changing World.* Burr Ridge, IL: McGraw-Hill/Irwin Professional Publishing.
8. SHRM Information Center. 1997. *Employment Applications: A Collection of Samples.* Alexandria, VA: Society of Human Resource Management.

▶ NOTES

1. Based on information in David J. Cherrington and Laura Z. Middleton, "An Introduction to Global Business Issues," *HR Magazine,* June 1995, 124–130.

2. Charlene M. Soloman, "Learning to Manage Host-Country Nationals," *Personnel Journal,* March 1995, 60–67.

3. R. A. Guzzo, K. A. Noonan, and E. Elron, "Expatriate Managers and the Psychological Contract," *Journal of Applied Psychology* 79 (1994), 617–626.

4. Reyer A. Swaak, "Today's Expatriate Family: Dual Careers and Other Obstacles," *Compensation & Benefits Review,* January–February 1995, 21–26.

5. Mark E. Mendelhall and Carolyn Wiley, "Strangers in a Strange Land: The Relationship between Expatriate Adjustment and Impression Management," *American Behavioral Scientist,* March–April 1994, 605–621.

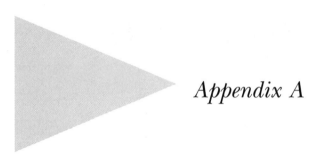

Appendix A

Current Literature in HR Management

Students are expected to be familiar with the professional literature in their fields of study. The professional journals are the most immediate and direct communication link between the researcher and the practicing manager. Two groups of publications are listed below:

A. Research-Oriented Journals. These journals contain articles that report on original research. Normally these journals contain either sophisticated writing and quantitative verifications of the author's findings or conceptual models and literature reviews of previous research.

Academy of Management Journal
Academy of Management Review
Administrative Science Quarterly
American Behavioral Scientist
American Journal of Psychology
American Journal of Sociology
American Psychologist
American Sociological Review
Annual Review of Psychology
Applied Psychology: An International
    Review
Behavioral Science
Behavioral Science Research
British Journal of Industrial Relations

Cognitive Studies
Decision Sciences
Group and Organization Studies
Human Organization
Human Relations
Industrial & Labor Relations Review
Industrial Relations
Interfaces
Journal of Abnormal Psychology
Journal of Applied Behavioral Science
Journal of Applied Business Research
Journal of Applied Psychology
Journal of Business
Journal of Business and Industrial
    Marketing
Journal of Business and Psychology
Journal of Business Communications
Journal of Business Research
Journal of Communications
Journal of Counseling Psychology
Journal of Experimental Social
    Psychology

Journal of Human Resources
Journal of Industrial Relations
Journal of International Business Studies
Journal of Labor Economics
Journal of Management
Journal of Management Studies
Journal of Occupational and
    Organizational Psychology
Journal of Organizational Behavior
Journal of Personality and Social
    Psychology
Journal of Social Policy
Journal of Social Psychology
Journal of Vocational Behavior
Labor History
Labor Relations Yearbook
Management Science
Occupational Psychology
Organizational Behavior and Human
    Decision Processes
Personnel Psychology
Psychological Monographs
Psychological Review
Social Forces
Social Science Research
Sociology Perspective
Sociometry
Work and Occupations

B. Management-Oriented Journals. These journals generally cover a wide range of subjects. Articles in these publications normally are aimed at the practitioner and are written to interpret, summarize, or discuss past, present, and future research and administrative applications. Not all the articles in these publications are management-oriented.

ACA Journal
Academy of Management Executive
Administrative Management
Arbitration Journal
Australian Journal of Management
Benefits and Compensation Solutions

Business
Business Horizons
Business Management
Business Monthly
Business Quarterly
Business and Social Review
California Management Review
Canadian Manager
Columbia Journal of World Business
Compensation and Benefits Review
Directors and Boards
Employee Benefits News
Employee Relations Law Journal
Employment Decisions Practices
Employment Relations
Employment Relations Today
Entrepreneurship Theory and Practice
Forbes
Fortune
Harvard Business Review
Hospital and Health Services
    Administration
HR Magazine
Human Behavior
Human Resource Executive
Human Resource Management
Human Resource Planning
INC.
Incentive
Industrial Management
Industry Week
International Management
Journal of Business Strategy
Journal of Pension Planning
Journal of Systems Management
Labor Law Journal
Long-Range Planning
Manage
Management Consulting
Management Planning
Management Review
Management Solutions
Management Today
Management World
Managers Magazine

Michigan State University Business
  Topics
Monthly Labor Review
Nation's Business
Organizational Dynamics
Pension World
Personnel Journal
Personnel Management
Psychology Today
Public Administration Review
Public Opinion Quarterly
Public Personnel Management
Recruiting Today
Research Management
SAM Advanced Management Journal
Security Management
Sloan Management Review
Supervision
Supervisory Management
Training
Training and Development Journal
Working Woman

C. Abstracts & Indices. For assistance in locating articles, students should check some of the following indices and abstracts that often contain subjects of interest.

ABI Inform
Applied Science and Technology Index
Business Periodicals Index
Dissertation Abstracts
Employee Relations Index
Human Resources Abstracts
Index to Legal Periodicals
Index to Social Sciences and Humanities
Management Abstracts
Management Contents
Management Research Abstracts
Personnel Management Abstracts
Psychological Abstracts
PsychLit
Reader's Guide to Periodical Literature
Sociological Abstracts
Work-Related Abstracts

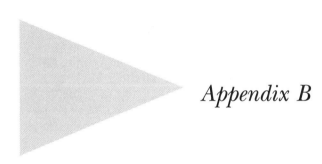

Appendix B

Important Organizations in HR Management

Academy of Management
Pace University
235 Elm Road
Briarcliff Manor, NY 10510-8020
(914) 923-2607

Administrative Management Society
4622 Street Road
Trevose, PA 19047
(215) 953-1040

AFL-CIO
815 – 16th Street, N.W.
Washington, DC 20006
(202) 637-5000

American Arbitration Association
140 W. 51st Street
New York, NY 10020
(212) 484-4800

American Compensation Association
14040 N. Northsight Blvd.
Scottsdale, AZ 85260
(602) 951-9191

American Management Association
135 W. 50th Street
New York, NY 10020-1201
(212) 586-8100

**American Society for Healthcare
Human Resources Administration**
840 N. Lakeshore Drive
Chicago, IL 60611
(312) 280-6111

American Society for Industrial Security
1655 N. Fort Meyer Drive
Arlington, VA 22209-3108
(703) 522-5800

**American Society for Public
    Administration**
1120 G Street, NW, Suite 500
Washington, DC 20005
(202) 393-7878

**American Society for Training and
    Development**
1630 Duke Street
Alexandria, VA 22312
(703) 683-8100

American Society of Pension Actuaries
1700 K Street, NW, Suite 404
Washington, DC 20006
(202) 659-3620

American Society of Safety Engineers
1800 East Oakton
Des Plaines, IL 60018
(847) 692-4121

**Association of Executive Search
    Consultants, Inc.**
151 Railroad Avenue
Greenwich, CT 06830
(203) 661-6606

Association for Health and Fitness
965 Hope Street
Stamford, CT 06902
(203) 359-2188

**Association of Human Resource
    Systems Professionals**
P.O. Box 801646
Dallas, TX 75380
(214) 661-3727

Bureau of Industrial Relations
University of Michigan
Ann Arbor, MI 48104

Bureau of Labor Statistics (BLS)
U.S. Department of Labor
3rd Street & Constitution Avenue, NW
Washington, DC 20210

**Canadian Public Personnel Management
    Association**
220 Laurier Avenue, West, Suite 720
Ottawa, Ontario K1P 5Z9
Canada
(613) 233-1742

Employee Benefit Research Institute
2121 K Street, NW, Suite 860
Washington, DC 20037
(202) 659-0670

Employee Management Association
5 West Hargett, Suite 1100
Raleigh, NC 27601
(919) 828-6614

Employee Relocation Council
1720 N Street, NW
Washington, DC 20036-2097
(202) 857-0857

**Equal Employment Opportunity
    Commission (EEOC)**
2401 E Street, NW
Washington, DC 20506

**Human Resource Certification
    Institute (HRCI)**
1800 Duke Street
Alexandria, VA 22314

Human Resource Planning Society
317 Madison Avenue, Suite 1509
New York, NY 10017
(212) 837-0632

Industrial Relations Research Association
7726 Social Science Blvd.
Madison, WI 53706
(608) 262-2762

Institute of Personnel Management
IPM House
Camp Road, Wimbleton
London SW19 4UX
England

Internal Revenue Service (IRS)
1111 Constitution Avenue, NW
Washington, DC 20224
(202) 566-3171

**International Association for Human
     Resource Information Management**
14643 Dallas Parkway, Suite 525
Dallas, TX 75240
(214) 661-3727

**International Association for
     Personnel Women**
194-A Harvard Street
Medford, MA 02155
(617) 391-7436

**International Foundation of Employee
     Benefit Plans**
18700 Blue Mound Road
Brookfield, WI 53008
(414) 786-6700

**International Personnel Management
     Association**
1617 Duke Street
Alexandria, VA 22314
(703) 549-7100

**International Society of Pre-Retirement
     Planners**
2400 South Downing Street
Westchester, IL 60153
(617) 495-4895

Labor Management Mediation Service
1620 I Street, NW, Suite 616
Washington, DC 20006

**National Association for the
     Advancement of Colored People
     (NAACP)**
4805 Mt. Hope Drive
Baltimore, MD 21215

**National Association of Manufacturers
     (NAM)**
1331 Pennsylvania Avenue, NW, Suite
     1500N
Washington, DC 20004
(202) 637-3000

**National Association of Personnel
     Consultants**
3133 Mt. Vernon Avenue
Alexandria, VA 22305-2640
(703) 684-0180

**National Association of Temporary and
     Staffing Services**
119 South Saint Asaph
Alexandria, VA 22314
(703) 549-6287

**National Employee Services &
     Recreation Association**
2400 S. Downing Avenue
Westchester, IL 60153

National Labor Relations Board
1717 Pennsylvania Avenue, NW
Washington, DC 20570
(202) 632-4950

**National Public Employer Labor
     Relations Association**
1620 I Street, NW, 4th Floor
Washington, DC 20006
(202) 296-2230

Occupational Safety and Health Association (OSHA)
200 Constitution Ave., NW
Washington, DC 20210
(202) 523-8045

Office of Federal Contract Compliance Programs (OFCCP)
200 Constitution Ave., NW
Washington, DC 20210

Pension Benefit Guaranty Corporation
P.O. Box 7119
Washington, DC 20044

Profit Sharing Council of America
200 N. Wacker Drive, Suite 1722
Chicago, IL 60606
(312) 372-3411

Society for Human Resource Management (SHRM)
1800 Duke Street
Alexandria, VA 22314
(703) 548-3440

U.S. Chamber of Commerce
1615 H Street, NW
Washington, DC 20062

U.S. Department of Labor
200 Constitution Ave., NW
Washington, DC 20210

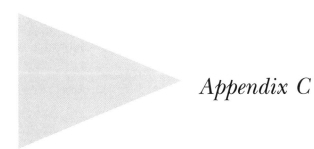

Appendix C

Guidelines to Lawful and Unlawful Preemployment Inquiries

Subject of Inquiry	It May Not Be Discriminatory to Inquire About:	It May Be Discriminatory to Inquire About:
1. Name	**a.** Whether applicant has ever worked under a different name	**a.** The original name of an applicant whose name has been legally changed **b.** The ethnic association of applicant's name
2. Age	**a.** If applicant is over the age of 18 **b.** If applicant is under the age of 18 or 21 if job related (i.e., selling liquor in retail store)	**a.** Date of birth **b.** Date of high school graduation
3. Residence	**a.** Applicant's place of residence; length of applicant's residence in state and/or city where employer is located	**a.** Previous addresses **b.** Birthplace of applicant or applicant's parents
4. Race or Color		**a.** Applicant's race or color of applicant's skin
5. National Origin and Ancestry		**a.** Applicant's lineage, ancestry, national origin, parentage, or nationality **b.** Nationality of applicant's parents or spouse

Subject of Inquiry	It May Not Be Discriminatory to Inquire About:	It May Be Discriminatory to Inquire About:
6. Sex and Family Composition		**a.** Sex of applicant **b.** Dependents of applicant **c.** Marital status **d.** Child-care arrangements
7. Creed or Religion		**a.** Applicant's religious affiliation **b.** Church, parish, or holidays observed
8. Citizenship	**a.** Whether the applicant is a citizen of the United States **b.** Whether the applicant is in the country on a visa that permits him or her to work or is a citizen	**a.** Whether applicant is a citizen of a country other than the United States
9. Language	**a.** Language applicant speaks and/or writes fluently, if job related	**a.** Applicant's native tongue; language commonly used at home
10. References	**a.** Names of persons willing to provide professional and/or character references for applicant	**a.** Name of applicant's pastor or religious leader
11. Relatives	**a.** Names of relatives already employed by the employer	**a.** Name and/or address of any relative of applicant **b.** Whom to contact in case of emergency
12. Organizations	**a.** Applicant's membership in any professional, service, or trade organization	**a.** All clubs or social organizations to which applicant belongs
13. Arrest Record and Convictions	**a.** Convictions, if related to job performance (disclaimer should accompany)	**a.** Number and kinds of arrests **b.** Convictions unless related to job performance
14. Photographs		**a.** Photographs with application, with resume, or before hiring
15. Height and Weight		**a.** Any inquiry into height and weight of applicant except where a BFOQ

Subject of Inquiry	It May Not Be Discriminatory to Inquire About:	It May Be Discriminatory to Inquire About:
16. Physical Limitations	**a.** Whether applicant has the ability to perform job-related functions with or without accommodation	**a.** The nature or severity of an illness or the individual's physical condition **b.** Whether applicant has ever filed a workers' compensation claim **c.** Any recent or past operations or surgery and dates
17. Education	**a.** Training applicant has received if related to the job under consideration **b.** Highest level of education attained, if validated that having certain educational background (e.g., high school diploma or college degree) is necessary to perform the specific job	
18. Military	**a.** What branch of the military applicant served in **b.** Type of education or training received in military **c.** Rank at discharge	**a.** Type of military discharge
19. Financial Status		**a.** Applicant's debts or assets **b.** Garnishments

Appendix D

HRCI Certification and Content Outline of the HR Body of Knowledge

▶ HUMAN CERTIFICATION TYPES

Professional in Human Resources (PHR) Requirements[a]
- A minimum of four years of HR professional experience,
- *or* an HR-related bachelor's degree and two years of HR professional experience,
- *or* an HR-related master's degree and one year of HR professional experience.
- **Students:** Special provisions for the PHR allow students to take the PHR exam within one year of graduation, even though they do not have the required experience. If they pass the examination, they receive a letter certifying examination results. Then they have four years in which to complete the specific experience requirements to earn certification. Full

certification is granted as soon as they submit evidence of meeting the work experience requirements.

Senior Professional in Human Resources (SPHR) Requirements[a]
- Eight years of professional HR experience,
- *or* an HR-related bachelor's degree and six years of HR professional experience,
- *or* an HR-related master's degree and five years of HR professional experience.

[a]For information regarding the above HR certification, contact the Human Resource Certification Institute, 1800 Duke Street, Alexandria, VA 22314 (703) 548-3440.

▶ HRCI CONTENT OUTLINE

Following each of the major functional subareas are the weightings for that subarea. The first number in the parentheses is the PHR percentage weighting and the second number is the SPHR percentage weighting. These weightings should help you allocate your time in preparing for each respective examination.

I.   **Management Practices (15%, 21%)**

   A.   *Role of HR in Organizations (2.78%, 3.91%)*

      1.   HR Roles: Advisory/Counselor, Consultant, Service, Control

      2.   Change Agent Role/Reengineering and Facilitating Both Content & Process

      3.   HR's Role in Strategic Planning

      4.   HR Generalist and HR Specialist Roles

      5.   Effects of Different Organizational Contexts and Industries on HR Functions

      6.   HR Policies and Procedures

      7.   Integration and Coordination of HR Functions

      8.   Outsourcing the HR Functions

   B.   *Human Resource Planning (2.04%, 2.87%)*

      1.   Environmental Scanning

      2.   Internal Scanning

      3.   Human Resources Inventory

      4.   Human Resource Information Systems

      5.   Action Plans and Programs

      6.   Evaluation of Human Resource Planning

   C.   *Organizational Design and Development (.65%, .99%)*

      1.   Organizational Structures

      2.   Organizational Development

      3.   Diagnosis and Intervention Strategies: Action Research, Sensing, Team Building, Goal Setting, Survey Feedback, Strategic Planning, Visioning, Sensitivity Training (T-groups), Grid Training

      4.   Role of Organizational Culture in Organizational Development

      5.   Role of International Culture in Organizational Development

      6.   Organizational Development in Response to Technological Change

   D.   *Budgeting, Controlling, and Measurement (1.08%, 1.56%)*

      1.   HR Budgeting Process

      2.   HR Control Process

      3.   Evaluating HR Effectiveness

   E.   *Motivation (.59%, .77%)*

      1.   Motivation Theories

      2.   Applying Motivation Theory in Management

   F.   *Leadership (.97%, 1.32%)*

      1.   Leadership Theories

      2.   Effect of Leadership In Organizations

      3.   Leadership Training

   G.   *Quality and Performance Management/TQM (1.82%, 2.41%)*

      1.   Performance Planning: Identifying Goals/Desired Behaviors

      2.   Setting and Communicating Performance Standards

      3.   Measuring Results and Providing Feedback

      4   Implementing Performance Improvement Strategies

      5.   Evaluating Results

   H.   *Employee Involvement Strategies (2.11%, 2.57%)*

      1.   Work Teams

      2.   Job Design and Redesign

      3.   Employee Ownership/ESOPs

      4.   Employee Suggestion System

      5.   Participative Management

      6.   Alternative Work Schedules

      7.   Role of HR in Employee Involvement Programs

   I.   *HR Research (.71%, 1.16%)*

      1.   Research Design and Methodology

      2.   Quantitative Analysis

      3.   Qualitative Research

   J.   *International HR Management (1.49%, 2.48%)*

      1.   Cultural Differences

      2.   Legal Aspects of International HR

      3.   Expatriation and Repatriation

      4.   Issues of Multinational Corporations

5. Compensation and Benefits for Foreign Nationals and Expatriates

6. The Role of HR in International Business

K. *Ethics (.77%, .96%)*

1. Ethical Issues

2. Establishing Ethical Behavior in the Organization

II. General Employment Practices (19%, 17%)

A. *Legal and Regulatory Factors: Definitions, Requirements, Proscribed Practices, Exemptions, Enforcement, Remedies, and Case Histories (6.38%, 5.29%)*

1. Title VII of the Civil Rights Act (1964) as Amended (1972, 1991)

2. Age Discrimination in Employment Act (1967) as Amended

3. Health, Medical, & Rehabilitation Statutes (e.g., Vocational Rehabilitation Act, Pregnancy Discrimination Act, Americans with Disabilities Act, Family & Medical Leave Act, HMO Act, etc.)

4. Vietnam-era Veterans Readjustment Act (1986)

5. Immigration Reform and Control Act (1986) as Amended (1990)

6. Employee Polygraph Protection Act (1988)

7. Uniform Guidelines on Employee Selection Procedures

8. Worker Adjustment and Retraining Notification Act (1988)

9. North American Free Trade Act

10. Common Law Tort Theories

11. Copyright Statutes

12. Compensation Laws and Regulations

13. Consumer Credit Protection Act, Wage Garnishment (1968), Fair Credit Reporting (1970)

14. Social Security/Retirement Legislation (e.g., ERISA)

15. COBRA (Consolidated Omnibus Budget Reconciliation Act) (1990); Omnibus Budget Reconciliation Act (1993)

16. Workers' Compensation and Unemployment Compensation Laws and Regulations

17. Legal and Regulatory Factors Affecting Employee and Labor Relations (e.g., NLRA, Taft-Hartley, Landrum-Griffin, etc.)

18. Federal Health, Safety, and Security Legislation (e.g., OSHA)

B. *Job Analysis, Job Description, and Job Specification (2.14%, 1.78%)*

1. Methods of Job Analysis

2. Types of Data Gathered in Job Analysis

3. Uses of Job Analysis

4. Job Descriptions

5. Job/Position Specifications

6. Validity & Reliability of Job Analysis, Job Description, & Job Specification

C. *Individual Employment Rights (1.72%, 1.67%)*

1. Employment-at-Will Doctrine

2. Exceptions to Employment-at-Will

3. Common Law Tort Theories

4. Job-as-Property Doctrine

5. Non-Compete Agreements

D. *Performance Appraisals (5.10%, 4.60%)*

1. Performance Measurement: The Criterion

2. Criterion Problems

3. Documenting Employee Performance

4. Category Rating Appraisal Methods

5. Comparative Appraisal Methods

6. Narrative Appraisal Methods

7. Special Appraisal Methods: MBO, BARS, BOS

8. Types of Appraisals

9. Rating Errors
10. Appraisal Interview
11. Linking Appraisals to Employment Decisions
12. Legal Contraints on Performance Appraisal
13. Documentation

E. *Workplace Behavior Problems (1.90%, 1.55%)*
1. Discipline
2. Absenteeism and Tardiness
3. Sexual Harassment
4. Drug and Alcohol Use
5. Off-duty Conduct

F. *Employee Attitudes, Opinions, and Satisfaction (2.01%, 2.11%)*
1. Measurement
2. Results Analysis
3. Interpretation
4. Feedback
5. Intervention
6. Confidentiality and Anonymity of Surveys

III. Staffing (19%, 15%)
A. *Equal Employment Opportunity/ Affirmative Action (3.56%, 2.99%)*
1. Legal Endorsement of EEO: Supreme Court Decisions
2. Equal Employment Opportunity Programs
3. Affirmative Action Plans
4. Special Programs to Eliminate Discrimination
5. Fairness Issues: Reverse Discrimination, Quota Hiring vs. Merit Hiring

B. *Recruitment (2.84%, 2.22%)*
1. Determining Recruitment Needs and Objectives
2. Identifying Selection Criteria
3. Internal Sourcing
4. External Sourcing
5. Evaluating Recruiting Effectiveness

C. *Selection (5.94%, 4.39%)*
1. Application Process

2. Interviewing
3. Preemployment Testing
4. Background Investigation
5. Medical Examination
6. Hiring Applicants with Disabilities
7. Illegal Use of Drugs and Alcohol
8. Validation and Evaluation of Selection Process Components

D. *Career Planning and Development (2.06%, 1.84%)*
1. Accommodating Organizational and Individual Needs
2. Mobility within the Organization
3. Managing Transitions

E. *Organizational Exit (4.60%, 3.56%)*
1. General Issues
2. Layoffs/Reductions-in-Force
3. Constructive Discharge
4. Retaliatory
5. Retirement
6. Employer Defenses against Litigation

IV. Human Resource Development (11%, 12%)
A. *HR Training and the Organization (3.06%, 3.72%)*
1. The Learning Organization, Linking Training to Organizational Goals, Objectives, and Strategies
2. Human Resources Development as an Organizational Component
3. Funding the Training Function
4. Cost-Benefit Analysis of Training

B. *Training Needs Analysis (1.52%, 1.52%)*
1. Training Needs Analysis Process
2. Methods for Assessing Training Needs

C. *Training and Development Programs (4.42%, 4.50%)*
1. Trainer Selection
2. Design Considerations and Learning Principles
3. Types of Training Programs

4. Instructional Methods and Processes
5. Training Facilities Planning
6. Training Materials

D. *Evaluation of Training Effectiveness (2.00%, 2.26%)*
1. Sources for Evaluation
2. Research Methods for Evaluation
3. Criteria for Evaluating Training

V. Compensation and Benefits (19%, 15%)

A. *Tax & Accounting Treatment of Compensation & Benefit Programs (.57%, .53%)*
1. FASB Regulation
2. IRS Regulations

B. *Economic Factors Affecting Compensation (2.09%, 1.77%)*
1. Inflation
2. Interest Rates
3. Industry Competition
4. Foreign Competition
5. Economic Growth
6. Labor Market Trends/ Demographics

C. *Compensation Philosophy, Strategy, and Policy (1.81%, 1.55%)*
1. Fitting Strategy & Policy to the External Environment and to an Organization's Culture, Structure, & Objectives
2. Training in and Communication of Compensation Programs
3. Making Compensation Programs Achieve Organizational Objectives
4. Establishing Administrative Controls

D. *Compensation Programs: Types, Characteristics, and Advantages/ Disadvantages (1.71%, 1.20%)*
1. Base Pay
2. Differential Pay
3. Incentive Pay

4. Pay Programs for Selected Employees

E. *Job Evaluation Methods (2.20%, 1.60%)*
1. Compensable Factors
2. Ranking Method
3. Classification/Grading Method
4. Factor Comparison Method
5. Point Method
6. Guide Chart–Profile Method (Hay Method)

F. *Job Pricing, Pay Structures, and Pay Rate Administration (2.14%, 1.49%)*
1. Job Pricing and Pay Structures
2. Individual Pay Rate Determination
3. Utilizing Performance Appraisal in Pay Administration
4. Reflecting Market Influences in Pay Structures
5. Wage Surveys

G. *Employee Benefit Programs: Types, Objectives, Characteristics, and Advantages/Disadvantages (3.42%, 2.17%)*
1. Legally Required Programs/Payments
2. Income Replacement
3. Insurance and Income Protection
4. Deferred Pay
5. Pay for Time Not Worked
6. Unpaid Leave
7. Flexible Benefit Plans
8. Recognition and Achievement Awards

H. *Managing Employee Benefit Programs (3.75%, 3.43%)*
1. Employee Benefits Philosophy, Planning, and Strategy
2. Employee Need/Preference Assessment Surveys
3. Administrative Systems
4. Funding/Investment Responsibilities

5. Coordination with Plan Trustees, Insurers, Health Service Providers, and Third-Party Administrators
6. Utilization Review
7. Cost-Benefit Analysis and Cost Management
8. Communicating Benefit Programs/Individual Annual Benefits Reports
9. Monitoring Compensation/ Benefits Legal Compliance Programs
I. *Evaluating Total Compensation Strategy & Program Effectiveness (1.32%, 1.26%)*
1. Budgeting
2. Cost Management
3. Assessment of Methods and Processes

VI. Employee and Labor Relations (11%, 14%)
A. *Union Representation of Employees (1.52%, 1.98%)*
1. Scope of the Labor-Management Relations (Taft-Hartley) Act (1947)
2. Achieving Representative Status
3. Petitioning for an NLRB Election
4. Election Campaign
5. Union Security
B. *Employer Unfair Labor Practices (1.68%, 1.91%)*
1. Procedures for Processing Charges of Unfair Labor Practices
2. Interference, Restraint, and Coercion
3. Domination and Unlawful Support of Labor Organization
4. Employee Discrimination to Discourage Union Membership
5. Retaliation
6. Remedies
C. *Union Unfair Labor Practices, Strikes, and Boycotts (1.96%, 2.60%)*
1. Responsibility for Acts of Union Agents
2. Union Restraint or Coercion
3. Duty of Fair Representation
4. Inducing Unlawful Discrimination by Employer
5. Excessive or Discriminatory Membership Fees
6. Strikes and Secondary Boycotts
7. Strike Preparation
D. *Collective Bargaining (2.94%, 4.06%)*
1. Bargaining Issues and Concepts
2. Negotiation Strategies
3. Good Faith Requirements
4. Notice Requirements
5. Unilateral Changes in Terms of Employment
6. Duty to Successor Employers or Unions: Buyouts, Mergers, or Bankruptcy
7. Enforcement Provisions
8. Injunctions
9. Mediation and Conciliation
10. National Emergency Strikes
E. *Managing Organization-Union Relations (.88%, 1.16%)*
1. Building and Maintaining Union-Organization Relationships: Cooperative Programs
2. Grievance Processes and Procedures
3. Dispute Resolution
F. *Maintaining Nonunion Status (.79%, .91%)*
1. Reasons
2. Strategies
G. *Public Sector Labor Relations (1.12%, 1.38%)*
1. Right to Organize
2. Federal Labor Relations Council
3. Limitations on Strikes
4. Mediation and Conciliation

VII. Health, Safety, and Security (6%, 6%)
A. *Health (2.41%, 2.22%)*

1. Employee Assistance Programs
2. Employee Wellness Programs
3. Reproductive Health Policies
4. Chemical Dependency
5. Communicable Diseases in the Workplace
6. Employer Liabilities
7. Stress Management
8. Smoking Policies
9. Recordkeeping and Reporting

B. *Safety (2.05%, 2.04%)*
   1. Areas of Concern
   2. Organization of Safety Program
   3. Safety Promotion
   4. Accident Investigation
   5. Safety Inspections
   6. Human Factors Engineering (Ergonomics)
   7. Special Safety Considerations
   8. Sources of Assistance

C. *Security (1.54%, 1.74%)*
   1. Organization of Security
   2. Control Systems
   3. Protection of Proprietary Information
   4. Crisis Management and Contingency Planning
   5. Theft and Fraud
   6. Investigations and Preventive Corrections

Source: © Human Resource Certification Institute

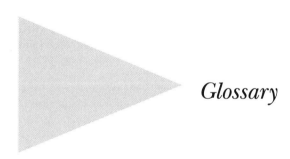

Glossary

4/5ths Rule Rule stating that discrimination generally is considered to occur if the selection rate for a protected group is less than 80% of the group's representation in the relevant labor market or less than 80% of the selection rate for the majority group.

401(k) Plan An agreement in which a percentage of an employee's pay is withheld and invested in a tax-deferred account.

A

Active Practice The performance of job-related tasks and duties by trainees during training.

Affirmative Action A process in which employers identify problem areas, set goals, and take positive steps to guarantee equal employment opportunities for people in a protected class.

Agency Shop A firm that requires employees who refuse to join the union to pay equivalent amounts equal to union dues and fees for the union's representative services.

Arbitration Process by which negotiating parties submit their dispute to a third party to make a decision.

Assessment Center A collection of instruments and exercises designed to diagnose a person's development needs.

Attitude Survey A special type of survey that focuses on employees' feelings and beliefs about their jobs and the organization.

Availability Analysis An analysis that identifies the number of protected-class members available to work in the appropriate labor market in given jobs.

B

Balance-Sheet Approach An approach to international compensation that provides international employees with a compensation package that equalizes cost differences between the international assignment and the same assignment in the home country.

Bargaining Unit All employees eligible to select a single union to represent and bargain collectively for them.

Behavior Modeling Copying someone else's behavior.

Behavioral Description Interview Interview in which applicants give specific examples of how they have performed or handled a problem in the past.

Behavioral Rating Assesses an employee's behaviors instead of other characteristics.

Benchmark Job Job found in many organizations and performed by several individuals who have similar duties that are relatively stable and that require similar KSAs.

Benchmarking Comparing specific measures of performance against data on those measures in "best practices" organizations.

Benefit Indirect compensation given to employees for organizational membership.

Bona Fide Occupational Qualification (BFOQ) A characteristic providing a legitimate reason why an employer can exclude persons on otherwise illegal bases of consideration.

Bonus A payment made on a one-time basis, which does not become part of the employee's base pay.

Broadbanding Practice of using fewer pay grades having broader ranges than traditional compensation systems.

Business Agent A full-time union official employed by the union to operate the union office and assist union members.

Business Necessity A practice necessary for safe and efficient organizational operations.

C

Career The sequence of work-related positions a person occupies throughout life.

Central Tendency Error Rating all employees in a narrow band in the middle of the rating scale.

Closed Shop A firm that requires individuals to join a union before they can be hired.

Co-Determination A practice whereby union or worker representatives are given positions on a company's board of directors.

Coaching Daily training and feedback given to employees by immediate supervisors.

Collective Bargaining The process whereby representatives of management and workers negotiate over wages, hours, and other terms and conditions of employment.

Commission Compensation computed as a percentage of sales in units or dollars.

Compa-Ratio Pay level divided by the midpoint of the pay range.

Compensable Factor Factor used to identify a job value that is commonly present throughout a group of jobs.

Compensation Committee Usually a subgroup of the board of directors composed of directors who are not officers of the firm.

Compensatory Time Off Time off given in lieu of payment for extra time worked.

Compressed Workweek Workweek in which a full week's work is accomplished in fewer than five days.

Conciliation Process by which a third party attempts to keep union and management negotiators talking so that they can reach a voluntary settlement.

Concurrent Validity Validity measured when an employer tests current employees and correlates the scores with their performance ratings.

Construct Validity Validity showing a relationship between an abstract characteristic and job performance.

Constructive Discharge Occurs when an employer deliberately makes conditions intolerable in an attempt to get an employee to quit.

Content Validity Validity measured by use of a logical, nonstatistical method to identify the KSAs and other characteristics necessary to perform a job.

Contractual Rights Rights based on a specific contractual agreement between employer and employee.

Contributory Plan Pension plan in which the money for pension benefits is paid in by both employees and employers.

Copayment Employee's payment of a portion of the cost of both insurance premiums and medical care.

Craft Union A union whose members do one type of work, often using specialized skills and training.

Criterion-Related Validity Validity measured by means of a procedure that uses a test as the predictor of how well an individual will perform on the job.

Critical Job Dimensions Elements of a job on which performance is measured.

Culture The societal forces affecting the values, beliefs, and actions of a distinct group of people.

Cumulative Trauma Disorders (CTDs) Muscle and skeletal injuries that occur when workers repetitively use the same muscles to perform tasks.

D

Decertification A process whereby a union is removed as the representative of a group of employees.

Defined-Benefit Plan Pension plan in which an employee is promised a pension amount based on age and service.

Defined-Contribution Plan Pension plan in

which the employer makes an annual payment to an employee's pension account.

Development Efforts to improve employees' ability to handle a variety of assignments.

Disabled Person Someone who has a physical or mental impairment that substantially limits that person in some major life activities, who has a record of such an impairment, or who is regarded as having such an impairment.

Discipline A form of training that enforces organizational rules.

Disparate Impact Situation that exists when there is a substantial underrepresentation of protected-class members as a result of employment decisions that work to their disadvantage.

Disparate Treatment Situation that exists when protected-class members are treated differently from others.

Distributive Justice Perceived fairness in the distribution of outcomes.

Diversity Differences among people.

Diversity Management Efforts concerned with developing organizational initiatives that value all people equally, regardless of their differences.

Downsizing Reducing the size of an organizational workforce.

Due Process The opportunity to defend oneself against charges.

Dues Checkoff Provision that union dues will be deducted automatically from payroll checks of union members.

Duty A larger work segment composed of several tasks that are performed by an individual.

E

Earned-Time Plan Plan that combines all time-off benefits into a total number of hours or days that employees can take off with pay.

Employee Assistance Program (EAP) Program that provides counseling and other help to employees having emotional, physical, or other personal problems.

Employee Stock Ownership Plan (ESOP) A plan whereby employees gain stock ownership in the organization for which they work.

Employment Contracts Agreements that spell out the details of employment.

Employment-at-Will (EAW) A common-law doctrine stating that employers have the right to hire, fire, demote, or promote whomever they choose, unless there is a law or contract to the contrary.

Equal Employment Opportunity (EEO) The concept that individuals should have equal treatment in all employment-related actions.

Equity The perceived fairness of the relation between what a person does (inputs) and what the person receives (outcomes).

Ergonomics The proper design of the work environment to address the physical demands experienced by people.

Essential Job Functions The fundamental job duties of the employment position that an individual with a disability holds or desires; they do not include marginal functions of the position.

Exempt Employees Employees classified as executive, administrative, professional, or outside sales, to whom employers are not required to pay overtime under the Fair Labor Standards Act.

Exit Interview An interview in which those leaving the organization are asked to identify the reasons for their departure.

Expatriate An employee working in a unit or plant who is not a citizen of the country in which the unit or plant is located but is a citizen of the country in which the organization is headquartered.

F

Federation A group of autonomous national and international unions.

Flexible Benefits Plan Benefits plan that allows employees to select the benefits they prefer from groups of benefits established by the employer.

Flexible Spending Account Account that allows employees to contribute pretax dollars to buy additional benefits.

Flexible Staffing Use of recruiting sources and workers who are not employees.

Flextime A scheduling arrangement in which employees work a set number of hours per day but vary starting and ending times.

Forced Distribution Performance appraisal method in which ratings of employees' performance are distributed along a bell-shaped curve.

Forecasting Identifying expected future conditions based on information from the past and present.

G

Gainsharing The sharing with employees of greater-than-expected gains in profits and/or productivity.

Garnishment A court action in which a portion of an employee's wages is set aside to pay a debt owed a creditor.

Glass Ceiling Discriminatory practices that have prevented women and other protected-class members from advancing to executive-level jobs.

Global Organization An organization that has corporate units in a number of countries that are integrated to operate as one organization worldwide.

Golden Parachute A severance benefit that provides protection and security to executives in the event that they lose their jobs or their firms are acquired by other firms and they are negatively affected.

Graphic Rating Using a scale that allows the rater to mark an employee's performance on a continuum.

Green-Circled Employee An incumbent who is paid below the range set for the job.

Grievance An alleged misinterpretation, misapplication, or violation of a provision in a union-management agreement.

Grievance Arbitration A means by which disputes arising from different interpretations of a labor contract are settled by a third party.

Grievance Procedure A formal channel of communications used to resolve grievances.

H

Halo Effect Rating a person high or low on all items because of one characteristic.

Handbilling Practice in which unions give written publicity to employees to convince the employees to sign authorization cards.

Health A general state of physical, mental, and emotional well-being.

Host-Country National An employee working in a unit or plant who is a citizen of the country in which the unit or plant is located but where the unit or plant is operated by an organization headquartered in another country.

HR Audit A formal research effort that evaluates the current state of HR management in an organization.

HR Generalist A person with responsibility for performing a variety of HR activities.

HR Research The analysis of data from HR records to determine the effectiveness of past and present HR practices.

HR Specialist A person with in-depth knowledge and expertise in a limited area of HR.

Human Resource Information System (HRIS) An integrated system designed to provide information used in HR decision making.

Human Resource (HR) Management The design of formal systems in an organization to ensure the effective and efficient use of human talent to accomplish organizational goals.

Human Resource (HR) Planning The process of analyzing and identifying the need for and availability of human resources so that the organization can meet its objectives.

I

Importing and Exporting The phase of international interaction in which an organization begins selling and buying goods and services with organizations in other countries.

Independent Contractors Workers who perform specific services on a contract basis.

Individual-Centered Career Planning Career planning that focuses on individuals' careers rather than on organizational needs.

Industrial Union   A union that includes many persons working in the same industry or company, regardless of jobs held.

J

Job   A grouping of similar positions having common tasks, duties, and responsibilities.

Job Analysis   A systematic way to gather and analyze information about the content and the human requirements of jobs, and the context in which jobs are performed.

Job Description   Identification of the tasks, duties, and responsibilities of a job.

Job Design   Organizing tasks, duties, and responsibilities into a productive unit of work.

Job Evaluation   The systematic determination of the relative worth of jobs within an organization.

Job Family   A grouping of jobs having similar characteristics.

Job Posting and Bidding   A system in which the employer provides notices of job openings within the organization and employees respond by applying for specific openings.

Job Satisfaction   A positive emotional state resulting from evaluating one's job experiences.

Job Specifications   Listing of the knowledge, skills, and abilities (KSAs) an individual needs to do the job satisfactorily.

Just Cause   Sufficient justification for actions.

K

Knowledge, Skills, and Abilities (KSAs)   Include education, experience, work skill requirements, personal requirements, mental and physical requirements, and working conditions and hazards.

L

Labor Markets   The external sources from which organizations attract employees.

Lockout   Shutdown of company operations undertaken by management to prevent union members from working.

Lump-Sum Increase (LSI)   A one-time payment of all or part of a yearly pay increase.

M

Managed Care   Approaches designed to monitor and reduce medical costs using good management practices and the market system.

Management by Objectives (MBO)   Specifies the performance goal that an individual hopes to attain within an appropriate length of time.

Management Rights   Those rights reserved to the employer to manage, direct, and control its business.

Mandated Benefits   Those benefits which employers in the United States must provide to employees by law.

Mandatory Issues   Those issues that are identified specifically by labor laws or court decisions as being subject to bargaining.

Market Price   The prevailing wage rate paid for a job in the immediate job market.

Mediation   Process by which a third party assists negotiators in their discussions and also suggests settlement proposals.

Mentoring   A relationship in which managers at midpoints in careers aid individuals in the first stages of careers.

Moonlighting   Work outside a person's regular employment that takes 12 or more additional hours per week.

Motivation   The desire within a person causing that person to act.

Multinational Enterprise (MNE)   An organization with units located in foreign countries.

N

National Emergency Strike   A strike that would affect an industry or a major part of it such that the national health or safety would be impeded.

Nepotism   Practice of allowing relatives to work for the same employer.

Noncontributory Plan Pension plan in which all the funds for pension benefits are provided by the employer.

Nonexempt Employees Employees who must be paid overtime under the Fair Labor Standards Act.

O

Organization-Centered Career Planning Career planning that focuses on jobs and on constructing career paths that provide for the logical progression of people between jobs in an organization.

Organizational Commitment The degree to which employees believe in and accept organizational goals and desire to remain with the organization.

Orientation The planned introduction of new employees to their jobs, coworkers, and the organization.

Outplacement A group of services provided to displaced employees to give them support and assistance.

P

Pay The basic compensation an employee receives, usually as a wage or salary.

Pay Compression Situation in which pay differences among individuals with different levels of experience and performance in the organization become small.

Pay Equity The concept that the pay for jobs requiring comparable knowledge, skills, and abilities should be similar even if actual duties and market rates differ significantly.

Pay Grade A grouping of individual jobs having approximately the same job worth.

Pay Survey A collection of data on existing compensation rates for workers performing similar jobs in other organizations.

Pension Plans Retirement benefits established and funded by employers and employees.

Performance Appraisal (PA) The process of determining how well employees do their jobs compared with a set of standards and communicating that information to those employees.

Performance Criteria Standards commonly used for testing or measuring performances.

Performance Management Systems Attempts to monitor, measure, report, improve, and reward employee performance.

Performance Standard The expected level of performance.

Perquisites (Perks) Special benefits-usually noncash items-for executives.

Piece-Rate System A productivity-based compensation system in which an employee is paid for each unit of production.

Portability A pension plan feature that allows employees to move their pension benefits from one employer to another.

Position A job performed by one person.

Predictive Validity Validity measured when test results of applicants are compared with subsequent performance.

Procedural Justice The perceived fairness of the process and procedures used to make decisions about employees, including their pay.

Production Cells Groupings of workers who produce entire products or components of products.

Productivity A measure of the quantity and quality of work done, considering the cost of the resources it took to do the work.

Profit Sharing A system to distribute a portion of the profits of the organization to employees.

Protected Class Those individuals who fall within a group identified for protection under equal employment laws and regulations.

Psychological Contract The unwritten expectations that employees and employers have about the nature of their work relationships.

Q

Quality Circle A small group of employees who monitor productivity and quality and suggest solutions to problems.

R

Ranking Listing of all employees from highest to lowest in performance.

Rater Bias Error that occurs when a rater's values or prejudices distort the rating.

Ratification Process by which union members vote to accept the terms of a negotiated labor agreement.

Realistic Job Preview (RJP) The process through which an interviewer provides a job applicant with an accurate picture of a job.

Reasonable Accommodation A modification or adjustment to a job or work environment that enables a qualified individual with a disability to enjoy equal employment opportunity.

Recency Effect An error whereby the rater gives greater weight to recent occurrences when appraising an individual's performance.

Recruiting Process of generating a pool of qualified applicants for organizational jobs.

Red-Circled Employee An incumbent who is paid above the range set for the job.

Reinforcement A concept based on the law of effect, which states that people tend to repeat responses that give them some type of positive reward and avoid actions that are associated with negative consequences.

Reliability The consistency with which a test measures an item.

Repatriation The process of bringing expatriates home.

Responsibilities Obligations to perform certain tasks and duties.

Retaliation Punitive actions taken by employers against individuals who exercise their legal rights.

Right-to-Work Laws State laws that prohibit both the closed shop and the union shop.

S

Safety Condition in which the physical well-being of people is protected.

Salary Payment that is consistent from period to period despite the number of hours worked.

Security Protection of employer facilities and equipment from unauthorized access, and protection of employees while on work premises or work assignments.

Selection The process of choosing individuals who have relevant qualifications to fill jobs in an organization.

Selection Criteria Standards that become the basis for selection.

Selection Interview Interview designed to assess job-related knowledge, skills, and abilities (KSAs) and clarify information from other sources.

Self-Directed Work Team An organizational team composed of individuals who are assigned a cluster of tasks, duties, and responsibilities to be accomplished.

Serious Health Condition A health condition requiring inpatient, hospital, hospice, or residential medical care or continuing physician care.

Severance Pay A security benefit voluntarily offered by employers to employees who lose their jobs.

Sexual Harassment Actions that are sexually directed, are unwanted, and subject the worker to adverse employment conditions or create a hostile work environment.

Special-Purpose Team An organizational team that is formed to address specific problems and may continue to work together to improve work processes or the quality of products and services.

Statutory Rights Rights based on laws.

Stock Option A plan that gives an individual the right to buy stock in a company, usually at a fixed price for a period of time.

Straight Piece-Rate System A pay system in which wages are determined by multiplying the number of units produced by the piece rate for one unit.

Strike Work stoppage in which union members refuse to work in order to put pressure on an employer.

Structured Interview Interview that uses a set of standardized questions asked of all job applicants.

Substance Abuse The use of illicit substances or the misuse of controlled substances, alcohol, or other drugs.

Suggestion System A formal method of obtaining employee input and upward communication.

T

Task A distinct, identifiable work activity composed of motions.

Tax Equalization Plan Compensation plan used to protect expatriates from negative tax consequences.

Telecommuting The process of going to work via electronic computing and telecommunications equipment.

Third-Country National An employee who is a citizen of one country, working in a second country, and employed by an organization headquartered in a third country.

Total Quality Management (TQM) A comprehensive management process focusing on the continuous improvement of organizational activities to enhance the quality of the goods and services supplied.

Training A learning process whereby people acquire skills or knowledge to aid in the achievement of goals.

Turnover Process in which employees leave the organization and have to be replaced.

U

Undue Hardship Condition created when making a reasonable accommodation for individuals with disabilities would pose significant difficulty or expense for an employer.

Union A formal association of workers that promotes the interests of its members through collective action.

Union Authorization Card Card signed by an employee to designate a union as his or her collective bargaining agent.

Union Security Provisions Contract provisions to aid the union in obtaining and retaining members.

Union Shop A firm that requires that an employee join a union, usually 30 to 60 days after being hired.

Union Steward An employee of a firm or organization who is elected to serve as the first-line representative of unionized workers.

Unit Labor Cost The total labor cost per unit of output, which is the average wages of workers divided by their levels of productivity.

Utilization Analysis An analysis that identifies the number of protected-class members employed and the types of jobs they hold in an organization.

Utilization Review An audit and review of the services and costs billed by health-care providers.

V

Validity The extent to which a test actually measures what it says it measures.

Vesting The right of employees to receive benefits from their pension plans.

W

Wage and Salary Administration The activity involved in the development, implementation, and maintenance of a base pay system.

Wages Payments directly calculated on the amount of time worked.

Well-Pay Extra pay for not taking sick leave.

Wellness Programs Programs designed to maintain or improve employee health before problems arise.

Workers' Compensation Provides benefits to persons injured on the job.

Index

ITP HIGHER EDUCATION
DISTRIBUTION CENTER
7625 EMPIRE DRIVE
FLORENCE, KY 41042

The enclosed materials are sent to you for your review by
CORY BEIMESCHE

SALES SUPPORT

Date	Account	Contact
02/08/99	684138	27

SHIP TO: Gloria Rembert
Mitchell Cmty College
Business Division
500 West Broad Street
Statesville NC 28677

WAREHOUSE INSTRUCTIONS

SLA: 7   BOX: Staple

LOCATION	QTY	ISBN	AUTHOR/TITLE
K-11A-001-02	1	0-324-00207-6	MATHIS/JACKSON HUM RES MGT:ESSN PERSPECTIVES1

INV# 144787203190
PO#
DATE: / /
CARTON: 1 of 1
ID# 0343631

PRIME-INDUCT
-SLSB

VIA: UP

PAGE 1 OF 1

BATCH: 0695406
026/034